Understanding Hezbollah

Contemporary Issues in the Middle East
Mehran Kamrava, *Series Editor*

Select Titles in Contemporary Issues in the Middle East

Democracy and the Nature of American Influence in Iran, 1941–1979
David R. Collier

Generations of Dissent: Intellectuals, Cultural Production, and the State in the Middle East and North Africa
Alexa Firat and R. Shareah Taleghani, eds.

Iraqi Migrants in Syria: The Crisis before the Storm
Sophia Hoffmann

Making the New Middle East: Politics, Culture, and Human Rights
Valerie J. Hoffman, ed.

The Mizrahi Era of Rebellion: Israel's Forgotten Civil Rights Struggle, 1948–1966
Bryan K. Roby

Ottoman Children and Youth during World War I
Nazan Maksudyan

Political Muslims: Understanding Youth Resistance in a Global Context
Tahir Abbas and Sadek Hamid, eds.

We Are Iraqis: Aesthetics and Politics in a Time of War
Nadje Al-Ali and Deborah Al-Najjar, eds.

For a full list of titles in this series, visit https://press.syr.edu/supressbook-series/contemporary-issues-in-the-middle-east/.

Understanding Hezbollah

The Hegemony of Resistance

Abed T. Kanaaneh

Syracuse University Press

First Edition 2021
21 22 23 24 25 26 6 5 4 3 2 1

∞ The paper used in this publication meets the minimum requirements of the American National Standard for Information Sciences—Permanence of Paper for Printed Library Materials, ANSI Z39.48-1992.

For a listing of books published and distributed by Syracuse University Press, visit https://press.syr.edu.

ISBN: 978-0-8156-3707-3 (hardcover)
978-0-8156-3716-5 (paperback)
978-0-8156-5521-3 (e-book)

Library of Congress Cataloging-in-Publication Data

Names: Kanaaneh, Abed T., author.
Title: Understanding Hezbollah : the hegemony of resistance / Abed T. Kanaaneh.
Description: First edition. | Syracuse, New York : Syracuse University Press, [2021] | Series: Contemporary issues in the Middle East | Includes bibliographical references and index. | Summary: "This book is concerned with the activism of the Lebanese Hizbullah movement towards strengthening its status in the Lebanese arena. It focuses on the Hizbullah's contribution to the development of the concept of Muqawamah (resistance) as part of a counter-hegemonic project"— Provided by publisher.
Identifiers: LCCN 2020047522 (print) | LCCN 2020047523 (ebook) | ISBN 9780815637073 (hardcover) | ISBN 9780815637165 (paperback) | ISBN 9780815655213 (ebook)
Subjects: LCSH: Hizballah (Lebanon) | Lebanon—Politics and government—1990–
Classification: LCC JQ1828.A98 K34 2021 (print) | LCC JQ1828.A98 (ebook) | DDC 324.25692/084—dc23
LC record available at https://lccn.loc.gov/2020047522
LC ebook record available at https://lccn.loc.gov/2020047523

Manufactured in the United States of America

To my parents,
Tawfiq and Salwa,
and to my family

Contents

Acknowledgments

This book would not have seen the light without the guidance and the continuous support of my supervisors, Eyal Zisser (Tel Aviv University) and Dai Filc (Ben Gurion University of the Negev), and for that I am grateful.

I would also like to thank Mahmoud Yazbak (University of Haifa) and Moshe Maoz (Hebrew University of Jerusalem) for their valuable comments on the initial version of the book, which helped to upgrade it. The original publication appeared as *Hezbollah v-higmonyat ha-muqawama* (Hezbollah and the Hegemony of *Muqawama* [Magnes Press, 2020]), and the current text reflects extensive revisions and adaptations.

I also thank Hamid Dabashi of Columbia University for his generous hospitality during my stay in the Middle East, South Asia, and Africa Department while I was working on the book. I am also grateful to Rhoda Kanaaneh and her family for their support during my stay in New York.

I am grateful to Malek Abisaab of McGill University for his support and his valuable comments.

I also thank the anonymous referees who endorsed and recommended this book.

My appreciation goes to Ruba Simaan for her contribution to translating the primary sources from Arabic and Hebrew into English and for her professional basic editing of the English manuscript.

My sincere gratitude goes to the team at Syracuse University Press for their professionalism in bringing this book into production.

Last but not least, I am grateful to my family for their support and patience: my parents, Tawfiq and Salwa; my brother, Ibraheem; my sister, Maha; my wife, Areen; and my kids, Yasar and Majd.

Understanding Hezbollah

Introduction

Toward a New Approach

Of central concern here are Hezbollah's activism toward strengthening its status in the Lebanese arena and its contribution to the development of the *muqawama* (resistance) into a cultural and a counterhegemonic project in the Lebanese arena. Hezbollah's resistance has become a weltanschauung, a cultural and a political tool that efficiently serves the interests of both Hezbollah and Lebanon, as perceived by the former.

Hezbollah is a relatively young organization compared to other players in the Lebanese arena. The organization started operating shortly after the Israeli invasion of Lebanon in 1982. Its entrance on the scene was preceded by a conceptual land reclamation carried out for several years by different revolutionary political streams and modernist clerics such as Musa al-Sadr, Muhammad Husayn Fadlallah, and others. Despite its relatively young age and the complexity of activities in the Lebanese arena, within two decades Hezbollah succeeded in realizing considerable achievements in the social and military arenas in Lebanon. Hezbollah's ability to credit itself with the Israeli withdrawal from southern Lebanon has enhanced its prestige and increased interest in it.

Gramscian and neo-Gramscian tools offer a way to follow up on Hezbollah's development and on its "Lebanonization"—the process of openness—as defined in the scholarly literature, which occurred at the end of the twentieth century and in the first decade of the twenty-first. This book provides a new explanation for Hezbollah's developmental process, from a purely military-religious organization into the main representative of a social group standing at the center of a unique counterhegemonic project that I call the "*muqawama* project."

It is evident that Hezbollah provides support mainly in Shi'ite regions; however, one cannot underestimate the willingness of Hezbollah and the organizations affiliated with it and with the *muqawama* project to provide services to all poor people residing in these regions, regardless of their ethnic, religious, and even national background. For example, Hezbollah's charity organizations are listed among the main supporters of the Palestinian refugees in the refugee camps in Lebanon.[1]

Hezbollah's unique *muqawama* project could not have developed without the cultivation of the ideological foundation by thinkers such as Muhammad Husayn Fadlallah, Ruhollah Khomeini, and 'Ali Shari'ati. Fadlallah's significant contribution was his definition of *muqawama* as a large-scale project not limited to just resistance operations against the Israeli occupation in southern Lebanon. He presented the *muqawama* as an Islamic and universal project within which all Muslim and non-Muslim disempowered populations could act as single unified actor.

Fadlallah's perception integrates with contemplations by Ruhollah Khomeini and 'Ali Shari'ati, who maintained that Islam is the real comprehensive and revolutionary ideology through which one can liberate disempowered populations wherever they are. This perception allowed Hezbollah at a later stage to shape the *muqawama* project, which has addressed many actors within the Lebanese arena, not just the Shi'ites, although it has grown up under the influence of the revolutionary stream of Shi'a Islam.

I argue here that comprehension of Hezbollah and its development will remain deficient unless we perceive the intra-Lebanese politics (and to a certain extent the regional politics in general) as the politics of hegemonic and counterhegemonic projects that compete with each other. This perception provides a new and different explanation for the alliances and coalitions that Hezbollah established during its second and third decades.

Hezbollah's *muqawama* project is counterhegemonic at multiple levels. First, it is directed against the elites who had dominated the Shi'ite community for a long time. Second and more important, it is directed on behalf of all marginalized groups in Lebanon against the Maronite–Sunni hegemony that deprived most Lebanese citizens—especially the Shi'ites who are perceived as a "proletariat" in Lebanon and are marginalized at the political and economic levels—of the opportunity to enjoy the available political and economic resources. Third, it is directed against the Israeli and US hegemony in the region and the world.

Through a special reading of the organization's history, this book attempts to provide answers to the relevant questions that concern researchers of the Middle East. For example, how could Hezbollah enter into negotiations and dialogue with Lebanese, regional, and international groups and authorities with whom it apparently shares no common ground? What was the impact of this dialogue on the organization? What is the essence of Hezbollah's *muqawama* project? What mechanism has the organization used to establish it? And so forth.

This book continues the work of Hamid Dabashi on the boundaries of the "liberation theology" discourse worldwide and in the Middle East. It also examines the challenges, the barriers, and the opportunities that affected the development of Hezbollah as a potential embodiment of the *muqawama*, which pushes the East–West and Islam–West dualities toward a resistive discourse that crosses ideological and geographical borders both inside and outside Lebanon and the Middle East.

A Note on the Literature

Most of the first phase of the literature on Hezbollah was concerned primarily with its military capabilities rather than with its cultural and political activities. These studies apparently were influenced by the organization's early years in the Lebanese arena, during which its main purpose was military resistance to the Israeli occupation of southern Lebanon rather than to play a role in the intra-Lebanese political arena. This trend, however, changed after the liberation of the largest parts of southern Lebanon, and the change became more pronounced after the Lebanon War (or July War) in 2006.

Some of these early studies perceived Hezbollah as an organization influenced mainly by countries such as Syria and Iran because it either did not have an independent operational ability or had a limited one. The impact of the organization's early years and reference to Hezbollah's military capacities can be found in academic studies written in the 1980s and 1990s, such as Ranstrup Magnus's *Hizb'Allah in Lebanon: The Politics of Western Hostage Crisis* (1997),[2] which emphasizes the kidnapping of Western citizens during the Lebanese Civil War and the role of Hezbollah and its leaders in this regard.

Waddah Sharara's *Dawlat Hizballah: Lubnan, mujtam'an Islamiyan* (The State of Hezbollah: Lebanon, an Islamic Society),[3] published in 1996, is an important book that deals with the historical development of the Shi'ite society in Lebanon and broadly addresses and highlights the organization's plan to render Lebanon an Islamic society and to reproduce the Iranian experience in Lebanon. Sharara maintains that all the changes Hezbollah has undergone are only cosmetic ones, directed toward achieving its desired goal.

Other studies describe Hezbollah as a protest movement undergoing a process of reconciliation with Lebanese society. According to this approach, Hezbollah is remarkably distant from the radical dimension that had characterized it early on. It has moved into a more pragmatic phase, which has enabled it to integrate into the intra-Lebanese political game and become an ordinary political party.

Studies of this phase in Hezbollah's history include *Al-Islamiyun fi mujtama' ta'adudi* (The Islamists in a Multicultural Society), published in 2000 by the Iranian scholar Masoud Asad Allahi, and the study by Eitan Azani published in 2005, *Hezbollah: The Story of the Party of God: From Revolution to Institutionalization*.[4] This research perceives Hezbollah as a protest movement and examines the impact of the different Lebanese, regional, and international systems on the organization's establishment and development. It emphasizes the close relationship between Hezbollah and Iran, but it simultaneously demonstrates the decisive influence of intra-Lebanese events (such as the Civil War, the Ta'if Agreement, and so forth) and of other regional players (Syria, Israel) on Hezbollah's development and on its transition from radical revolutionism to pragmatism.

Hezbollah's development is depicted in the Lebanese scholar Ghassan 'Azi's book *Hezbollah: Min al-hilm al-idioloji . . . ila al-waqi'yya al-siyasiyya* (Hezbollah: From the Ideological Dream . . . to Political Pragmatism, 1998) and in Augustus Norton's book *Hezbollah: A Short History* (2007).[5]

In *Hezbollah: Politics and Religion* (2002), Amal Saʿd-Ghrayeb analyzes the development of Hezbollah's pragmatic attitudes and its ability to navigate, in a changing reality, between its Islamist ideological basis and the political pragmatism that has characterized its later stage. Saʿd-Ghrayeb foresees that Hezbollah will further emphasize its Lebanese patriotism and nationalism at the expense of its Islamist ideological foundations.[6]

One of the most important books that attempts to construct a general profile of Hezbollah is *In the Path of Hizbullah* (2004) by the Lebanese researcher Ahmad Nizar Hamzeh.[7] In it, Hamzeh outlines the organization's development, structure, and ideological-religious basis and emphasizes especially the relationship between Hezbollah and the Iranian religious leadership. He argues that Hezbollah is progressing toward establishing an Islamic state in Lebanon more quickly than expected. This prediction now seems to have been wrong; nevertheless, this has not diminished the book's value or Hamzeh's argument that Hezbollah serves as a role model to other organizations and movements in the Arab and Islamic world, mainly among the Palestinians.

Eyal Zisser allocates a considerable part of his book in Hebrew, *Lebanon: Dam bArzim* (Lebanon: Blood in the Cedars, 2009), to the discussion of Hezbollah's historical, ideological, and conceptual development, and he highlights the organization's forms of action within the intra-Lebanese political arena and its attempt to utilize and redirect its military achievements toward dominating and remodeling that arena.[8]

It is worth referring to Michael Milstein's monograph in Hebrew about the *muqawama*, Muqawama: *ʿAliyato shil itgar ha-hitnagdot vi hashbaʿato ʿal tfisat ha-bitahon ha-liʾumi shil Yisraʾil* (Muqawama: The Emergence of the Resistance Challenge and Its Influence on the Perception of Israeli National Security, 2009).[9] Milstein's research indeed refers to *muqawama* from an Israeli strategic-military perspective, but he addresses the uniqueness of the term in the Middle Eastern context and sketches the changes that the term has undergone over the years with the emergence of a "new resistance," which, according to Milstein, is more Islamist and fundamentalist. Milstein integrates into this category different parties that, in my opinion, should not be put together (for example, the mujahideen in Afghanistan and Hezbollah in Lebanon).

In the past few years, the Lebanese researcher Yousef al-Agha (a.k.a. Joseph Alagha) has written a number of books about Hezbollah and its ideological development. Two of them call for a specific mention here: *The Shifts in Hizbullah's Ideology: Religious Ideology, Political Ideology, and Political Program* (2006) and *Hizbullah's Identity Construction* (2011).[10] Al-Agha discusses the important contribution of resistance to the development of the organization's unique identity; however, he does not analyze the *muqawama* as a meeting point between the organization and other movements. Nor does he analyze it as the most important point for the organization (as I suggest in due course in this book) to enter into a process of negotiations and development of a joint political project with the different players in the Lebanese and regional arenas.

In their book *Rethinking Hizballah: Legitimacy, Authority, Violence* (2012), Samer Abboud and Benjamin Muller attempt to analyze Hezbollah in terms of international relations.[11] They challenge key elements of the presumptions present in the field of international relations, which they regard as a discipline dominated by a Western viewpoint that disregards the uniqueness and the contributions of Middle Eastern scholarship. They present the case of Hezbollah as a sort of challenge to the Weberian perception of the state monopoly over the use of force.

A more recent study, *Hezbollah: From Islamic Resistance to Government* (2016), by James Worrall, Simon Mabon, and Gurdon Clubb, attempts to provide a broader picture of Hezbollah's development toward openness and the complexity of its position in light of its involvement in Syria and given the Arab Spring, which started in Tunisia and spread to other places in the Arab world.[12] These researchers, who specialize in the study of terrorism and armed groups, put into perspective the reference to Hezbollah as a terrorist organization contra its transition to different methods and politics as a result of its enhanced self-confidence and its central position in intra-Lebanese, regional, and even international politics.

An important work by Rula Jurdi Abisaab and Malek Abisaab, *The Shi'ites of Lebanon: Modernism, Communism, and Hizbullah's Islamists* (2014), includes an attempt to trace the relational dialectics between the Shi'a in Lebanon and Iraq, on the one hand, and the Communist and leftist movements, on the other.[13] They maintain that the new modern movement of activist clergymen and the Communist movements and leftist organizations in both Iraq and southern Lebanon have mutually affected each other. They add that Shi'ite political Islam has not fully denounced the socialist revolutionary principles of the leftist movements, which are not completely secular and have not denounced religion. The movements' development process has been based somewhat on the Shi'ite culture and on popular perceptions and beliefs that relate the imams, especially 'Ali and Husayn, to revolutionism and activism aspiring to establish social justice worldwide.

In *Hezbollah: The Political Economy of Lebanon's Party of God* (2016), Joseph Daher attempts to offer a new Marxist analysis for the phenomenon of Hezbollah. Daher argues that Hezbollah and "Islamic movements in general . . . are neither revolutionary nor progressive groups, but are parties led by political interests that can be explained through a materialist approach, and not simply by a focus on ideology."[14] Although Daher's argument regarding the usage of a Marxist approach is correct, in my opinion he does not take all of the other variables at play into consideration. The mechanical equation between Hezbollah and the other Islamic movements is extremely problematic, as I show in this study.

In contrast to Daher, in terms of understanding Hezbollah's development from a "radical" phase to a new "Lebanonized" stage, Bashir Saade argues in *Hizbullah and the Politics of Remembrance: Writing the Lebanese Nation* (2016) that change has not affected Hezbollah's ideology, writing that "the politics of remembering has enabled Hizbullah to develop and to defend the main project to which it owes its existence: resistance against Israel." He adds that "Hizbullah has managed to negotiate its political presence in Lebanon and beyond through a thorough reworking of national narratives. In so doing, it has set new political frameworks within which Lebanese actors are to relate both to each other and to external enemies."[15]

Whereas Daher has ignored Hezbollah's ideological development, Saade's approach overlooks the economic and infrastructure dimensions of the party's "main project[,] to which it owes its existence." In contrast to Saade, I do believe that Hezbollah has gone through an important change in its political, economic, and even religious views. I illustrate later in the book, especially in chapters 4 and 5, the main changes that have moved the party from a small group into a vast movement at the core of a nascent "historical bloc."

Several studies have referred in particular to the organization's media image and strategies. Lina Khatib, Dina Matar, and Atef Alshaer examine in *The Hizbullah Phenomenon: Politics and Communication* (2014) the development of the organization's political strategy and the reflection of that political strategy in its communication strategy.[16] They place a special emphasis on the central position that the secretary-general occupies in the organization's communication strategy.

In *Channels of Resistance in Lebanon: Liberation, Propaganda, Hezbollah, and the Media* (2011), a study based on her doctoral thesis, Zahera Harb examines how Hezbollah's television channel al-Manar (the Beacon) surveyed the late period of the Israeli occupation of southern Lebanon between 1997 and 2000, comparing it to the Lebanese channel Télé Liban's coverage of the war in 1996 (or, as the Israelis called it, Operation Grapes of Wrath).[17]

Most of these more recent studies address in different ways the change that Hezbollah has been undergoing, while sharing the conclusion that Hezbollah has embarked on a process of rendering its radical positions more pragmatic. Yet, although examining Hezbollah's development, they still associate the *muqawama* concept with the organization's radical and military dimension, not with its intra-Lebanese activities relating to social, economic, educational, and other dimensions of the *muqawama* project, as I emphasize in this book. Studies that refer to these dimensions also subjugate them to the organization's supreme military goal.

These studies do not sufficiently highlight the cultural, historical, and social dimensions of Hezbollah's activism and do not refer to the hegemonic politics that Hezbollah is trying to bequeath to Lebanese society, sometimes successfully and sometimes less so. Most of these studies are limited to Iran's influence on Hezbollah and Hezbollah's military nature.

I argue that the Lebanese arena, which is replete with different streams and forces, affects Hezbollah's ability to reproduce the Iranian model in Lebanon. I also argue that the *muqawama* project, around which Hezbollah is trying to establish a historical bloc in Lebanon, is independent and cannot be controlled. This project is different from what most of the studies mentioned have depicted as the organization's original goal; it constitutes a new and relatively open arena that allows a deeper understanding of Hezbollah's development, at least in the past two decades.

Theoretical Framework

In this book, I suggest considering the term *muqawama* (resistance) as a signifier allowing the establishment of a historical bloc composed of various forces and articulating them into a new hegemonic project led by Hezbollah. This historical bloc comprises not only political parties and forces but also different social organizations and players, such as civil society organizations that serve large sectors beyond their "natural" target groups. It establishes a "*muqawama* society" that depends mainly (not merely) on poor or "oppressed" populations, which are the backbone of this counterhegemonic project.

I refer to "hegemony" as a nonfinal and a nonclosed project. It is a mode of thinking, organization, and life perception in a given society. A certain hegemonic project would nevertheless include within it its own culture a worldview that unites different social groups; a common language that reflects and molds the different social groups, movements, and political parties; and institutions that consolidate and design the nascent hegemony.

Hegemony and Other Theoretical Concepts

The concept of hegemony first emerged in the Russian socialist philosophy in the late nineteenth and early twentieth centuries following the social democratic movement debate on the ability of the proletariat—still too weak and numerically limited—to lead the awaited revolution when capitalism was still in its infancy. The debate also concerned the role that the proletariat should play in the struggle to establish a liberal democratic regime that would constitute a basis for the proletarian and socialist revolution, according to Marxist orthodoxy.[18]

The debate generated two main responses. The orthodox response, supported by Georgy Plekhanov, was that each social class was responsible for fulfilling a specific role. The bourgeoisie had to lead the democratic revolution against the imperial authority. The proletariat then had to assume responsibility for the next stage (the socialist revolution), take over the reins of leadership in the country, leaving the bourgeoisie behind, and establish the socialist phase of human development.

In contrast, Vladimir Lenin's response referred to the concept of hegemony as a socialist strategy. Lenin opined that the proletariat should fulfill a dual historical role through a representative political party. It should replace the weakened Russian bourgeoisie and lead the democratic revolution that the people of the Russian Empire had longed for. Then it would be able to pursue its revolution and reach the socialist stage.

Lenin assigned the proletariat an unprecedented role that had not existed previously in Marxist orthodoxy; however, as both a socialist philosopher and strategist, he was fully conscious of this class's numerical weakness in Russia. He believed that in order for the proletariat to fulfill its assigned role, the struggle should move from the economic dimension to a political one. It should recruit the masses in order to gain the support of the majority and then represent that majority, who would rebel against both exploitation and the country that enslaved its "people."[19]

Lenin believed that the main revolutionary subject was the proletariat; however, he also believed that the proletariat should align with the peasantry, become a "hegemonic" party in this alliance, and lead the "people" in their revolution against the Russian czarist absolutism.[20] Lenin believed that another force existed in the transition to the political dimension, which comprised various possible alliances between different social classes.

The Gramscian Approach

The Italian philosopher Antonio Gramsci is most associated with the concept of hegemony and its transformation from a tactic into a means of comprehending contemporary society's historical development. Imprisoned during the fascist period (1922–43), Gramsci (d. 1937) wrote his famous "prison notebooks," a series of thirty-three notebooks in which he analyzed the reasons behind the collapse and failure of the revolutionary movement in Italy especially and in western Europe generally. In these notebooks, Gramsci developed his own concept of hegemony. Through this concept, one could analyze the existing capitalist structure and the methods of action that the social class seeking hegemony within the society should adopt.

Gramsci's notion of hegemony has numerous innovations. The main innovation is the transformation of hegemony from a strategy of the proletariat, as suggested by Lenin, into a tool that allows comprehension and analysis of the capitalist state and its mechanisms, mainly in the "West."[21] According to Gramsci, hegemony is both a state and a process. Hegemony can emerge in both state institutions and civil society and by means of the process of struggle of the "historical bloc" comprising different forces.

Blitzkrieg versus Trench Warfare. According to Gramsci, czarist Russia was a centralist state in which the czar and the ruling group held all the power. In 1917, the Russian government had become totally isolated and used force and violence to exert control. Thus, the revolutionary movement could easily attack the czar's palace to deliver a fatal blow to the czarist regime. Gramsci named this tactic "blitzkrieg." In contrast, the Western countries were more developed than czarist Russia and had a more complex state structure composed of the standard state institutions as well as a diverse and complex civil society in which the bourgeois hegemony was also instilled, or, as Gramsci stated:

> At least in the case of the most advanced states . . . "civil society" has become a very complex structure and one which is resistant to the catastrophic "incursion" of the immediate economic element (crises, depressions, etc.). The superstructure of civil society is like the trench-systems of modern warfare. In war it would sometimes happen that a fierce artillery attack seemed to have destroyed the enemy's entire defensive system, whereas in fact it had only destroyed the outer perimeter.[22]

Therefore, the revolutionary strategy in the more-developed countries required a "trench warfare"—in the sense that the struggle of the proletariat and its political representative would be long lasting—so that they could organize a "historical bloc" that would lead the struggle. This tactic would enable gradual control over all positions to instill the alternative proletarian hegemony in the society. According to Gwyn Williams in his classic essay on Gramsci's concept of hegemony, a project becomes hegemonic when its "concept of reality is diffused throughout society in all its institutional and private manifestations, informing with its spirit all taste, morality, customs, religious and political principles, and all social relations, particularly in their intellectual and moral connotation."[23]

The Historical Bloc. According to Gramsci, the main revolutionary subject was not the social class but the historical bloc. He borrowed this term from the French philosopher George Sorel, the father of revolutionary syndicalism, who attempted, with others in the late nineteenth and early twentieth centuries, to understand "why the socialist revolutions [were] hindered from spreading in the world."[24] Sorel moved the focus from the social classes to the "blocs" that develop around a given myth. He chose the *general strike* as the myth that consolidates the historical bloc in its constant war against bourgeois decadence and culture.

Gramsci combined Sorel's "bloc" with Lenin's "hegemony" and uniquely presented the "historical bloc" as the active subject in contemporary human history. According to Gramsci, the historical bloc forms when different social groups unite around a hegemonic project and is the force behind the project. The historical bloc is a dialectic concept in that it embodies the interaction between its different components in the goal of achieving unity at a broader scale.[25]

According to Gramsci, the social class that leads the historical bloc is dynamic; it goes through a process of mutual influence with the other parties and the other subordinate groups in the same bloc. Hence, the historical bloc is not the sum of its parts; rather, it is a new synthesis. Here lies the major innovation suggested by Gramsci: in contrast to the orthodox Marxists before him, he did not consider the social class as the ultimate subject but rather the historical bloc made up not only of social classes and political parties but also of social movements and different subordinate groups.[26]

Gramsci moved the focus from the economic to the ethical, cultural, and political. He explained that the intellectuals should lead the "general will" of the historical bloc. An intellectual and ethical leadership would formulate a more exalted synthesis, which the ideology would help to transform into an organizational mortar that would consolidate a historical bloc. Gramsci defined the intellectual not just as a pursuer of truth;

he maintained that a "social group, coming into existence on the original terrain of an essential function in the world of economic production, create[s] together with itself, organically, one or more strata of intellectuals which give it homogeneity and an awareness of its own function not only in the economic but also in the social and political fields."[27]

Organic intellectuals are therefore a historical product associated with the emergence of new social groups. Gramsci considered these intellectuals integral to the hegemonic project and as its main architects, alongside the crowd taking part in the joint historical bloc. Moreover, he maintained that in the modern era one does not refer to the individual intellectual but rather to the collective intellectual, as in a political party, a newspaper editorial team, or a university.[28] This clarification matches Gramsci's distinction that in the modern era one does not refer to the Machiavellian prince but rather to the "new prince": "The modern prince, the myth-prince, cannot be a real person, a concrete individual. It can only be an organism, a complex element of society in which a collective will, which has already been recognized and has to some extent asserted itself in action, begins to take concrete form."[29]

Gramsci designated a major place for the intellectuals in the formation and design of the historical bloc and in disseminating its worldview and transforming it into a collective popular-national will.

By moving the focus from the economic to the ethical and political dimensions of society, Gramsci highlighted that the social class needs to be "leading" before its rise to power. He even deemed leading a prerequisite to the rise to power: "A class is dominant in two ways, namely it is 'leading' and 'dominant.' It leads the allied classes, it dominates the opposing classes. Therefore, a class can (and must) 'lead' even before assuming power." He added that "there can and there must be a 'political hegemony' even before assuming government power, and in order to exercise political leadership or hegemony one must not count solely on the power and material force that is given by government."[30]

The social class can establish its leadership so that it can integrate into the debate and synthesis not only other social classes but also different groups in society. Together, they should build and enhance a common popular-national will around which more forces will gather to occupy the hegemonic position of power, not only in civil society but also in the political realm.[31] Gramsci accentuated a leadership that helps the masses to express, deepen, and strengthen their self-engagement in sociopolitical transformation.[32]

A hegemonic social group is thus one that succeeds in leading the popular, national, and patriotic struggles for the purpose of attaining leadership at the national level and not just within the historical bloc.[33]

Although Gramsci's understanding of hegemony is the foundation of my analysis of Hezbollah, I also use a reading of his main ideas developed by Ernesto Laclau and Chantal Mouffe.[34] Laclau and Mouffe attempted to liberate the Gramscian concept of hegemony from its class essentialism and to instill in it more recent insights provided by critical and poststructuralist theories.

From Laclau and Mouffe's perspective, a subject's position is not determined by a single axis (for example, the class axis, according to the Marxist tradition). Instead, other axes—such as ethnicity, gender, nationality, class—can define a subject's position. For a collective subject (a historical bloc) to be built, a process of articulation is needed. Articulation means that relationships between the different social groups are not a necessary consequence of a common essence but rather of a praxis and a political struggle leading to different consequences: "Any practice establishing a relation among elements such that their identity is modified as a result of the articulatory practice."[35] Laclau and Mouffe perceive hegemony as a special kind of articulation.

According to Laclau and Mouffe, the state of hegemony is changeable and dynamic and enables different sorts of connectedness to emerge. It also allows a society to stabilize around a hegemonic project that enhances a historical bloc, which develops contingently through a process of political struggle. The historical bloc from this perspective is not supposed to develop around a sole predetermined axis of struggle; rather, it can emerge despite the presence of different axes of struggle, according the political praxis that characterizes every society. A certain historical bloc occurs through the building of a "chain of equivalences," perceived by Laclau and Mouffe as a mechanism that allows linkage between different meanings of the same signifier, thus connecting between the needs and/or demands and/or worldviews of different social groups.[36] As demonstrated in this book, the *muqawama* is the model of such a signifier.

Hegemony in This Book

Researchers who have rediscovered the Gramscian approach and its relevance to the Middle East have recently discussed the question whether Gramsci's theoretical development can be applied beyond both the European countries and the context of the early twentieth century. In the introduction to their collected volume *The Postcolonial Gramsci*, Neelam Srivastava and Baidik Bhattacharya emphasize that the Gramscian analysis served as a basis for the development of Edward Said's theory of Orientalism and for the emergence of the subaltern studies that have prevailed in South America, India, and elsewhere.[37]

Thomas Butko has made an interesting attempt to analyze political Islam using Gramscian tools by comparing Islamic intellectuals—such as Hassan al-Banna, Abul Ala Maududi, Sayyid Qutb, and Ruhollah Khomeini—and Gramsci.[38] A prominent weak point in Butko's analysis is his perception that the Islamist ideology could be a unifying ideology of the historical bloc that would replace the existing hegemony. However, the Gramscian notion of building such a hegemonic project emphasizes that the leading group must be open to joint negotiations and articulation with other forces so that together they can create a broader and new general will. The intellectuals discussed by Butko were not so open to such a project.

Although certain Islamist movements' ability to lead a historical bloc that promotes a particular hegemonic project should not be negated, to do so these movements should either detach themselves from their "religious essentialism" or undermine it and attach themselves to another signifier, such as the *muqawama*, around which they can build the desired counterhegemonic project.

In due course, I demonstrate how the *muqawama* has become a signifier that has enabled the establishment of a historical bloc comprising different forces that maintains its own counterhegemonic project. I hereby refer to the will of one group—Hezbollah—to consolidate Lebanese society in particular and the region in general around the resistance as a watershed between the different projects in Lebanon and the whole region. Moreover, from the perspective of Hezbollah and the other forces that constitute this nascent historical bloc, the *muqawama* is an essence, a culture, and a worldview. Through it, the social, political, economic, and religious arena of Lebanon and the whole region can be redefined.

The development of Lebanese history can be understood more explicitly if one adopts the perspective of hegemonic action and struggles. Within this arena, the socioeconomic dimension is one of several axes that unite competing hegemonic historical blocs and projects, while the sectarian-religious and social democratic axes also intersect and separate at different historical points.

My use of hegemonic politics as a tool for analyzing Lebanese politics and history suggests a new understanding of the popular slogan "Lebanon's strength lies in its weakness." Until the Arab Spring, Lebanon had been the weakest state in the Middle East according to the Weberian notion of the state and the site where hegemonic politics developed and succeeded in subjugating the citizens (probably owing to the state's weakness).

Given its diverse centers of power and multiple players, on the one hand, and its developed civil society (that is, developed relative to the other Middle Eastern states), on the other hand, the Lebanese state has facilitated hegemonic politics. It requires the political-social player to integrate into alliances and continuous negotiations with other groups. The political social player's aims are to attain control, broaden its impact, and to take over more positions in the long-term "trench warfare," not through the "blitzkrieg" that is more common in other Middle Eastern states, where the civil societies are not well developed and power is concentrated in the hands of the ruler.

Division of Chapters

In the first chapter, I focus on the development of the *muqawama* concept worldwide but particularly in the Middle Eastern context. The concepts I refer to in this chapter include jihad, *istishhad*, *fida'*, *sumud*, *muman'a*, and, of course, *muqawama*. I also conduct a historical review of the development of *muqawama* in Palestine before moving on to Lebanon, the focus of the book.

The second chapter conducts a historical review of Lebanon. The uniqueness of this chapter lies in the use of Gramscian perspectives in the attempt to understand the history of Lebanon. In addition to the historical, social, and political review, I attempt to draw the history of Lebanon as one of hegemonic projects that dominated Lebanon at the political and conceptual levels throughout the decades immediately following the establishment of the Lebanese state in the early 1940s up until the collapse of the first hegemonic project, the "project of merchants and bankers." The review of this first project includes an economic, social, and symbolic analysis and refers to, inter alia, the ideas of two intellectuals leading this project, Michel Chiha and Charles Corm. This part of chapter 2 ends with an analysis of the reasons behind the collapse of the merchants and bankers' hegemony and of the hegemony headed by the Maronite elite, which led to a bloody civil war.

I then move to a brief review of the historical roots of Hezbollah in Lebanon and to the history of Shi'ites in Lebanon, especially within the dominant hegemony in Lebanon. At the end of chapter 2, I briefly review the personal history of young clergymen who started to flourish among the Lebanese Shi'a from the late 1960s to the early 1970s and who would later become the organic intellectuals who established and led Hezbollah and the organization's hegemonic project.

The third chapter analyzes the conceptual basis on which Hezbollah's young leadership developed. In this chapter, I chose five outstanding intellectuals of the political Shi'a from the twentieth century who laid out the ideas on which Hezbollah is based: Muhammad Baqir al-Sadr, Ayatollah Ruhollah Khomeini, 'Ali Shari'ati, Musa al-Sadr, and Muhammad Husayn Fadlallah.

In this third chapter, I review and analyze some of the writings of these intellectuals, highlighting the breaking point between their philosophy and that of the classical Twelver Shi'a, which placed a special emphasis on the *taqiyya*, concealment of the twelfth imam, and on distance from direct political activism as long as he is concealed. I also refer to the convergence and divergence points between these intellectuals' thought and that of other secular, socialist, and revolutionary movements of the Third World.

In the fourth chapter, using the concepts and history developed in the preceding chapters, I examine the main components of Hezbollah's *muqawama* project in Lebanon. I argue that this project has three main layers that have undergone changes in the same way that Hezbollah itself has transformed: the religious layer and the revolutionary-resistive interpretation of Shi'a Islam; Lebanese and Arab nationalism, in addition to its relations to and perceptions of Lebanese religious pluralism; and the socioeconomic layer as well as economic and status-based social positions.

In the fifth chapter, I review the mechanisms for the dissemination of Hezbollah's alternative hegemonic project. To achieve this goal, I review the books that Hezbollah has published as well as the educational system, youth movements, novels, TV channels, press, social media, internet sites, and even computer and internet games it disseminates to implement its *muqawama* project among the public in Lebanon and the region. At the end of this chapter, I take a look at the organization's current secretary-general, Hassan Nasrallah. Through what Nasrallah has said at various times over many years, I present the organization's development since the early 1980s up to the second decade of the twenty-first century and the organization's transition from a state of introversion to a state of extroversion in which it has established an alternative hegemonic project that is integrated in the debate and the negotiations with other parties in the Lebanese arena.

In the conclusion, I attempt to combine all of the book's main insights. I also address the impact of recent events, especially the Syrian Civil War and Hezbollah's involvement in it in alignment with the ruling regime, on the progress or the disintegration of Hezbollah's *muqawama* project inside and outside Lebanon.

1

The Essence of *Muqawama*

Language, according to Antonio Gramsci, is among the most important arenas in which the hegemonic project develops. He maintains that "every language represents an integral conception of the world and not simply a piece of clothing that can fit indifferently as form over any content."[1] In their neo-Gramscian processing of the hegemonic project, Ernesto Laclau and Chantal Mouffe maintain that the historical bloc around which a certain hegemonic project is established develops by a "chain of equivalences" that link demands, definitions, and identities. They interpret the "chain of equivalences" as a mechanism that connects between the different meanings of the same signifier, thus allowing a connection between the needs, demands, and worldviews of different social groups.[2]

In this chapter, I trace the history of the current formation of the *muqawama* signifier that developed in the Middle East arena and its continuous interaction with other signifiers deriving from the same semantic field, which serves as a conscious and symbolic basis for the historical bloc that established the hegemonic project. I also examine the concepts of jihad, *istishhad*, *fida'*, *muman'a*, and, ultimately, *muqawama*.

Jihad

The word *jihad* derives from the Arabic root ج.ه.د. According to the encyclopedic dictionary *Lisan al-'Arab* (Dictionary of the Tongue of the Arabs), its meaning is *juhd*—that is, "effort," "activity," or "diligence."[3] A *mujahid* is a person who makes or invests in efforts. Another word derived from the same root is *mujtahid*—an Islamic cleric who works diligently on the interpretation of the Shari'a, the Qur'an, and the words of God. Jihad is an action, mostly military, that targets the infidels—those who do not follow the words of God. Therefore, jihad makes all possible effort to elevate the words of God and enhance the prestige of Islam. Some Western authors and Orientalists have translated the term *jihad* as "holy war," but this translation is very problematic,[4] as I demonstrate later.

Jihad in Islam

The term *jihad* has been used since the times of Prophet Muhammad. The wars that the Prophet declared or fought were considered jihad because they aimed to expand the boundaries of the Islamic state and subsequently the Islamic empire and to protect the state or empire from hostile attacks.[5] Thus, the use of the term *jihad* to denote the fight against infidels and the expansion of Dar al-Islam (the House of Islam) has lasted for centuries. However, the practice of jihad has changed over the different historical periods given the controversies and the arguments that the Islamic empire has witnessed since the eighth century CE.

With the rise of the Western colonial empires such as Britain and France, the defensive and resistive meaning of *jihad* gained an additional momentum owing to the thinkers who proposed reformist approaches to *fiqh* (Islamic jurisprudence), such as Jamal al-Din al-Afghani in the nineteenth century. He emphasized that a state of peace and harmony is the natural condition that should prevail between Islamic states and the other religions, but Muslims are forced into the defensive jihad because of European colonialism.[6] He prepared the ground for legitimizing the resistive operation against colonialism throughout the Islamic world.

In the 1950s and the 1960s, different Islamic thinkers, such as Sayyid Qutb in Egypt and al-Maududi in Pakistan, developed a more radical and modernist perception of jihad.[7] This perception was based on the writings of Ibn Taymiyyah dating back to the fourteenth century, who had issued fatwas (religious rulings) permitting Muslims to rebel against their leader. These fatwas also enabled Muslims to deem their leader an infidel and to declare jihad against him if he did not implement the Shari'a properly in the state.[8] Al-Maududi and Sayyid Qutb updated these fatwas and adapted them to the twentieth century. They founded the newest version of Islamic and jihadist fundamentalism in the Sunni world. To remove the last barrier standing in the face of jihad against a

Muslim leader in a Muslim state, such as Egypt, modernist jihadists took the extreme step of declaring that these leaders were infidels even though they were Muslims.[9]

A significant difference exists between the Shi'ite and the Orthodox Sunni movements in the perception and practice of jihad. The Sunni Muslims continue using jihad to describe the Islamic wars against the infidels, giving these wars a religious-jihadist form even when Muslims initiated them. However, the Shi'ite 'ulama' (religious scholars) have been extremely prudent in their use of the term. They allow the declaration of jihad only if the Muslims are led by the Prophet Muhammad or by one of the twelve infallible imams, who are considered the legitimate leaders of the Islamic *umma* (nation). Because the twelfth imam, Imam al-Mahdi, is a "hidden imam," the Shi'ites maintain that Muslims are not allowed to declare jihad.[10]

This is the position of the Shi'ite 'ulama' pertaining to the conservative Akhbari school of the Shi'ite *fiqh*. In contrast, the interpretations associated with the 'ulama' of the Usuli school emphasize *ijtihad al-'ulama'*. According to this interpretation, the ban on declaring jihad in the absence of the hidden imam applies only to offensive jihad. Those who follow the Usuli school maintain that Muslims are obliged to defend themselves and to declare defensive jihad when the Islamic *umma* or land is endangered or attacked by external forces.[11] This position is important for the Islamist-Shi'ite interpretation of *muqawama* in the late twentieth century, as I demonstrate later.

Al-Jihad al-Akbar *versus* al-Jihad al-Asghar

The meaning of the concept of jihad in the Islamic tradition is not limited to war. The 'ulama' refer repeatedly, in accordance with their goals, to the Prophet's hadith (his words, actions, and habits) when he welcomed the Muslim warriors upon their return from invasions (*ghazwa*): "'A great welcome awaits those who terminated the lesser jihad and are looking forward towards the greater jihad.' When asked about the greater jihad, Prophet Muhammad answered: 'It is the jihad of man against himself.'"[12]

The main idea behind *al-jihad al-akbar* (the greater jihad) is that every Muslim has to invest in himself or herself, to control his or her desires, and to attempt to defeat the satanic forces hidden within himself or herself. From the ʻulama'ʼs perspective, this form of jihad is a prerequisite for undertaking *al-jihad al-asghar* (the lesser jihad), in which weapons and swords are used.[13]

Istishhad

The only terms in the history of Islam whose emotional baggage approximates that of the term *jihad* are *shahid*, *istishhad*, and the other words deriving from the root ش.ه.د. The original meanings of the words derived from this root are associated with seeing and witnessing. To be a *shahid* means to be a witness, and "al-Shahid" is one of the many names of God in Islam, which means that God is the witness of humans' deeds.[14] However, the term *shahid* also means "he who dies for God's sake."[15] In later periods, the term has also been applied to the one who dies for the sake of the homeland or for a certain ideology.

The term *shahid* appears fifty-five times in the Qur'an, though in different variations. It refers mostly to God; in other places, it refers to his messengers (in particular the Prophet Muhammad and Jesus), to believers, and once even to infidels. In most instances, it means "witness," not "holy martyr."[16]

The use of the term *shahid* in the sense of a person who dies for God's sake derives from the hadith rather than from the Qur'an, as in "no man would enter heaven and aspire to leave it except for the *shahid*, who strives to re-die for God's sake ten times after he knows how elevated his status is in heaven" (Muslim, Asaheeh). The perception of the *shahid* as a holy martyr has been based on various interpretations; for example, it is thought that a *shahid* sides with God in favor of justice and truth until he is killed.[17] This use of the term brings to mind the use of the Greek term *martyr* in early Christianity, which means "witness" in Greek and is used in a similar sense of holy death in Christianity.[18]

The terms *shahid* and *shahada* have a special connotation within Shiʻa Islam, relating to the "*istishhad* al-Husayn," the martyrdom of Husayn. Husayn, the third imam in the Shiʻa faith and the grandson of the Prophet Muhammad, is referred to in Shiʻite parlance as *sayyid al-shuhada'* (master of martyrs). The Shiʻites organize annual memorials and *ta'zeya* (condolence rites) in mosques and *husayniyat* (special buildings that are designated for this purpose) to commemorate the massacre of Husayn and his family at Karbala' by Yazid, the Umayyad caliph.

According to the Shi'a faith, the other imams in history died as *shuhada'* (martyrs), except for the twelfth imam, the hidden imam. The Shi'ite ideology has transformed *shahada* into a way of life; they believe that *al-shuhada'* establish a continuity and a connection with the different imams and prophets.[19]

The use of the term *shahid* to describe those killed for the sake of the homeland and not only for God is a significant and central overlapping point between different Islamic forces, such as Hezbollah, and the nationalist or patriotic forces in the Arab world generally and in Lebanon particularly.

Fida'

The word *fida'* means "the salvation or the ransoming of a prisoner."[20] The Qur'an includes the verse "and We ransomed him with a great sacrifice" (Sura Assafat, verse 107), in which God refers to the cancellation of the sacrifice of Ismail, the son of Abraham, and the substitution of a lamb.

Later, the term *fida'i* became a synonym of *mujahid*. In the dictionary *Al-mu'jam al-wasit* (The Intermediate Lexicon), it is interpreted as follows: "He [the *fida'i*] is the *mujahid* for the sake of Allah or the homeland and sacrifices himself for this cause."[21] However, when the title "al-Fadi" (the Savior) is used in Arabic, it refers to Jesus, who is deemed the savior of all believers from the original sin.

The Palestinian resistance and armed struggle from the 1960s to the 1980s appropriated the term *fida'i* to refer to those who sacrifice themselves for the sake of the homeland. On the one hand, this term has a stronger nationalist and patriotic connotation than *mujahid*. On the other hand, having Muslim and Christian religious roots, it was suitable for the Palestinian unity embodied in the *fida'yin* movement. In 1972, the executive committee of the Palestine Liberation Organization (PLO) decided to adopt the hymn "Fida'i" as the Palestinian national hymn. This initiative highlights the significance of the term and its symbolism in the history of the Palestinian people.[22]

Sumud

The gerund *sumud* derives from the root ص.م.د. Nouns derived from the same root include *samd*, "the thick soil" or the highest place on a piece of land (although not as high as a mountain);[23] *samda*, a rock that is deeply rooted in the ground;[24] and *mismad*, the strong female camel that can endure hunger and thirst.[25] The metaphoric meaning of *sumud* is "steadfastness in the face of the enemies" or "endurance in the confrontation of a counterforce."

The term *sumud* gained its political meaning, emotional load, and strong connotation of passive resistance following the war of 1948 and the Palestinian Nakba (Catastrophe). As defined by Helena Lindholm-Schulz, "the concept of '*Sumud*' has gone far beyond a rhetorical embellishment and has become a strategy of survival and even an organizational policy."[26] Palestinians who remained in their lands within Israel following the end of the war in 1948 employed the term mainly as a political strategy and goal. Given the new state's unquestionable military superiority, the Palestinians became destitute under Israeli rule. As part of a largely displaced nation, they lacked a unified and strong political leadership. In response, the new leadership that emerged among Palestinians in Israel, especially the Communist Party of Israel, emphasized among the Arab population the refusal of the submissive narrative adopted by members of the traditional Palestinian leadership inside Israel. The *sumud* narrative was a sort of compromise or a walk on a tightrope by the Palestinian population that remained in Israel between their desire to remain faithful to their people and their continuous struggle to gain their civil rights in the new state.

Palestinians in the West Bank and Gaza Strip adopted a similar strategy following the Israeli occupation in 1967. To avoid the trauma of 1948, when the Palestinians were driven out of their lands and became refugees, they decided at the beginning of the occupation to adopt a strategy of *sumud*, passive resistance. This resistance "related to the land and agriculture as well as [to] indigenousness. The ideal image of the Palestinian was the *fellah*, the peasant, who stayed put on his land and refused to leave."[27] This strategy added another dimension—along with the *fida'i* who was involved in the active and military *muqawama* in his place of residence—to the perception of the Palestinian resistance.

Upon the Israeli occupation of southern Lebanon, the strategy of *sumud* was approved by Shi'a clergy, including Ayatollah Muhammad Husayn Fadlallah and Muhammad Mahdi Shamseddine, who had also perceived it as a passive resistance that the residents of southern Lebanon should adopt in the face of the Israeli military presence on their land.[28] *Sumud* provided a supportive and comfortable ground for the development of a more active resistance in the area.

Muman'a

The noun *muman'a* derives from the root م.ن.ع. The verb *man'a*, which comes from the same root, means "to prevent someone from obtaining something,"[29] and *al-mana'a* means "immunity against diseases."[30] The phrase *qal'a mani'a* can be translated as "a fortress that cannot be invaded or reached";[31] and the adjective *mumani'* means "opponent."

The concept of *muman'a* emerged from these meanings. A relatively new political concept, it was established by the Syrian leadership in the 1990s after the collapse of the Soviet Union, which was Syria's strongest and main ally during the Cold War. *Muman'a* is passive resistance and steadfastness against the pressures exerted by the strong forces operating in the international arena, such as the United States and Israel. Boycott or rebellion against the New World Order, whose dominant force is the United States, is included in the interpretation of this concept.[32] With the passage of time, the official representatives of Syria sought to connect the term with the *muqawama* forces, who adopt active resistance strategies, and simultaneously to highlight the role of Syria in the *muqawama* forces' activities.[33] From their perspective, Syria's uniqueness "lies in its ability to maintain its status as a radical anti-Israeli base . . . that does not conform to the American position and is not moving toward the normalization of relations with Israel."[34] In this sense, Syria is a sort of a *mumani'a*, a logistical home front for the resistance, the *muqawama*.

However, when Hezbollah's current deputy secretary-general Sheikh Na'im Qasim interprets the *muqawama*, he divides it into two stages or historic periods: in the first stage, the aim is liberation from the Israeli occupation, and the second stage moves on to the *muman'a*.[35] In other words, Sheikh Qasim maintains that the *muman'a* is another phase in the *muqawama* project, which aims not only at defeating the present occupation forces but also at standing steadfast in the face of the strongest global force—namely, Western imperialism led by the United States. Upon dividing the *muqawama* project into phases, Hezbollah's deputy secretary-general introduced into the global equation other forces, apart from Iran and Syria, that are in the vanguard of the *muman'a* axis in the region: Hugo Chávez's Venezuela, Communist Cuba, North Korea, and other countries and forces whose unity is based on their opposition to US foreign policy.

Muqawama

Unlike the concepts of jihad and *istishhad*, the concept of *muqawama* does not have roots in Islamic history, nor does it appear in the Qur'an. The root of the word *muqawama* is ق.و.م. Words that derive from this root have different meanings. The word *qiyam*, for example, means "standing up"; "resurrection, adherence, and preservation of something"; and "the confrontation of enemies to prevent them from achieving their goal."[36] *Muqawama* means "resistance."

The idea of *muqawama* did not exist as a political idea before the twentieth century. Even when the reformist Sheikh Jamal al-Din al-Afghani wrote on colonialism in the nineteenth century, he used the term *muqawama* in its technical sense—that is, closer to "material-natural resistance" rather than as a political concept with broader cultural connotations and meanings.[37] Al-Afghani instead used the term *nuhud*, which also refers to "standing up" and "resurrection"; and in the period of al-Afghani's writings, one of the direct connotations of *nuhud* was al-Nahda (the Renaissance) in Europe and later in other regions of the world. As a reformist cleric and one of the Islamic renaissance leaders, Al-Afghani suggested that the colonized nations, especially those in the Islamic world, could not achieve real renaissance (*nahda*) without *nuhud*, confronting and terminating colonialism.

Al-Afghani introduced different examples of nations that had confronted powerful colonialism and defeated it—among them, the colonists in what became the United States who confronted British colonialism as well as the Greeks, Serbs, Romanians, and Bulgarians who confronted Ottoman colonialism, even though they were small nations facing a tremendous force. In the latter example, a humanistic and universalistic position is noticeable, with al-Afghani sympathetically describing the *nuhud* of the Greeks and Serbs against the (Muslim) Ottoman colonialism of the late nineteenth century.[38]

When al-Afghani referred to the Islamic nations, he added the concept of jihad to the mechanical concept of the *muqawama* (which in his usage is not backed by a comprehensive perception of a *muqawama* society, nurtured by its culture) and to the broader concept of *nuhud*. He interpreted jihad as *muqawama* and *nuhud* against all the colonial forces—in other words, he applied the defensive interpretation of jihad.

Michael Milstein maintains that the term *resistance* emerged during World War II as a collective attribute of the clandestine organizations that operated in Europe against the Nazi forces.[39] These organizations contained different groups from France, the Balkans, and the Soviet Union. Because of this historical background, in all languages the term *resistance* has the positive connotation of a struggle to achieve national liberation against rampant colonial forces—a positive connotation that has led to the universal legitimacy of the *muqawama* concept versus other concepts originating in the Islamic world.

Milstein outlines the geographic journey of the term *resistance*. He indicates that the Algerian National Liberation Front, which was founded in the mid-1950s and struggled against French colonialism, was the main agent of the transition of *muqawama* (as a political term) from Europe into the North African arena and then into the Middle East.[40] Mu'een Ahmad Mahmoud also associates the roots of the *muqawama* and the operations of the *fida'yin* in the Middle East with World War II, after which the Algerian Revolution and the Vietcong forces in South Vietnam appropriated the concept of resistance. The concept subsequently reached the Palestinian organizations, which began operating in an organized way in the mid-1960s.[41]

Mahmoud, Milstein, and others agree that the establishment of the *muqawama* concept in the Middle East is the outcome of propaganda efforts by the Palestinian factions. Israel's defeat of the Arab regimes in the Six-Day War in 1967 and their subsequent weakening enabled the Palestinian factions to free themselves to a certain extent from official Arab domination, which further enhanced the *muqawama* concept associated with their activism.

The Resistance in Palestine

For decades, Palestine has been deemed the watershed case in which resistance forces differed from collaborators and from those who reconciled with the colonial forces in the region. Although *muqawama*, both as a concept and as a culture, did not develop in Palestine and is not unique to Palestine, no other nations have practiced *muqawama* for so long. Therefore, the development of the concept in Palestine and among Palestinian actors in the Middle East is uniquely important.

The Great Revolt, 1936–1939

Although the conflict over the control of Mandatory Palestine did not start in the 1930s, the Great Revolt (or "the revolution," in Palestinians' discourse) was undoubtedly an important landmark in the history of consolidating the Palestinian nation and a resistive national Palestinian identity.

The Great Revolt in Palestine erupted on April 15, 1936, when two Jews were killed by Arab Palestinians. Although the murder was apparently committed from criminal rather than national motives, it sparked violence, which turned into a comprehensive Arab rebellion joined by thousands of Arab Palestinians from all social backgrounds and geographical areas.[42] The revolt started with a general strike in the Arab areas of Mandatory Palestine, and its expansion to the port of Jaffa was a severe blow for the mandatory authorities. Al-Lajna al-Qawmiyya (National Committee) was established to coordinate the movements of the Palestinian masses in the strike and to formulate the main national demands being made by the Arab Palestinian people.[43]

That period witnessed the emergence of new groups of rebels who attacked the British forces and sometimes Jewish forces and settlements.

One of the rebellion's leaders was Sheikh 'Izz al-Din al-Qassam. The Marxist-Palestinian historian Emile Touma does not disregard the religious characteristics of these groups but at the same time indicates that they were more progressive than the traditional Palestinian leadership of that time in that they directed their operations mainly toward the British and depended more on popular forces, the lower social classes, and the Palestinian peasants than on urban landowners and effendis.[44]

It is worth emphasizing the persistent use of the term *jihad* to describe the Palestinian rebels' operations during the revolt; in addition, the groups of Palestinian rebels and the two hundred Syrian fighters who arrived in Palestine to take part in the revolt were called *mujahidun*.[45] Moreover, Palestinian leaders who were exiled to Damascus established a body called al-Lajna al-Markaziya lil-Jihad al-Watani fi Falastin (Central Committee for the National Jihad in Palestine).[46] Historians from different streams agree on the religious dimension of the revolt; however, the term *jihad* also obtained a national dimension (although nationalism had not yet matured), as reflected in the inclusion of the word *watani* (national) in the committee's name and in the consideration of the "establishment of an independent secular Arab state" in Mandatory Palestine as the main goal for all political operations conducted by the Palestinians during these early years.[47]

The Great Revolt was an important landmark in the development of the Palestinian people's self-consciousness, and it symbolized the national and social discontent among the poor classes and the peasants regarding the submissive approach taken by the urban Palestinian leadership, who were funded mainly by the British. The *mujahidin*'s revulsion toward the urban culture was also reflected in the expansion of the revolt outside the big cities, to the villages, and in the transformation of the peasant and the traditional *kuffiyyah* (scarf) into the main symbols of the nascent Palestinian nationalism. Many years later, upon the emergence of the Palestinian national movement in exile, the *kuffiyyah* became anew the main symbol of the Palestinians' national resistance.

The brutal suppression of the Great Revolt, the people's exhaustion, and the rifts that occurred between the different Palestinian forces and parties brought the rebellion to an end, with 15,000 Palestinians wounded, 5,600 detained, and 5,000 dead.

The Arab–Israeli War of 1948: The Arab Regimes' First Failure

The most significant political developments in Palestine occurred at the end of 1947 and the beginning of 1948, when the British declared their intention to leave Mandatory Palestine. Both the Palestinians and the Jews found themselves obliged to deal with the new reality of facing one another without any other force between them.

Following the United Nations' Partition Plan adopted in 1947, which aimed to create independent Arab and Jewish states and to internationalize Jerusalem and Bethlehem, Arab military operations, like those conducted during the Great Revolt a decade earlier, commenced. Although the local Arab population had neither unified armed forces nor an organized army at that time, the mufti Hajj Amin al-Husayni declared the establishment of Jaysh al-Jihad al-Muqaddas (Army of the Holy Jihad), which comprised approximately five thousand volunteers. The Arab countries for their part declared the establishment of the Jaysh al-Inqadh (Arab Liberation Army), which comprised three to four thousand volunteers led by Fawzi al-Qawuqji,[48] the Syrian officer who had also commanded the volunteer forces during the 1936–39 Arab revolt in Palestine.

The Arab armies joined the war just before David Ben-Gurion declared the establishment of the State of Israel. Diverse literature points to the coordination forged between King Abdullah of Transjordan, head of the Arab armies' unified command, and the Zionist movement. Most war efforts were first led by the Palestinian *fallahin* (peasants), who initiated unorganized resistance operations in each village to withstand the organized attacks by the Hagana forces and other Zionist military organizations. Again, the peasants called the resisters the *mujahidin*, thereby strengthening the national resistive connotation of the word generated during the Arab revolt in Palestine.

During the Arab–Israeli War of 1948, many disagreements occurred between the Palestinians and the volunteers of Jaysh al-Inqadh and the Arab armies. Some volunteers despised the Palestinians and regarded them as uncivilized peasants,[49] and this disdain contributed to the development of a Palestinian national distrust of the Arab regimes.

Within a short period, the Palestinians became refugees as 800,000 out of 950,000 Palestinians living within what became the new State of Israel fled or were expelled outside the borders, a reality that shaped anew the politics and the history of the Middle East. In addition to the Palestinians who became refugees outside their homeland, some became refugees when they left their villages even though they did not leave the boundaries of the new state, and others remained in their villages. Although each village has its own story, our main concern here is the development of a new perception of *muqawama*. This perception, also called *sumud*, has become a unique type of resistance—the steadfast determination to remain in the motherland and to develop Palestinian nationalism.

The Arab Palestinians in Israel

Upon the signing of the cease-fire agreements between Israel and the Arab countries in 1949, approximately 156,000 Palestinians remained within the boundaries of Israel. Once a majority in Mandate Palestine, the Palestinians now became a minority not considered an integral part of the state. Although they remained in their homeland, they were defeated as they lacked a national leadership and were devoid of real forces or urban centers. In addition, it was not guaranteed that they could stay in the new state. Indeed, about one-sixth of the Palestinians who remained in Israel were internal refugees—individuals and families who were not allowed to return to the places of residence from which they were displaced.[50]

The Palestinians who remained in Israel suffered from double marginalization in comparison to the exiled Palestinians. The new state had no time or interest to take care of the "enemies" who remained in its boundaries. When Israel realized that it had to deal with them sooner or later, its main goal was to prevent them from rejoining its external enemies; thus, for two decades Arab areas and towns in Israel were subjected to martial law, which imprisoned people in their homes. The Palestinian citizens of Israel were not allowed to leave their villages without the approval of each region's military governor.[51] The Palestinians who were expelled from the new state were dispersed throughout different Arab countries, and others stayed on their lands in the Gaza Strip under Egyptian control and in the West Bank under King Abdullah and then King Hussein of Jordan.

Over the years, it became apparent that the Palestinians' remaining in Israel contributed to the development of a new aspect of Palestinian nationalism. The idealization of this choice occurred coincidentally with the formation of the term *baqa'* (survival) and the more loaded concept of *sumud*, which added to the term *baqa'* an active dimension, the "political awareness of a nation," and the accentuation of the popular stratum's or the peasants' aspect of the Palestinian national identity.

There is no doubt that the Communist Party of Israel, which replaced the traditional leadership of the Palestinian population over the years, played a major role in enhancing the motif of *sumud* among the Palestinian minority in Israel. The leadership of the Communist Party was politically obliged to maneuver between two main axes that formed the identity of the Palestinian minority in Israel: being an integral part of the Palestinian Arab people and becoming (or struggling to become) part of Israeli civic experience. *Sumud* was the formula that merged these two extremes within the Palestinian experience, with a leftist discourse reflecting the challenges faced by the Palestinian peasants who remained in Israel to fight the injustice practiced against them.

The principle of *sumud* appeared not only in the political platform of the Communist Party but also in the *adab al-muqawama fi Falastin al-muhtalla*, the resistance literature in Occupied Palestine, as described by the exiled Palestinian author Ghassan Kanafani. Examples of this literature are the stories of Emile Habibi and the poems of Tawfiq Zayyad, Samih al-Qasim, and Mahmoud Darwish (who immigrated to Beirut in the 1970s and joined the PLO).

The *sumud* narrative began with an incident in Nazareth on Israel's tenth anniversary. On May 1, 1958, Communist Party activists clashed with police and security forces, while the traditional leadership of the Palestinian population participated in Israel's tenth anniversary to "show the world that the Palestinians live happily and enjoy democracy in Israel."[52] Tawfiq Kanaaneh, a Communist activist who was sentenced to a four-year prison term for participating in this demonstration, wrote in his autobiography that the Communist Party activists and their friends employed slogans demanding the end of martial law and recognition of the rights of the Palestinian minority in Israel.[53]

The act of *sumud* reached its culmination on Land Day, which started with a general strike on March 30, 1976, to protest against the confiscation of lands belonging to Palestinians in Galilee: "The stand of the Arab population against the government and the first 'Land Day,' organized in 1976, was a crossroad between the minority and the majority. . . . On the basis of a proper analysis of the changing socioeconomic reality, the Communist Party estimated that the mid-1970s created the circumstances needed for changing the protest techniques. The essence of this change was the transition from the stage of relative passivity to a stage of vigorous political activism."[54] This activism did not turn into an armed *muqawama*, however, for the Palestinian citizens still wanted to achieve their civil rights in Israel while at the same time to remain part of the Palestinian people.

Sumud as a political narrative and a component of Palestinian identity also appeared in other places, such as the West Bank and the Gaza Strip, which were occupied by Israel following the Six-Day War. In these cases, most Palestinians' choice not to leave their lands and become refugees was perceived as a lesson learned from the national trauma of the Nakba as "the ideal Palestinian became the peasant, the farmer who stayed home and refused to leave."[55] The *samidun* (pl., "the steadfast") endured the humiliations of the occupier and adhered to their lands—a bitter lesson learned from the Arab–Israeli War of 1948 and the Nakba.

The Six-Day War: The Arab Regimes' Second Failure

If the Palestinians had expectations of the Arab regimes, those expectations were shattered following the Six-Day War, also known as al-Naksa (the Setback) among Arabs. Within six days, the Israeli army succeeded in defeating the Egyptian, Jordanian, and Syrian armies and in occupying the Golan Heights, Sinai, and the rest of the territories that had been part of Mandatory Palestine.

This event created a dramatic historical change in the region. Yazid Sayigh indicates that the Naksa created opposing trends in the Arab world: although the Israeli army strike subdued the Arab regimes' attitude toward Israel, the new occupation further complicated the Middle Eastern conflict and reduced the possibility of reaching peace agreements in the region.[56] Baruch Kimmerling and Joel Migdal claim that the Israeli–Palestinian conflict now donned the same features it had before the end of the British Mandate—a struggle between two communities, each claiming ownership of the same land.[57]

Either way, the Palestinians returned to live under the same regime for the first time since 1948. More importantly, the war demonstrated anew the inability of the Arab regimes (some of which were republics) to liberate Palestine and return the Palestinian refugees to the lands from which they were displaced or expelled. As a consequence of this failure, Palestinian underground and resistive organization intensified. The Six-Day War not only was a tremendous strike against the Arab regimes but also damaged the concept of Arab unity and the realization of a comprehensive Arab nationalism, which had originated with the Egyptian leader Gamal Abdel Nasser. These conditions prepared the arena for a renewed blossoming of Palestinian nationalism.

The main symbol of the new nationalism was the figure of the *fida'i*. The revolutionary generation began establishing armed resistance organizations that were inspired by the revolutionaries of the Third World, such as Che Guevara, Ho Chi Minh, and Mao Zedong, and mainly by the achievements of the Algerian National Liberation Front.[58]

Muqawama *as an Alternative*

The Palestinian organizations formed in the mid–twentieth century were divided into two major movements. The first movement believed in the Arab nationalism as a platform for the liberation of Palestine and was part of the *harakat al-qawmiyun al-Arab*, Arab nationalist movement, which led to the development of different movements and parties in Arab countries (in Palestine, it gave rise mainly to al-Jabha al-Sha'biyya li-Tahrir Falastin [Popular Front for the Liberation of Palestine] and, at a later stage, al-Jabha al-Dimuqratiyya li-Tahrir Falstin [Democratic Front for the Liberation of Palestine]). Palestinian activists in this Arab nationalist movement believed that the way to Tel Aviv passed through the capitals of the Arab countries and through the unification of the Arab world into one political entity. It was obvious that this movement was greatly influenced by Nasser's rise to power.[59]

Activists of the second movement, which started in the mid-1960s, believed that in the equation of Arab unity and the liberation of Palestine, the latter should precede the former. The young core members who led this movement, which became a central power among the Palestinians, believed that they could not rely on the Arab regimes to solve the Palestinian issue.[60] These youth, including Yasser Arafat, Khalil al-Wazir, Salah Khalaf, and Mahmoud Abbas, formed the leadership of the Palestinian people and generated a renewed Palestinian nationalism based on the ethos of resistance and armed struggle.

Undoubtedly, the defeat of the Arab regimes in the Six-Day War indirectly benefitted the Fatah movement (its name coming from the reverse acronym of Harakat al-Tahrir al-Watani al-Filastini, or Palestinian National Liberation Movement) established in the late 1950s and early 1960s. The first postwar armed conflict between Fatah members and Jordanian soldiers and the Israeli army at the Israeli–Jordanian border eventually created the symbol of the new Palestinian (and Arab) resister, the *muqawim*, who became the only hope after Israel's crucial strike against the Arab armies. Known as the Battle of al-Karama (Battle of Honor), this battle was the starting point of restoring the Arab honor that had been lost with the Six-Day War.

Fatah, which formed the core of the Palestinian National Liberation Movement, was considerably influenced by the revolutionary terminology that began to spread in the Third World in this period, from Vietnam in the East to Cuba and Latin America in the West, with a central resistance base in Algeria. But at that time Fatah stood apart from the other resistance movements, mainly the leftist ones, that had started to develop among the Palestinian refugees in the refugee camps and in the West Bank. Fatah was greatly influenced by the relationships between some of its members, especially Yasser Arafat, and the Muslim Brotherhood in Egypt (some Fatah members were even part of the brotherhood), developed mainly during the *muqawama* operations in the Gaza Strip and the Suez Canal zone between 1950 and 1954.[61] As opposed to the different movements by which it was inspired, Fatah tried to revive the figure of the

Palestinian rebel and *mujahid* of the 1936–39 Arab revolt in Mandatory Palestine, during which the new Palestinian nationalism developed.

The various elements that influenced Fatah's identity are manifested in its announcement on January 1, 1965, of its first military operation: "After relying on Allah and since we believe in our right to struggle for regaining our land, and in the sacred Jihad, and in the Arab revolutionary forces from the Atlantic Ocean to the Gulf and in the support provided by the free and virtuous people around the world, one of our Action force units conducted an operation in the Occupied Territories on the night of December 31, 1964."[62]

In this first announcement of the first Palestinian *muqawama* movement after the Nakba, jihad is clearly perceived as a major motif borrowed from Islamic culture, wherein the national sense of jihad acquired during the 1936–39 revolt is revived. Yet additional axes around which the main Palestinian resistance movement developed can also be identified in this statement. The first was Palestinian independence, to which Fatah aspired; according to the announcement, the movement's military activism was based on the Palestinians' national right "to struggle for regaining our land" and not on Arab nationalism. The second axis of Palestinian *muqawama* was the connection between Islamic history reflected in the use of the term *jihad* and the new revolutionary forces all over the world.

This connection was considerably affected by the relationships forged between the leaderships of Fatah and Algeria, which had gained independence a few years earlier in 1962 following a persistent struggle against the French colonial regime. Fatah was aware of the great potential revealed in the independent operations of the Algerian resistance and of the appropriation of the *muqawama* concept as a strategy for reminding the whole world in general and the Europeans in particular of the European resistance and guerilla movements that struggled against the German Nazi occupation during World War II. For Fatah, it was a conscious and planned strategy: the foreword to one edition of the journal *Filastinuna* (Our Palestine) published by Fatah made a direct comparison between the resistance to the tragedy of the Palestinians' marginalization and Europeans' resistance to the Nazi occupation.[63]

Fatah was not the only movement that cultivated the *muqawama* strategy within the framework of the renewed Palestinian nationalism. The Popular Front for the Liberation of Palestine, the Democratic Front for the Liberation of Palestine, and other organizations and movements perceived *muqawama* as the only effective way of revitalizing the Palestinian people and regaining their lost homeland. In its establishment statement in 1967, the Popular Front indicated that "the armed *muqawama* is the only effective way that cannot be avoided by the masses in order to confront the Zionist enemy. . . . These masses are the essence and the leaders of *al-muqawama*, and through this means they can eventually achieve success."[64]

Whereas Fatah was influenced mainly by the Algerian *muqawama* and tried to combine the Palestinian national–Islamic history with the national revolutionism of the Third World, the leftist Palestinian movements received their main inspiration and support from the different resistance movements that operated in the Third World, such as Vietnam, Cuba, and China, but did not attach importance to Islamic history or rhetoric.

Fatah was clearly different from the other resistance movements in its interpretation of the concepts of *muqawama* and *thawra* (revolution). Fatah used both terms mainly in their national sense and perceived itself as a national liberation movement that could not discuss the revolution in its class-based and Marxist form as long as a political state in which a natural class-based society could form was lacking. Fatah believed that just as Arab unity could be achieved only after the liberation of Palestine, class-based issues and revolutions could be relevant only after a real state were established in the liberated homeland.[65] In contrast, the other resistance movements and fronts used the concept of *thawra* in its Marxist sense—or, at least, they believed so. They thought that the Palestinian *muqawama* movement pioneered the revolutionary movements in the Arab world and that they should cooperate with these revolutionary forces to start class-based revolutions in the Arab countries, mainly those neighboring Israel, in order to bring about the liberation of Palestine.

2

The Shattered Hegemony and the Beginning of Hezbollah

This chapter outlines the main features of Lebanon and its sociopolitical history as arenas which have decisively contributed to the consolidation of the unique *muqawama* project in its current form as represented by Hezbollah. To achieve this, I refer to the centrality of the Maronite elites in the establishment of Lebanon and the formation of a hegemonic project—"the merchants' and bankers' republic"—that lasted for decades thereafter. I also refer to the marginal position that Shi'ites occupied for many decades in Lebanese history. Then I move on to a brief review of the historical roots of Hezbollah in Lebanon and to the history of Shi'ites within the dominant state of hegemony in Lebanon at its very beginning.

Lebanon: A Historical, Social, and Political Background

Lebanon developed its Christian character during Ottoman rule, the emirates period, and through the establishment of "Greater Lebanon" in 1920 under the French Mandate, which enhanced the Christian Maronite dominance. The ruling and economic elite for many years was the Christian elite, dominated by the Maronites. Therefore, Lebanese identity, from its beginning up to the Civil War in 1975, had a clear Maronite character.[1]

France aimed to establish a political entity loyal to French interests in the region.[2] Therefore, for many years it invested much effort in fostering economic relationships; in fact, the French investments in Syria and Lebanon before World War II reached two hundred million French francs, a hundred million of that allocated to Mount Lebanon and Beirut.[3] It also fostered religious and cultural relationships with the Maronites and leaders of other religious groups in Lebanon—that is, in the region destined to be the Lebanese state.

The declaration of "Greater Lebanon" was not necessarily the only means of satisfying the Maronite elite's requirement of establishing a state that would constitute a national home for the Maronite community. Part of the Maronite elite led by advocate Émile Eddé, president of the state under the French Mandate, were in favor of a state established in a smaller area but with more stability at the sectarian level and with a clear Maronite dominance. What they had in mind was Mount Lebanon or the Ottoman Mutasarrifate, where Maronites constituted a majority of 58 percent and 80 percent when combined with the other Christian communities living there. But the total percentage of Christians in Greater Lebanon dropped to 54 percent, with the Maronites constituting only 29 percent of the new state's population.[4] The decline in the percentage of Christians in the new homeland did not stop with the expansion of the borders but continued with the passage of time due to demographic changes, immigration, and high fertility rates among Muslim communities, as reflected in the population census of 1932 (the last to be conducted until today), which showed that the percentage of Christians had declined to about 50 percent.[5]

In addition to its Maronite Christian character, Lebanon was shaped by the Greater Lebanon concept. Greater Lebanon included all the regions that were historically ruled by Emirs Fakhr al-Din ibn M'aan (d. 1633) and Bashir II (d. 1840), the mythological fathers of the Lebanese state, whose emirates extended from Beirut and Mount Lebanon to Tripoli and 'Akkar in the North, the Biqa' Valley in the East, and Jabal 'Amel in the South.[6] These regions were crucial for providing the new state with the vital economic and geopolitical conditions for survival. Indeed, immediately following Lebanon's independence, these regions provided 83 percent of the taxes, and the taxes were invested mainly in Mount Lebanon.[7]

The new state also depended on an alliance between the Maronite elite, led by Bechara al-Khoury, the first president of Lebanon, and the Sunni elite composed of merchants and leaders from the coastal cities, represented by Riad al-Solh; together, they built the foundations for the establishment and survival of the Lebanese state. This alliance was the basis of the three-decade hegemonic project that prevailed in Lebanon during both turbulent and peaceful times from its independence until the Civil War.

This hegemonic project had two main layers: the distributive/socioeconomic layer and the conscious/symbolic one. It was characterized by radical liberalism at the economic/commercial level, in which all intervention by the state in regularizing the free market, especially foreign trade, was rejected and a minimalistic state was especially emphasized. As Michel Chiha, the businessman and the organic intellectual of the "merchants republic," explained the liberal state, "We need measured laws and a management that is solely concerned with basic needs: minimum procedures that are regulated by law, maximum opportunities and open horizons."[8]

Two prominent ideologists, Michel Chiha and Charles Corm, formed the ideological backbones of the hegemonic project in Lebanon. Each adopted in his own way the ethos that served as the basis for this project: Lebanon was the heir of the Phoenicians and a nation of merchants and bankers, the "Switzerland of the East." Through this conscious/symbolic axis, Chiha, Corm, and others greatly succeeded in linking the (imagined) history of the Lebanese people with the present and in articulating the distributive/socioeconomic dimension by means of the conscious/symbolic dimension of the same project. This articulation was made by the organic intellectuals of the ruling group (the merchants and bankers) within the historical bloc that created the hegemonic project. These intellectuals relied on parties (such as al-Hizb al-Dusturi, the Constitutional Party), associations (such as al-Finiqyun al-Judod, or New Phoenicians), newspapers (such as *al-Hayat* [Life]), as well as individuals to enhance the dominance of their hegemonic project.

It is worth noting that the historical bloc whose center was occupied by merchants and bankers, especially in Beirut and the other coastal cities, also included subordinate groups such as the Maronite and Sunni middle class. These groups developed simultaneously with the advancement of trade in Lebanon. Landowners and feudal chiefs, especially those of the Shi'ite community in the South, were also integrated into the hegemonic project by being allowed to maintain their status quo in their communities and by being assigned undisputed ruling positions. Furthermore, a minimalistic state was supported at the social and economic levels, with nonintervention in internal politics, intracommunal relations (in the South and the Biqa'), and a minimal share in the ruling regime at the national level.

The Project's Conscious Layer: The Ideological Basis of the Merchants' Republic

The main perception of Lebanon in the first years following its establishment as an independent state concerned its uniqueness. This perception was based on the idea that Lebanon was the "Phoenicia" of modern times, that the Lebanese people had "a global message to the human race," like that of the Phoenicians thousands of years ago, and that trade was an integral part of Lebanese identity, constituting a bridge between nations and especially between East and West.

According to the prevailing national perception, Lebanon was not merely the Phoenicia of modern times but also the "Switzerland of the East" because it was a small country neighboring larger ones and had both economic competences and an intensely evolving banking sector—the natural result of a tremendous development in trade. Hence, the natural alliance between the commercial and financial bourgeoisies rendered Lebanon one of the major financial crossroads in the world. This status was further enhanced by the ultraliberal economic perceptions and beliefs adopted by Lebanese economic and political elites,[9] in contrast to the socialist and semisocialist positions taken in adjacent countries such as Syria, Nasserite Egypt, and Iraq after the revolution of 1958.

These ultraliberal perceptions derived from the unique history of the Lebanese elites, especially the Maronites. It was also a result of the historical development of Mount Lebanon and the coastal cities since the nineteenth century. This unique history includes the development and enhancement of trade between Mount Lebanon and Europe, France in particular, as well as the latter's great investment in Beirut and Mount Lebanon. Equally important was the emergence of a Lebanese bourgeoisie largely dependent on its relationships with the Western empires, who were competitively eager to gain greater power in the Ottoman Empire.[10]

The supporters of the popular-national belief that Lebanon was the Switzerland of the East compared the Swiss pluralism to the Lebanese religious pluralism and the beautiful mountainous landscape of Switzerland to that of Lebanon. The transformation of Lebanon into a first-class tourist destination, replete with ski resorts, helped foster this image.[11]

Chiha and Corm were two organic intellectuals of the ruling groups in Lebanon in the first decades following its independence, and each fostered the Phoenician, Swiss, and Mediterranean ethos. Both were members of the "Phoenician alliance," an association of intellectuals, in particular Maronite bourgeoisie from Beirut, who wanted to detach Lebanon from its Arab history and establish a new-old national identity based on the ancient Phoenicians.

Charles Corm was born in 1894 to a Lebanese bourgeois family. He believed that the Lebanese people were descendants of ancient Phoenicians and that they had a global mission to fulfill and a global message to disseminate. In 1934, at the age of forty, Corm abandoned his commercial affairs to dedicate himself fully to his cultural and ideological affairs, aiming to channel his energies into disseminating the Phoenician doctrine in Lebanon.[12] He established the New Phoenicians, an association of Maronite bourgeois intellectuals, who published the "Phoenician periodical" in order to segregate Lebanon from the surrounding Arab countries and to emphasize the uniqueness of the Lebanese identity.[13] Corm wrote his articles and poetry in French and avoided using Arabic in order to emphasize the differences between the Lebanese people and the neighboring Arab world. He perceived Lebanon's future as that of a state with a solid Christian and Maronite majority. In theory, Lebanon would be multireligious, but in practice the Maronites would be dominant in the state not only because of their numerical and cultural superiority but also because of their unique relationship with France in particular and with Europe in general.[14]

Corm believed that the greatness of the Lebanese people as descendants of the ancient Phoenicians was related not to the Phoenicians' military power but to their intellectual power—the vividness and appeal of their exceptional culture.[15] Like the Phoenicians who brought light to the world through the introduction of a written alphabet, their Lebanese descendants had also been assigned a cultural message they should disseminate to the whole world—this was the mission of the Lebanese people, according to Corm and his peers. The New Phoenicians praised the immigration of the Lebanese people to every corner of the world. Unlike other intellectuals who criticized emigration, Corm and his peers deemed these journeys as an integral part of the dissemination of the Lebanese message and of the adventurous and free Lebanese spirit and as one step toward the spread of genuine religious beliefs.[16]

The most influential figure in the formulation and establishment of the intellectual and ideological infrastructure of Lebanon between independence and the Civil War was Michel Chiha. He had great influence on Lebanese history and the national Lebanese perception, which constituted the conceptual basis for the hegemonic project prevailing in Lebanon for three decades. Chiha was a typical example of the organic intellectual of his social group in the transformation of the project from theory into practice.

Michel Chiha was born in 1891 to a Catholic bourgeois family. He studied at Saint Joseph University in Beirut, which, alongside the American University in Beirut, was a leading university in Lebanon. These two institutions were among the hegemonic mechanisms (as Gramsci defined them) that produced a group of intellectuals who maintained the hegemonic project that dominated Lebanon for decades. Chiha was one of the owners of the Phar'on-Chiha Bank (Banque Pharaon & Chiha), which his father established with the in-laws. Owing to his familial and occupational background, Chiha thus represented the central social class leading the historical bloc toward the establishment of the first Lebanese Republic. This background molded his ideology and thus the basis for the Lebanese Constitution that he formulated with other experts. Chiha was a businessman, a politician, a thinker, a journalist, and a poet.

Unlike Corm, Chiha did not believe that the Lebanese people were the direct descendants of the Phoenicians but rather simply the heirs of Phoenician culture, for they lived in the same geographical area that the Phoenicians lived in and were therefore inspired by the Phoenicians' cultural and economic spirit.[17] Chiha's thinking included a clearly geographical determinist dimension; he believed in the crucial influence of geographical location on people and on their perceptions and missions. Chiha fostered the Lebanese people's special attitude toward the Phoenicians in order to develop a unique Lebanese national identity.[18]

The Mediterranean identity played a major role in Chiha's ideological perception. Chiha, a businessman, a merchant, and the representative of the businessmen and merchants' class in Lebanon, believed that Lebanon's geographical location dictated its fate as a merchants' country open to the whole world—especially the Western part of world. This openness was not limited to trade but also included cultures and ideologies. Lebanon, which embodied the myth of the merchants' country and revived the Phoenician era, was an open country that inherently believed in freedom and liberalism in the exchange of goods, ideas, cultures, and services.[19] Or, as Chiha himself stated, "Lebanon would survive not only by trading goods and services, but also by exchanging ideas; and this would be achieved only through freedom of thought and pluralism."[20]

This openness was also reflected in Chiha's attitude of containment—that is, the need to maintain a special relation—with regard to neighboring Arab countries and the Arab world in general, as opposed to Corm, who attempted to detach Lebanon from the Arab world and from its Arab history. Chiha, who saw Lebanon's trade potential and the role it could play as a bridge connecting East and West, encouraged and legitimized the establishment of special relationships between Lebanon and the Arab world.[21] With his brother-in-law Bechara al-Khoury, the first postindependence president of Lebanon,[22] he agreed that Lebanon had an "Arab face." This perception was indicated in the Lebanese National Pact and in the historical compromise between the Christian (especially Maronite) bourgeoisie and the Sunni merchants and bourgeoisie, represented at that time by Riad al-Solh, who later became the first prime minister of Lebanon after its independence.

Chiha believed in the ability to guarantee Christian dominance within the Christian–Sunni bourgeois alliance not through an external French intervention but rather through a constitution that both groups of elites agreed upon and that would preserve the essential interests of all Lebanese sects' elites.[23]

The New Phoenician ideology and the comparison whereby Lebanon was the "Switzerland of the East" had considerable impact on the ideological infrastructure of independent Lebanon—or, as it was called by different scholars, the First Republic of Lebanon, the republic of merchants and bankers. Beginning in the mid-1970s, the blood-soaked Civil

War, however, led to the shattering of the Lebanese model suggested by Charles Corm, Michel Chiha, and others. Yet for a better understanding of Lebanese history and the hegemony that prevailed in Lebanon for a few decades, light should be shed on the socioeconomic background that served as a basis for the emergence of the Lebanese national perception suggested by Corm and Chiha.

The Republic of Merchants and Bankers: Phoenicia and the Switzerland of the East

The "New Phoenicia" and "Switzerland of the East" comparisons did more than accentuate the cultural aspect of Lebanon as perceived by the elites and generally believed among the Lebanese people inside and outside the country. They also described the economic structure of the new Lebanese state—a state founded on two economic bases. The first was that Lebanon was a country of commerce and a bridge between the industrial West and the East, which was a source of raw materials, especially the petroleum of Persian Gulf Arab states, which appeared in the international arena as a major source of energy in the first half of the twentieth century. The second base was the fact that Lebanon underwent a major change in its economic structure and became one of the most influential centers of banking, capital trading, and stock exchange in the Middle East and the whole world.

Lebanon was a capitalist-liberal island in the semisocialist sea of the neighboring Arab countries, especially Syria. The Lebanese historian Philip K. Hitti described well the uniqueness of Lebanon in those years, and in the spirit of the times he wrote the following paragraph in his book *Lubnan fi al-tarikh* (Lebanon in History):

> As opposed to Syria, Lebanon is a state of commerce and transit between East and West. Lebanon is a state of merchants who are not very different from their Phoenician ancestors. Therefore, Lebanon has from ancient times favored free trade, and the policy of free trade is the basis for its prosperity and wealth, for Lebanon is a small country, located on an aerial and terrestrial crossroad between East and West and between North and South. As Lebanon is not rich with natural resources—if we do not include the magnificent landscape, the beautiful climate, the strategic location and the expertise, intelligence, and diligence of its

merchants—Lebanon is indeed founded on its being an agent of export, import, and distribution in international trade.[24]

In the very first years following its independence in 1943, Lebanon went through an accelerated process of economic progress and prosperity. It also underwent another significant process in which it replaced its longtime political guardian France with the United States of America, the emerging Great Power after World War II.[25]

Different scholars maintain that the accelerated progress of Lebanon's liberal and capitalist economy was enhanced by several key factors.[26]

The huge financial investments the Allies made in Lebanon during World War II led to capital accumulation in Lebanon, rendering it the country with the highest per capita income among all Arab countries.[27]

The Lebanese economic system "profited" from the Palestinian Nakba (Catastrophe) and the establishment of the State of Israel by inheriting the former economic position of Palestine and its ports, especially the Port of Haifa.[28] Lebanon also absorbed middle- and upper-class Palestinian refugees with a capital of fifty million Palestinian pounds,[29] in addition to 120,000 Palestinian refugees. Although the latter were deemed a heavy economic burden for Lebanon, they nevertheless constituted a cheap, skilled, and educated labor force.[30]

The customs union between Lebanon and Syria was cancelled, and Lebanese merchants were freed from their "Big Sister's" (i.e., Syria's) tendency to raise taxes and customs in order to protect local merchants and industries against the free global tendency of the Lebanese bourgeoisie, who supported a more liberal approach and favored the enhancement of relationships with Western countries.

Lebanon benefitted from an additional regional element: the discovery of enormous oil reserves in the Gulf states, the gradual flow of oil money into the region, and the role assigned to Lebanon as a mediator and agent for Arab countries vis-à-vis industrialized Western countries.[31] All this made a great contribution to the development of the banking sector in Lebanon and to the absorption of Gulf states' capital by this sector—a consequence of Lebanon's readiness and advanced economic and financial system, in contrast to other countries in the region. The significant impact of Gulf states' money on the development of the banking sector in Lebanon is reflected in the increase in the number of banks in Lebanon from nine in 1945 to ninety-three in 1966.[32]

In the 1950s and upon the adoption of the Nasserite semisocialist approach in certain Arab countries, such as Syria and Iraq, Lebanon benefitted from the subsequent emigration of wealthy people from those countries. They found refuge in Lebanon, known for its radical economic-liberal nature and its democratic ambiance relative to the other countries in the region.[33]

These factors, alongside others, accelerated economic progress in Lebanon and constituted a sort of socioeconomic infrastructure for the conscious axis of the Lebanese bourgeoisie's hegemonic project. The Lebanese economy developed at a rate of 7 percent in the 1950s and 6 percent in the 1960s and early 1970s. Yet it was clear that this development was dependent mainly on the services sector, which grew at a tremendous pace, as opposed to the manufacturing sectors, agriculture and industry. The number of workers in the latter sectors also changed accordingly. In 1957, 68 percent of the labor force was integrated in different manufacturing sectors, mainly agriculture, but this rate dropped to 44 percent in 1970. In contrast, the rate of workers in the services sector increased from 32 percent in 1957 to 56 percent in 1970.[34] This increase corresponded with the conscious decision made by the Lebanese state's leadership after independence to highlight the need to build Lebanon as a service economy and as a commercial and financial crossing point[35] and thus to realize the ethos of Lebanon as the "Switzerland of the East" and the New Phoenicia. In fact, it is probably this ethos that reinforced the ruling group's policies and interests rather than the other way round.

However, Lebanon's immense progress and growth, known at that time as "an economic miracle," did not benefit all the Lebanese people. Wealth was concentrated in the hands of thirty families who constituted a sort of oligarchy that aggressively controlled the state, syphoning into their bank accounts most of the income generated by the ultraliberal Lebanese economy for which they had advocated.[36]

These families and many others accumulated their wealth through three main resources. The first was the prosperous silk economy, at the center of which Lebanon remained during the Mutasarrifate period. The second was the profits that these families accumulated during World War II, especially between 1940 and 1944, when the Allies issued 76 million pounds sterling in Syria and Lebanon. The third was the massive wealth accumulated by family members who immigrated to West Africa, the Americas, and the Arab states of the Persian Gulf.[37] The wealth of fifteen of these families was estimated at 245 million Lebanese pounds, nine times the Treasury of the Lebanese state in 1949.[38]

Within the groups constituting the historical bloc that led the hegemonic project of Lebanon in the mid–twentieth century, a hierarchical structure was established, headed by the commercial bourgeoisie, which always had the upper hand in all tensions and controversies with the industrial bourgeoisie. For instance, in the late 1940s and early 1950s the industrial bourgeoisie sought to raise the rate of customs in order to protect local industries from imported industries, but the commercial bourgeoisie fought to prevent such a procedure. The scale eventually tipped in favor of the merchants after they received support from the Lebanese government and officials, thus reinforcing the ethos of the "bankers and merchants' republic."[39]

All Lebanese people were not equally advantaged by the economic well-being and the abundance of money in the country at the time, however. These resources were concentrated in specific sectors, in specific geographical areas, and among certain classes. Beirut and Mount Lebanon witnessed the most impressive prosperity and benefitted the most from this economic growth. The growth led to internal (and external) migration within Lebanon, and Beirut attracted larger numbers of Lebanese workers and residents from the marginalized areas in the South, the Biqa', and the North, leading to an increase in Beirut's population from 50 percent of the whole country in 1959 to more than 61 percent in 1970.[40]

This mass movement from the Lebanese periphery to the capital city caused tremendous social and economic challenges for the Lebanese state. The internal migration to Beirut created a "poverty belt" in the city's suburbs and surrounding areas that included Lebanese residents from all areas and religions as well as the Palestinian refugees in the camps of Tel al-Za'tar eastward and of Sabra, Shatila, and Bourj al-Barajneh westward.[41]

Amid this turmoil, the changes that occurred among the Shiʿite community were particularly interesting.

The Shiʿite community was mostly rural, dominated by traditional leaders and landowners. It was partially integrated in the hegemonic project to guarantee "industrial calmness" in the periphery, while patron–client relationships with the Shiʿite peasants were established in the Biqaʿ and southern Lebanon. In the 1970s, the Shiʿite community settled in urban areas, mainly in Beirut's southern suburbs; and following a long process that started in the early 1970s, its members began to liberate themselves from the control mechanism practiced by traditional leaders in rural areas,[42] a self-liberation that contributed to the disintegration of the hegemonic project initiated in the peripheries.

These social and demographic changes started to undermine the hegemonic project that had prevailed for three decades. The economic alterations within Lebanon and the regional developments outside it (such as the defeat of the Arab states in the Six-Day War in 1967; the events of Black September, which led to the movement of PLO and the Palestinian factions from Jordan to Lebanon; and the Israeli reprisals against the Palestinian resistance bases and against civilians in southern Lebanon) were extremely challenging for the merchant republic and the national Lebanese perception.

Sectarianism in Lebanon was a very effective tool for religious leaders and chiefs. It helped them preserve their hegemony and that of the Lebanese elites, merchants, bankers, and landowners under the veil of the progressive Lebanese, the "Swiss" of the Middle East and the open-minded Phoenician, all of whom benefitted from the free market's profits that had permeated different parts of Lebanon. However, sectarianism soon exploded in the elites' face. The free and wild market economy continued to concentrate the profits of economic prosperity in the hands of a small group of elites and their cronies, and these elites had sectarian features. The strongest thirty families controlling the state's economy, as mentioned previously, were religiously divided into twenty-four Christian families and six Muslim families (four Sunni, one Shiʿite, and one Druze).[43]

The Lebanese system, which maintained, according to Chiha, that merchants and bankers should be allowed to lead the state for the benefit of everyone, assigned the leaders of different religious communities roles as reconcilers in the Parliament. The Parliament was more of a balanced council than a genuine "legislature" capable of interfering in the state's economic policies. This situation was preferable for the leaders of the merchants and bankers project, who referred to ultraliberalism as a single, comprehensive approach.

The Maronites' Political, Social, and Economic Dominance in Lebanon

The Lebanese National Pact and Constitution, based on the Mandatory Constitution of 1926, provided the main framework for Lebanese political life throughout the period preceding the Civil War (that is, up to 1975). The National Pact was never a written document but rather a "gentlemen's agreement" between the *zu'ama'* (sectarian leaders) of the two major communities at that time—the Maronites represented by Bechara al-Khoury and the Sunnis represented by Riad al-Solh. It was on the one hand a compromise between the two communities and on the other a dam to hold back the radical camps within these communities. One such camp from the Maronite side called for definite rejection of any connection between Lebanon and the neighboring Arab world, but a camp from the Muslim side refused to recognize Lebanese independence.

This compromise preserved to a certain extent the privileges that Christians in general and Maronites in particular enjoyed in Lebanon. Government posts were distributed according to sector: the president was to be a Maronite, the prime minister a Sunni, and the Parliament's Speaker a Shi'ite. It was also decided to divide the Parliament's seats in a five-to-six ratio between the Christians and other religious communities; thus, the former were guaranteed a permanent majority in the Parliament. Such Christian dominance in Lebanon was not limited to the political arena. It was also manifested in the distribution of key positions and high bureaucracy in the state, where the five-to-six ratio also applied.

Among the apparent factors igniting this barrel of explosives in Lebanon was the quasi-complete congruence between the sectarian and socioeconomic gaps in Lebanese society. In 1961, research conducted by a delegation of the French organization (the Institut de recherche et de formation en vue du dévéloppement) upon the request of Lebanese president Fu'ad Chehab showed that 4 percent of the Lebanese population controlled 33 percent of the national income, whereas 50 percent received only 18 percent of it. Kamal Hamdan quotes the summary of this report and writes: "Development started and proceeded only in Mount Lebanon, whereas the other areas remained faltering: the North lacked developmental initiatives, and the South witnessed a withdrawal."[44] (Note that most of the residents of Mount Lebanon were Maronite, most of the residents in the North were Sunni, and the Biqa' and South were populated mainly by Shi'ites.)

The congruence between sectarian and socioeconomic gaps also appears in the data of the industrial survey conducted by the Central Bureau of Statistics in Lebanon in 1971. The survey showed that major commercial and industrial institutions were owned and operated mainly by Christians, with only a smaller number of similar institutions owned and operated by Muslims of different communities. For example, 75 percent of commercial companies and institutions with more than fifty employees were owned by Christians, the remaining 25 percent of like institutions owned by Muslims. Two-thirds of bank managers were Christian, as were three-quarters of the owners of commercial and insurance companies. Moreover, out of the largest twenty-five financial institutions in Lebanon seventeen were owned by Christians and only seven by Muslims.[45]

These figures do not indicate a complete congruence between religious and class divisions. Moreover, there is no doubt that each religious community also experienced internal class divisions. Research cited by Theodor Hanf shows that in the Christian community the industrial and commercial bourgeoisie constituted 4 percent, the middle class 67 percent, the proletariat 21 percent, and the "lower" stratum of the proletariat about 8 percent. In contrast, the division among Muslims was 2 percent bourgeoisie, 56 percent middle class, 23 percent proletariat, and 19 percent low proletariat.[46]

These figures prove that there was internal class division within each of the major religious groups in Lebanon. Nonetheless, an in-depth segmentation of these figures to examine the types of jobs occupied by members of the Christian middle class, as opposed to their Muslim counterparts, shows that middle-class Christians were mostly professional workers and educated clerks, whereas middle-class Muslims were mostly semiskilled laborers. According to this research, the lower strata of the proletariat, including agricultural workers and temporary workers in the services sector, alongside the unemployed, were mostly Muslim, especially Shi'ite.[47] This division in turn explains why most Shi'ites prior to the Civil War went through a process of socialization and politicization by the different radical parties, trade unions, and farmers' movements, which explicitly called for a renewed division of the state's wealth and resources. These figures also explain the Christian and Sunni middle class's devotion to the pre–Civil War hegemonic order and their persistence as a subordinate group within the merchants' project.

At the economic level, this merchants' project benefitted the Maronite middle class, followed by its Sunni counterpart, more than the other sectarian groups. At the ideological level, members of these social classes (the graduates of private universities in Lebanon) gained an advantage from the idea that they were successors of the glorious history of the Phoenicians and were the "Swiss of the Middle East." They adopted the chain of equivalences that the leaders and intellectuals of the hegemonic project established between the signifier of the merchants and the Lebanese people: Phoenician history and the "Swiss" present of Lebanon.

The "divorce" that occurred between the Muslim masses and their leaders may be attributed in part to the distancing between the Muslim Sunni elite and the Muslim masses,[48] many of whom, especially within the Shi'ite community, belonged to the proletariat and the low proletariat. This group experienced enhanced feelings of detachedness toward the constitutive ethos and strategy in Lebanon, mostly because they did not have a share in the wealth. This detachment did not occur so clearly among Christian Maronites, for the polarization between the bourgeois elite and the middle class, constituting two-thirds of the community, was not as sharp among the Maronites as within the Muslim community.

This polarity in the Lebanese system, the thwarting of all attempts to modify the economic system through state intervention (especially under president Fu'ad Chehab in the 1960s), and Lebanon's leaders' exaggerated loyalty to "liberalism" and the principles of extreme free trade pushed the popular strata to doubt and resent the nature of the hegemony that had governed Lebanon for decades. These internal trends were also influenced by such external factors as the escalating Israeli–Palestinian conflict, the Arab–Israeli conflict near Lebanon, and the movement of the Palestinian factions' leaders into Lebanon. The ethos that "Lebanon's power lay in its weakness"[49] and that it was the "Switzerland of the East" was called into question. Other counterhegemonic projects also started to mature, undermining the hegemony in Lebanon at both the sociopolitical and the economic levels.

Sectarian and socioeconomic disparities, alongside these regional conditions and changes, led to the outbreak of the bloody Civil War. It was to last for fifteen years and has been widely described as "a war of all against all" (as Thomas Hobbes would have put it), ultimately requiring international external intervention.

The Shattering of Hegemony: The Civil War

The historian Ussama Makdisi argues that sectarianism as a political system is a modern story that opened the way for changing political structures. He accentuates the fact that the violence of 1860 in Lebanon did not take place only between different sects (the Maronites and Druze, for example) but also within sects in their attempt to define their own boundaries.[50]

To a certain extent, we can understand the Lebanese Civil War, which started in the 1970s, by taking the same approach: it was not a religious war. In its different phases, members of all religious groups fought against each other, and at certain points fights erupted within individual religious groups. In 1975, internal tensions in Lebanon and Lebanese society, which the hegemonic project had failed to mitigate, developed into a war that continued until 1990. The war ended with the signing of the Ta'if Agreement between the disputing parties and with more than 70,000 causalities, around 100,000 injured, more than 820,000 refugees expelled from their villages in Lebanon, and around 900,000 people fleeing the countrywide conflict.[51]

A combination of factors led to the eruption of the Civil War. Social motives greatly contributed to turning increasing socioeconomic tensions into an extensive battle. It is also worth referring to the awakened social activism in Lebanese society. During the years from 1946 to 1970, only one general strike was declared, whereas in the immediate pre–Civil War years, with the deterioration of the socioeconomic situation and the revival of different trade unions, three strikes were declared just between 1970 and 1975.[52] The greater number of strikes was accompanied by a rise in the inflation rate in Lebanon from 2 percent in the 1960s to 18 percent in 1974.[53]

The Marxist thinker Mahdi 'Amel argued that the bourgeoisie would attempt to provide a sectarian cover to the class struggle in order to maintain and strengthen its position of control. He accentuated the internal class negations inside each sect and in Lebanese society as a whole. He assumed that the sectarian approach would help the dominant elite of each sect to maintain its control over popular forces within each community.[54]

However, socioeconomic problems do not sufficiently explain the Lebanese Civil War, which derived mainly from the intersection between socioeconomic gaps, religious disparities, Maronite Lebanese dominance, and the beginning of the gradual disintegration of the merchants and bankers' hegemonic project. All this resulted from the ruling group's abstention from introducing internal reforms and improvements to the Lebanese model or from leading a "passive revolution" that would make needed corrections to the Lebanese system without making substantial changes.

Moreover, in the mid-1960s new players—namely, the PLO and other Palestinian militant organizations—came into the complex Lebanese arena and started to use southern Lebanon as a stronghold for their ongoing struggle against Israel. This was especially the case after King Hussein's loyal forces expelled the Palestinian factions from Jordan in the events of Black September.

To sum up the main reasons for the outbreak of Civil War in Lebanon, one might refer to the intersection between the socioeconomic tensions that peaked in the 1970s, the enhanced feelings of oppression among marginalized communities owing to the Lebanese system, and the radicalization process that different religious groups underwent. Added to these intersecting factors were ongoing pressures exerted by different external forces, both regionally and globally, in the Lebanese arena and the transformation of Lebanon into a space for squaring accounts between different regional forces.

The Palestinians in Lebanon and the Shi'ites: Pockets of Resistance to Hegemony

Like the other Arab countries neighboring Mandatory Palestine, Lebanon absorbed a portion of the Palestinian refugees expelled after the declaration of the State of Israel in 1948. More than 100,000 Palestinian refugees passed the border into southern Lebanon. They were mostly from the northern Galilean villages, neighboring Acre, Bisan, Nazareth, Safad, Tiberias, and Haifa's suburbs.[55] In the first years following the arrival of the Palestinian refugees in Lebanon, their relationships with the residents of southern Lebanon, especially the Shi'ites, were very positive.[56] At that time, though, a relationship between the Palestinian refugees and the Lebanese Christian community was not established.[57]

Ironically, the Palestinian Nakba provided an opportunity for the Lebanese state to develop economically for two main reasons. First, the services sector witnessed an unprecedented development when Arab countries cut off relationships (at least open ones) with the new Israel. Thus, Beirut replaced Haifa as the main port for Arab countries and the main point of contact between Arab countries and Europe, Asia, and parts of Africa.[58] The second factor was the arrival of both wealthy investors and Palestinian workers, the latter providing a cheap labor force. The Palestinians brought about fifty million Palestinian pounds into the Lebanese economic circuit, but along with this added wealth came 120,000 refugees who required care.[59]

Lebanon, dominated by the Maronite elite and the ultraliberal capitalist approach, treated the Palestinian refugees as it did its own citizens, seeking to absorb them according to the refugees' abilities to integrate and enhance the hegemonic project of that time. The state thus divided the refugees according to two main criteria: socioeconomic status and religious affiliation. The Christian refugees obtained Lebanese citizenship "quite easily" in contrast to their Muslim counterparts. The latter obtained

Lebanese citizenship more easily if they were wealthy or bourgeois and thus able to pay large sums of money to lawyers to handle their citizenship requests.[60]

In the first years following their arrival in Lebanon, Palestinian refugees maintained mostly a neutral political position. They demonstrated this neutrality by their abstention from participating in the events of 1958, which constituted a general rehearsal of the civil war that would erupt less than two decades later.[61] The same year witnessed confrontations between supporters of Camille Chamoun—an ethno-Maronite pro-Western nationalist and a prominent representative of the merchant-and-banker coalition hegemonic project—and a coalition of pro-Eastern and pro-Arab nationalism forces of the Nasserite school under the leadership of Kamal Jumblatt. The specific reason for the confrontation was Chamoun's attempts to extend his tenure as president for an additional term in violation of the Lebanese Constitution.[62]

At the same time, a special relationship was established between Palestinian refugees and the Shi'ite community, two communities positioned on the margins of the hegemonic project that prevailed in Lebanon—a relationship that proved hospitable to the refugees and provided them with support upon their arrival in the southern towns. The clear majority of the Palestinians arrived in Lebanon after they had lost their land and property in Mandatory Palestine and subsequently had a low socioeconomic status, the same as that endured by the Shi'ite community in Lebanon for years.

As Rula Jurdi Abisaab and Malek Abisaab have shown in their research, a very old and deep relation between the people of North Palestine and South Lebanon—especially the Shi'ites—was established well before the independent Lebanese state: "For the southerners, it was Haifa not Beirut that was the center of commercial activities. Many had relatives in Haifa or traveled to it for business."[63]

The Shi'ite community was the most marginalized in Lebanon. Its rates of poverty and unemployment were the highest, and it remained on the margins of Lebanese society and the hegemonic project of the merchants and bankers' republic. Yet despite the Shi'ites' sympathy toward the Palestinians, the latter's arrival in the Shi'ite areas of southern Lebanon harmed the Shi'ites economically because the Palestinians agreed to work in agriculture and simple jobs for wages lower than the already low wages paid to Shiʿite workers.[64]

The Palestinians gradually became a burden on the Lebanese state and a disturbance to its delicate sectarian balance. Unlike other countries in the region, such as Jordan, which granted the Palestinians Jordanian citizenship and allowed them to integrate and move forward, Lebanon deprived the vast majority of Palestinians of citizenship and hindered their integration.[65] The Palestinians eventually succumbed to the living conditions in the refugee camps despite their dire economic situation; they worked so hard that some of the Lebanese called them *hameer* (donkeys). ʿAin al-Hilweh refugee camp, the largest of all Palestinian refugee camps in Lebanon, was called "the zoo."[66]

Considering the continuous humiliation thus inflicted on Palestinian refugees, who had at first thought that their crisis was temporary and that they would ultimately be able to return to their homes and lands (as promised by the Arab regimes prior to the war in 1948), they started to organize themselves militaristically and politically in Lebanon, and the *muqawama* narrative started to mature among them. This trend received a special boost upon the establishment of the PLO and the Palestinian National Liberation Movement (Fatah) in the mid-1960s.

Following the total failure of the Arab armies in 1967, Palestinian organizations decided to take their fate into their own hands and adopted a strategy of *muqawama* and armed struggle against Israel. The Lebanese arena, previously always a calm zone in the Arab–Israeli conflict, began to heat up as Palestinian organizations started to operate there. It is likely that ongoing pressures, the humiliation of the refugees, and Lebanon's opposition to granting them Lebanese citizenship or allowing them to integrate into Lebanese society caused this unique counteraction on the part of Palestinian organizations. At first, they were able to remain neutral within a state split between two forces: one supporting the Palestinian *muqawama* (including mainly leftist parties and other forces among Muslim communities) and another—especially national forces with a Maronite dominance—resisting any attachment to the Arab surroundings.

The Palestinian *muqawama* forces and the *fida'yin* established their first bases in the area of al-ʿArkoub in southeastern Lebanon, which became known as "Fatah Land."[67] Although some Lebanese youth joined and operated within the Palestinian *muqawama* in the South in its very first years, the Christian right-wing forces did not approve of the Palestinian military presence in Lebanon and felt that it posed a threat to the Lebanese ethos and to the stability of the Lebanese system. The first confrontation between the PLO and the Lebanese state (dominated by the Christian hegemony) occurred in 1969, leading ultimately to the intervention of Egyptian president Nasser and the signing of the Cairo Agreement between the PLO and Lebanon. This agreement was the first document in which the Lebanese state recognized the right of the Palestinian *muqawama* to use Lebanese lands to launch operations against Israel. And the PLO recognized the sovereignty of the Lebanese state over its lands and committed to maintaining the security and internal affairs within the refugee camps, the homes for tens of thousands of Palestinians.[68]

The Palestinian military presence in Lebanon was further enhanced following the events of Black September in Jordan, when Palestinian organizations were involved in armed confrontations with the regime of King Hussein. As King Hussein gained the upper hand, most of the Palestinian *muqawama* organizations and movements in Jordan eventually moved to Lebanon, which also bordered Israel but where the central government's control was loose.[69]

The Shi'ites and the Palestinians suffered disregard and neglect by the Lebanese state. They were resentful toward the state's structure and the right-wing Maronite dominance[70] and toward the dominant hegemony in Lebanon: the ethos of the "Switzerland of the East." Their shared destiny was also apparent when the two populations became the targets of reprisal operations carried out by Israel against the Palestinian *muqawama* population, which had assimilated in the South and other places in Lebanon, mainly around Beirut. The poor neighborhoods of Beirut and its environs were inhabited by Palestinians and Shi'ites who had fled from the South, first because of the South's economic deterioration and neglect and later because of Israeli attacks targeting the South.[71] The Israeli attacks did not differentiate between Palestinians and Shi'ites. In the 1970s, Israel and its ally in Lebanon, the Lebanese officer Sa'd Haddad, founder of the Jaysh Lubnan al-Hur (Army of Free Lebanon, the militia that was later called the Jaysh Lubnan al-Janubi, South Lebanon Army or SLA), tried to recruit Shi'ite volunteers under the leadership of Christian officers and under Israeli guidance to carry out operations against the Palestinian organizations. This attempt, however, failed.[72]

Palestinian refugee camps and the Palestinian *muqawama* organizations' military camps became in due course training centers for the first Shi'ite militant movement, Harakat al-Mahrumin (Movement of the Deprived),[73] led by Imam Musa al-Sadr, and its military wing Amal (meaning "hope" in Arabic but also the acronym of Afawaj al-Muqawama al-Lubnaniyya, or Battalions of the Lebanese Resistance).[74] At first, the Harakat al-Mahrumin wore the mantle of a social reform movement; in fact, however, it was the first political movement whose leaders and main supporters were Shi'ite. Yet it was not exactly a religious movement because it never prioritized the Shari'a over the State of Lebanon.

The Palestinians, mainly Fatah and the PLO, tried to avoid involvement in the Lebanese Civil War because the Jordanian experience and the events of Black September were still vivid in their memory.[75] However, the more radical parties within the PLO (the Popular Front, the Democratic Front, and others) pulled the Palestinians and the *muqawama* movements into the war to fight alongside the Lebanese radical Left and the revolutionary forces and to create large-scale revolutionary change in Lebanon (and thus, it was hoped, subsequently in the Arab world).[76]

During the Civil War, which transformed into an all-out war, the relationships between the Palestinians and certain Shi'ite leaders ran aground. Amal, which became the strongest Shi'ite movement, perceiving itself the representative of Shi'ite interests, could not endure Israeli harassments against the Shi'ites in the South that were a consequence of operations carried out against Israel by Palestinian organizations. Despite its support for the Palestinian parties in their resistance against Israel—that is, despite its lip service to the *muqawama* ethos—Amal eventually began working against the Palestinians, particularly against the PLO.[77]

These operations, however, did not put an end to the relationship between Shi'ites and the Palestinian resistance movements. In fact, this period enhanced the perception of a shared destiny between the Palestinian resistance forces and the new resistance movements that had begun to simmer among the Shi'ites. Both were inspired by the radical, resistive Islam that had begun to develop in Lebanon following the fracture between the dominant stream in Amal and the Muqawama al-Islamiyya fi Lubnan (Islamic Resistance in Lebanon) movement, which fought alongside the Palestinians in the 1980s and pulled the *muqawama* flag from their hands.

Who Were the Shi'ites in Lebanon?

The historian Kamal Salibi maintains that the Shi'ites in Lebanon are descendants of Yemeni and Hijazi Arab tribes. The Yemeni Awza'a tribe settled in the region of Baalbek in the Biqa' Valley, and the Yemeni 'Aamilya tribe settled in today's southern Lebanon. Salibi also refers to another tribe that settled in southern Lebanon, the Bani Matawil, originally from South Hijaz. They gave their name to the Shi'ites of southern Lebanon, who were thus called the "Matawila." It is important to note that these tribes came from Yemen and the Hijaz a long time before the emergence of Islam in the seventh century CE.[78]

The prevalent explanation among Lebanese Shi'ites is that they originate from the activism of the Prophet's companion Abu Dharr al-Ghiffari, who introduced Shi'ite perceptions into Lebanon and Syria.[79] Some historians consider this figure one of the first "socialists" in Islam owing to his defense of the poor and critique of the third caliph, 'Uthman bin 'Affan, whose rule witnessed the development of an Arab aristocracy in the new Islamic state. Rodger Shanahan argues that Lebanese Shi'ites' tendency in their oral accounts to associate themselves with Abu Dharr al-Ghiffari aims to accentuate the authenticity of their Islam.[80]

In addition to Lebanese Shi'ites' (and certain researchers') emphasis on their link to Abu Dharr al-Ghiffari, they also insist on accentuating their Arabism and the fact that they originated from the Arab tribes of the Arabian Peninsula and Yemen. In so doing, they refute researchers who cast doubt on Lebanese Shi'ites' Arab identity and maintain that they were originally Persians. Rula Jurdi Abisaab, in contrast, argues that certain Shi'ite tribes in Lebanon—the Bani Hamdan tribe and the 'Amel tribe, after whom Jabal 'Amel in southern Lebanon was named—are originally from Yemen and were present in the region during the early centuries of Islam.[81]

After the establishment of the Ottoman Empire and its control over the whole extent of what would later be called the Lebanese state, an attitude of hostility and skepticism prevailed between the Sunni Orthodox Ottoman authorities and the empire's Shiʿite minorities. This attitude was further enhanced by the rivalry between the Ottoman Empire and Safavid Iran, which had made Twelver Shiʿa Islam the religion of state.[82] In the early years of this rivalry, Lebanese Shiʿite clerics and families began migrating from Lebanon to Iran because of the hospitable treatment they enjoyed in the new Safavid state and its need to establish and instill Shiʿa Islam—hence the deep historical relationship between Iran and the Lebanese Shiʿites.[83]

For hundreds of years, Shiʿites in Lebanon swung between emerging buds of resistance inherent to the Shiʿite worldview and fear and prudence (*taqiyya*), which had a long history because of different regimes' strict attitude toward the Shiʿites. The Lebanese Shiʿites' collective awareness was particularly scalded during the rule of the Acre-based Ottoman governor Ahmad Pasha al-Jazzar, "the Butcher," in the eighteenth century CE, who massacred Shiʿites and punished them for their alliance with Sheikh Zahir al-ʿUmar, the former governor of Acre who had aspired to achieve independence from the Ottoman Empire.[84]

The Shiʿites' political and social situation worsened, and members of the Shiʿite community continued to live on the margins of the Ottoman Empire until the empire's final days in the early twentieth century. The Istanbul central government's skeptical attitude toward this community, which was known to diverge from sanctioned religious orthodoxy, led to further exclusion of Lebanese Shiʿites from power centers. This exclusion only worsened their inferior status vis-à-vis other communities upon the establishment of Greater Lebanon in 1920.[85]

The Shiʿite elite were then divided in their response to the new entity. Many Shiʿite notables from the South rejected the idea of "Greater Lebanon." They believed that the new state would keep them marginalized in comparison to Mount Lebanon, where the Maronite community was concentrated and its elite had solid relations with and interests in France. Some of the southern notables complained that they felt used and that despite the fact that the residents of the South paid taxes, little if any had been spent on them or on their region compared to what was spent on Mount Lebanon. Not all Shi'ite notables voiced this position, however. Some believed that their own economic and political interests would be promoted by joining and supporting the idea of Greater Lebanon.[86]

Shi'ites on the Margins of the "Bankers and Merchants' Republic"

The Shi'ites constituted a large portion of the poor population in Lebanon, especially among the peasants in southern Lebanon and the Biqa'. A large percentage of the downtrodden workers in the suburbs of Beirut was also Shi'ite.

The Shi'ite economy in Lebanon depended for many years on a simple family-based agricultural economy. This economy contributed to strengthening familial bonds and enhancing internal unity among the Shi'ite families. However, Muhammad Murad maintains that it was based on *iqta'* (feudalism) as it enhanced the patron–client relations between poor families and the families of the *zu'ama'*, the traditional leaders, whose status had been inherited since Ottoman rule.

Because the Shi'ite *zu'ama'* could obtain permits to grow tobacco—the main crop in the southern areas—and owned the largest plots of land in the South and the Biqa', they had relations with both the peasants and the state authorities, hence their ability to maintain the peasants' interests and to sell their produce to the authorities.[87]

The Shi'ite families of southern Lebanon, whose economy depended on agriculture (about 90 percent of the labor force in the South worked in agriculture until the 1950s),[88] helped the *zu'ama'* to control the peasantry and impose their authority. And through the *zu'ama'*, the central government controlled the South with relative efficiency. This system of dominance—that is, the subjugation of the Shi'ite community to the dominant ruling group, especially the Maronite elite—guaranteed the ruling hegemonic system already in the first year after Lebanon's independence.[89]

This hegemonic system preserved the interests of the Shi'ite *zu'ama'* by maintaining their leadership in their communities without creating substantial change to the political representation in general and among the Shi'ites in particular. The Maronite–Sunni elite, however, kept the

Shi'ite community, including its leaders, on the margins of the hegemonic project, away from the real centers of power, and minimized their role in Lebanon's imagined community and history.[90]

Like the Shi'ites themselves, subjugated to the hegemonic project of the mostly Maronite and Sunni merchants and bankers, agriculture was also dominated by the hegemony of trade—the financial market and service economies that developed in Lebanon at that time.[91] Potent groups, commercial chains, and banks also entered the agricultural sector and controlled it through loans; the sale of fertilizers, pesticides, and agricultural machinery; and ownership over the domains of refrigeration, packaging, and distribution. For example, twenty-five of the owners of the biggest freezing works dominated two-thirds of the apple market, and twenty owned 81 percent of the citrus market, of which three dominated one-third of that market. Two other companies held monopolies on the import of fertilizers and pesticides in Lebanon.[92]

The concentration of the agricultural sector in the hands of a small number of merchants and the control of the importers over agriculture gradually oriented Lebanese agriculture toward international markets and mechanization, thus urging many workers to relocate to cities in search of other sources of income. Whereas 50 percent of the Lebanese people worked in agriculture in the 1950s, the rate had dropped to 20 percent by 1975, when the Civil War broke out.[93] That same year, 60–65 percent of the villagers in southern Lebanon and 40–45 percent in the Biqa' left their homes and migrated. Of them, the clear majority (75 percent) moved to Beirut and to the internal areas of Lebanon, while the remainder immigrated to the Gulf Arab states and to other countries around the world.[94]

The second-highest concentration of Shi'ites in Lebanon was to be found in Biqa' Valley communities based on tribal values and "tribalism,"[95] the roots of which are founded on the special relations between different members of each cluster of peasant families. Rula Abisaab and Malek Abisaab note that "members of each cluster endorsed the informal authority of a senior leader or 'chief' from among its wealthier and more influential families," and the lands that a senior leader owned seemed to be shared, although unequally. This system, they argue, differed significantly from the societal arrangements in the South, where peasants worked on the land of unrelated families. It is for this reason that the Biqa'i Shi'ites came to be perceived as organized into "tribes."[96]

At the same time, families' income, especially from the 1950s on, depended on cannabis and the illegal drug trade, thus circumventing state dominance.[97] However, this work-around enabled ruling groups in the Lebanese state to further marginalize the Shi'ites in this area, isolating them from Beirut and the rest of the country.

The Shi'ite community's exclusion from the political, economic, and social center of Lebanon (Beirut) further deepened its social marginality and economic subjugation. Even when Shi'ites started migrating and settling in Beirut in the mid–twentieth century, the key positions were already occupied by members of other communities who had arrived there earlier.[98]

Nevertheless, Dahyih, the southern suburb of Beirut that over the decades had absorbed hundreds of thousands of Shi'ites who fled the dire economic reality in the South and the Biqa', became a new center for the Shi'ites. Their migration increased as aggressions between the PLO forces—who dominated vast areas in southern Lebanon—and Israel flared up in the late 1970s. The Shi'ites' move into Beirut, however, did not guarantee that they would share control and hegemony in Lebanon but rather merely reiterated their subjugation and marginality. The community remained in the impoverished suburbs around Beirut, unable to infiltrate into the city's core that represented the ruling hegemonic project in Lebanon of the past few decades.

This extensive migration of the Shi'ite population changed the traditional patronage relations within the community and led to a deep identity crisis.[99] The Shi'ites integrated into the Lebanese equation at a relatively late phase of the twentieth century, yet their integration was coupled with a demand for compensation for the years of their forced exclusion from this equation.

New versus Traditional Forces

In the elections held in the late 1960s and early 1970s, the Shi'ite *zu'ama'* still dominated the representation of the Shi'ite community in the Lebanese Parliament, despite the extensive migration from the South to Beirut.

Augustus Norton provides two explanations for the continued dominance by the Shi'ite *zu'ama'*. The first is that most of the immigrants at that time were not acquainted with any other form of social governance and were still captives of the system they knew in the South. The second is related to the nature of the Lebanese political system at that time, which determined that citizens should vote in the district where they were born, not in their place of current residence.[100]

The tremendous economic power of the heads of the Shi'ite honorable families and their control over their people's sources of income enhanced their political position and crowned them as the exclusive community leaders for decades—until, that is, the emergence of new popular movements and parties, which started to compete with them for the reins of leadership.

New developments—including socioeconomic change, ongoing migration from the South and the Biqa' to Beirut, the emergence of Palestinian resistance organizations in the Lebanese arena in general and the Shi'ite arena in particular, and the alliances developed between these organizations and the new parties (especially the radical leftist parties)—led to the gradual erosion of status for the Shi'ite *zu'ama'*; their position of leadership was gradually occupied by new forces. Nor did emerging resistance to the political order prevalent in Lebanon in general spare the dominant traditional Shi'ite forces. Resistance to the Lebanese regime and to the long-term exploitation of the poor Shi'ites thus penetrated to the internal relations within the Shi'ite community.

The erosion of the status of the notables and the *zu'ama'* in the Shi'ite community was owing in large part to the appearance of Musa al-Sadr,[101] an Iranian cleric of Lebanese origins, who arrived in 1959 to serve as the mufti of Tyre in southern Lebanon. He began rousing the Shi'ites and transforming them into a consolidated community that demanded its rights according to the sectarian Lebanese equation.[102] From the beginning, the Lebanese saw al-Sadr as the envoy of the Iranian shah in Lebanon; this impression was further enhanced by the fact that his selection, like the selections of other clerics operating outside Iran, had to be approved by SAVAK, the secret police of the shah's regime.[103] In any event, before the end of the shah's regime in 1979 and before al-Sadr's disappearance in

Libya in 1978, his relations with the shah worsened, and he began to establish new relations with clerics who opposed the shah's regime.

Al-Sadr provided an active interpretation of Shi'ite tradition, symbols, and myths, and he gradually succeeded in disseminating a reformative but not revolutionary message. He did not suggest changing the system fundamentally but rather enhanced the feelings of deprivation among members of the Shi'ite community, thus introducing an alternative to the traditional politics of the notables and *zu'ama'* in the Shi'ite arena. However, for the radical leftist parties, which had established a solid base in the Shi'ite community at that time,[104] "it [Shi'ite politics] was a politics of polarization, of feudalism, on the one hand, and extremism, *al-tataruf*, on the other hand. Finding a new way was an urgent necessity."[105] Al-Sadr proposed to the Shi'ites in Lebanon and to the whole country a new national perception that would reposition the Shi'ites at a higher status but without full abolition of the existing Lebanese system. He operated according to the traditional rules of the Lebanese game and accepted the Maronite dominance, yet within the framework of the same rules he called for granting his community a bigger share of the pie.

Al-Sadr thus largely reflected "political Maronism" but in a Shi'ite version, for he did not call for the cancellation of the Lebanese sectarian system. Rather, he advocated the introduction of certain amendments in favor of the Shi'ites. Therefore, it was not surprising that Amal, the movement he established and that continued his legacy after his disappearance from the Lebanese arena in 1978, was later involved in a blood-soaked confrontation with the Palestinian organizations. Amal had concluded that the Palestinians were *ghuraba'* (strangers) who brought destruction to Lebanon with their ongoing fight against Israel.[106] The Maronite right-wing movements in Lebanon had reached the same conclusion.

Supporting the Amal movement thus meant supporting the return of the Lebanese state and the Lebanese army to the South and preventing the Palestinian organizations from using the South as a base for their operations against Israel.[107] In fact, the Amal movement was a conservative movement that sought to rebuild the Lebanese state with only a few cosmetic changes.[108]

This conclusion apparently brought Nabih Berri, who became the leader of the Amal movement during the Civil War, to agree to join representatives of the Hizb al-Kata'ib al-Lubnaniya (Lebanese Phalanges Party) and other representatives of the Maronite elite in the Hay'at al-Inqath al-Watani (Salvation Committee) declared by President Elias Sarkis. Berri's decision to take this position was among the main contributors to the split within the Amal movement and the establishment of a more radical offshoot with a stronger Islamist emphasis influenced by the Iranian Revolution and, no less importantly, with a stronger emphasis on resistance.

The Beginnings of Hezbollah

By the late 1970s and early 1980s, the Shi'ite community had matured and was ready for a new and radical force from within. It had undergone an accelerated process of urbanization and migration from the periphery to Beirut, with all the accompanying implications: a social and economic blow to as well as the disintegration of the traditional frameworks that had organized the social life in the Shi'ite villages and of the traditional patronage relations within the community, thus leading to a deep identity crisis.[109]

As a result, the Shi'ite community was ripe for political radicalization by the radical leftist parties and later through cooperation and coexistence with the Palestinian resistance organizations in Lebanon.[110] Moreover, it is evident that the events that decisively influenced the Shi'ite community were the Israeli invasion of Lebanon in 1982 and subsequent occupation of southern Lebanon, the Islamic Revolution in Iran in 1979, and Ayatollah Ruhollah Khomeini's dispatch of Iranian Revolutionary Guardsmen to the Biqa' in 1982.[111]

However, the leftist movements and parties could not maintain dominance among the Shi'ite community, although up to the 1990s a large portion of the activists in these organizations was Shi'ite (for example, 41 percent of the participants of the Communist Party's congress in 1993 were Shi'ite).[112] This loss of dominance occurred for many reasons, including the eruption of the Civil War, which enhanced sectarianism;[113] the revival of radical Islam and the entry of the Iranian Revolutionary Guards into the Biqa' to recruit and train Shi'ite militias; the disagreements within the leftist movements; the ongoing intervention of regional forces in Lebanese events; the emerging tensions between Palestinian organizations (allies of the leftist parties) and the residents of southern Lebanon as a result of Israeli reprisals; the southern Lebanese residents' feeling that the Palestinians were taking over the region; and so forth.

Moreover, the appearance of a new and unique cleric in the Lebanese arena, Musa al-Sadr, played a decisive role in the introduction of a "third way." Waddah Shararah and Fu'ad Ajami describe well the Shi'ite community's revulsion and hostile attitude in the 1940s, 1950s and 1960s toward the Shi'ite traditional clerics in Lebanon. The general perception was that these clerics were "submissive and conservative" and totally dependent on the benevolence of the *zu'ama'*. Shi'ite society felt resentful and angry toward the clerics, who were deemed honorable only under the auspices of the *zu'ama'*.

Ajami quotes a secular Shi'ite at that time who later became a great admirer of Musa al-Sadr and rather scathingly described the traditional cleric of the time in Lebanon: "Our cleric wrapped himself with a mantle, put his head on his hand, and fell asleep. When he woke up, all he could do was tell others to go to sleep. He lived a passive life; and you should not be misled by his gestures, for they would lead you backward. A cleric would be the reason for two miseries: the first when he remains behind; and the second when he makes other follow him. . . . [A] cleric's head is full of baseless thoughts, miracles, and myths."[114]

Musa al-Sadr played a decisive role in the introduction of a "third way." Al-Sadr was a charismatic, independent, and political cleric, and, according to Waddah Shararah, although he was not a "first-class" cleric, his strength lay in his social and political activism, his direct and continuous relations with the Shi'ite community, and his establishment of a network of regional and intra-Lebanese relationships.[115] Within Gramsci's framework, Musa al-Sadr would be deemed a new kind of cleric who embodied the "organic intellectual" of a certain social group and who operated within and organized this group. After his disappearance, other Shi'ite clerics continued his legacy and contributed to the development of the Shi'ite community's religious-political awareness and unity.

In addition to the intra-Lebanese developments, the Israeli invasion of southern Lebanon in 1982 made a decisive contribution to the birth of a new radical Shi'ite force and to the emergence of the Lebanese national resistance.[116] The first representative of that resistance was the Jabhat al-Muqawama al-Wataniyya al-Lubnaniyya (Lebanese National Resistance Front), established by the Lebanese Communist Party and the Munazamat al-'Amal al-Shuyu'i fi Lubnan (Communist Action Organization in Lebanon). Representation was later transferred to al-Muqawama al-Islamiyya fi Lubnan (Islamic Resistance in Lebanon), which was ideologically different from the secular, leftist, and Palestinian forces in the newly built *muqawama* arena in Lebanon.

An additional factor that led to the emergence of this new player in the Lebanese Shi'ite arena was the success of the Iranian Revolution, which made Imam Khomeini, with all that he symbolized, the leader of the Islamic Republic of Iran.[117] Iranian support for the clerics who split from the Amal movement in Lebanon was decisive.[118]

In contrast to Amal, which demanded a share of the sectarian pie in Lebanon, Hezbollah introduced itself from its start in the early 1980s as a radical organization seeking to change the intra-Lebanese structure fundamentally. This goal was reflected in the name of the nascent organization, Hezbollah: Al-Thawra al-Islamiyya fi Lubnan, or Party of God: The Islamic Revolution in Lebanon. In other words, the organization aimed to create a fundamental change in the political system in Lebanon and to establish a revolutionary Islamic regime on the model of Iran. This revolutionary aspiration was natural in the context of the Civil War, which was at its peak when the movement first emerged and which pushed all Lebanese movements and organizations to their extreme.

Hezbollah's first public appearance in the Lebanese arena, with the publication of "The Open Letter" in February 1985, was preceded by the birth of several organizations and movements representing radical Islam among Lebanese Shi'ites, including al-Jihad al-Islami (Islamic Jihad) and al-'Adala al-Thawriyya (Revolutionary Justice). Hezbollah eventually became an umbrella organization, taking different movements and organizations under itself.[119] In an interview cited by Rodger Shanahan, Hezbollah's secretary-general Hassan Nasrallah mentioned that the Committee of Nine, constituting Hezbollah's founding leadership, comprised the following elements: three independent clerics; three members of the Hizb al Da'wa al-Islamiyya (Islamic Da'wa Party) in Lebanon, whose ideological roots were in Iraq (especially in the philosophy of Muhammad Baqir al-Sadr); and three members of the Islamic Amal movement headed by Husayn Musawi.[120] The latter group had split from the Amal movement after the disappearance of Musa al-Sadr and the entry of Nabih Berri, al-Sadr's successor—along with that of the leader of the Lebanese Phalanges Party, Bachir Gemayel—to the Salvation Committee upon the request of President Elias Sarkis.[121]

In the 1980s, the revolutionary enthusiasm and the atmosphere of crisis that characterized Lebanon in general and the Shi'ite community in particular led many youths of different ideological backgrounds to unite and create substantial and revolutionary change in their reality. They included 'Abbas al-Musawi and Subhi al-Tufayli from the Da'wa Party; Hassan Nasrallah, Ibrahim Amin al-Sayyid, Na'im Qasim, Muhammad Yazbak, and others from Amal; 'Imad Mughniyya and Abu Hassan Khader Salameh from Fatah; and 'Abdel Hadi Hamadah from the Lebanese Communist Party.[122]

The New Leaders: Organic and Frustrated Intellectuals

Elie Kadourie raises an interesting hypothesis regarding nationalism as the product of a group of frustrated intellectuals who lacked access to centers of power in the states and great empires that preceded the emergence of the national concept and the great force it acquired both before and after World War I. In brief, these intellectuals suggested the idea of nationalism as a tool by which they could divide the great empires into smaller "national units" in order to have a share of influence and power.[123]

This perception might be used with a few adaptations to analyze the appearance of the young clerics destined to lead Hezbollah in Lebanon and the Shi'ite community in general out of sociopolitical marginality in the Lebanese arena and into its center. This goal ultimately was not achieved through nationalist ideas, however, but through ideologies of radical Islam in the spirit of Ayatollah Khomeini and with the decisive intention to create a genuine social change in Lebanon.

This group of young enthusiasts had common features. All were in their twenties and thirties when Hezbollah was established in the late 1970s and early 1980s. They were clerics positioned at the bottom of the Shi'ite clerical hierarchy as well as the first clerics in their families. They did not belong to the traditional clerical families, who came mostly from southern Lebanon, but were in general from the Biqa' and Beirut, with only a few from the South.

Another common denominator among these young leaders was that they all were influenced by the philosophy of Muhammad Baqir al-Sadr in Iraq and his radical and activist Islamic thought manifested in the Iraqi Da'wa Party (which operated secretly during the regime of the Ba'th [Renaissance or Resurrection] Party in Iraq). Many of Hezbollah's young leaders spent a few years in the religious school of Najaf in Iraq, which was at that time a vigorous arena for religious Shi'ite activism. This activism was inspired by Baqir al-Sadr and Khomeini,[124] both of whom suggested a more activist and radical Islam, which drew Shi'ite youth in Iraq and the Arab world away from radical secular organizations and parties. Rula Jurdi Abisaab argues that these clerics resemble Gramscian organic intellectuals "who are rooted in society and who serve and promote the interests of the lower class."[125]

In the 1970s, Lebanese students had to flee Iraq after the Iraqi authorities banned the activism of the Da'wa Party and expelled all non-Iraqi Shi'ite clerics from the country. This expulsion led to the return of a "critical mass" of approximately one hundred young, energetic, and radical clerics to stormy Lebanon, and they immediately started creating substantial and radical changes, which peaked with the Civil War in the mid-1970s.

One of these young clerics was 'Abbas al-Musawi, born in 1952 to a secular family in the village of al-Nabi Sheeth in the Biqa' Valley. In the late 1960s, he met Musa al-Sadr and joined the Ma'had al-Dirasat al-Islamiyya (Islamic Studies Institute), which al-Sadr had established in Tyre. A year and a half later Musawi traveled to Najaf to study under Muhammad Baqir al-Sadr. Nine years later, having reached the level of Dars Kharij in his studies, he had to leave Iraq because of the persecution of Shi'ites by the Iraqi authorities at that time. In 1978, when he returned to Lebanon, he established a *hawza* (a seminary for religious studies) in Baalbek, a region that did not have many clerics.[126]

Subhi al-Tufayli, who would later be elected the first secretary-general of Hezbollah, was also born in a village in the Biqa' Valley, Brital. He, too, was the first cleric in a secular, multiple-child family, whose breadwinner was a soldier in the Lebanese army. Tufayli was the only one among his siblings to pursue theological studies. He left for Najaf in 1965 and joined the disciples of Muhammad Baqir al-Sadr. He stayed there for nine years until an arrest warrant was issued against him by the Iraqi authorities in 1974, and he was forced to return to Brital. Upon his arrival there, he joined a group of clerics who opposed Musa al-Sadr. In 1976, al-Tufayli left Lebanon for Qom, Iran, on the eve of the revolution there. Al-Tufayli did not finish his studies, although he reached the level of Dars Kharij. He involved himself in activism against the shah in Iran, and following the success of the revolution, he returned to Lebanon to contribute to the exportation of revolution there.[127]

Sheikh Muhammad Yazbak, also the first cleric in his family, was born in Baalbek, Lebanon, in 1950. He left for Najaf and studied there for seven years. After his expulsion from Iraq, he helped 'Abbas Musawi establish the *hawza* in Baalbek.[128]

Southern Lebanon was also the home of some of Hezbollah's founding leaders whose profiles generally match those of the leaders so far reviewed. One young leader was Sheikh Raghib Harb, later called "Sheikh al-Shuhada'" after being assassinated by Israel on February 16, 1984.

Harb was born in the village of Jebchit in southern Lebanon. He studied in the Ma'had al-Shar'i al-Islami (Islamic Shari'a Institute, established by Muhammad Husayn Fadlallah) in Beirut. A few years later he moved to Najaf to pursue his studies. However, four years after that, in 1974, he was expelled from Iraq. He returned to Lebanon and became the imam of his village, Jebchit. He gradually succeeded in recruiting a group of young religious Shi'ites who separated from Amal after the disappearance of Musa al-Sadr.[129]

Hezbollah's current secretary-general, Hassan Nasrallah, was born in 1960 to a family originally from southern Lebanon. The eldest son among nine children, he was born and raised in the poor Karantina slum in Beirut. In the 1970s, young Hassan left for Najaf, where he studied in the religious school of Muhammad Baqir al-Sadr. There, he met 'Abbas Musawi, and they became close friends. Nasrallah succeeded in completing the first part of his studies, but in 1978 he was expelled from Iraq and returned to Lebanon. He joined the Amal movement and for a while was a member of the movement's political bureau. Following the Israeli invasion of Lebanon in 1982, however, and the internal dispute that erupted in the Amal movement regarding its leader's participation in the Salvation Committee, Nasrallah left with a core group and joined the founders of Hezbollah.[130]

The founding leader with the most exceptional background was Husayn Musawi. He was originally a teacher of Arabic literature who had received a secular education in Lebanon. Musawi was the deputy of Nabih Berri, the leader of the Amal movement, but he resigned following Berri's entry to the Lebanese state's Salvation Committee in 1982. Musawi then established the Islamic Amal movement and claimed determinedly that it was the real Amal movement, preserving the tradition of Imam Musa al-Sadr. He took over part of Amal's estate in the Biqa' and, with the help of others, succeeded in establishing the military and logistic arm of the nascent Hezbollah.[131]

Other examples of Hezbollah's leaders clearly represent the far-reaching changes in the Shi'ite community in Lebanon and the development of a new strata of young clerics who deemed religion a radical refuge from their reality and marginality in the Lebanese arena. As maintained by Waddah Shararah, these young clerics were born to families that had missed the formal, secular, and Western Lebanese education train, and upon pursuing religious studies, they acquired the tools to take revenge upon the Shi'ites who had arrived first in Beirut and had successfully integrated into the "original" Lebanese project of the bankers and merchants' republic.[132]

The new clerics were inspired by the activist clerics who matured in the 1950s, 1960s, and 1970s and led a genuine revolution in how Shi'ite clerics were perceived. In Lebanon, the most prominent of these activist clerics was definitely Musa al-Sadr, who prepared the ground for the consolidation of a stronger Shi'ite community with a distinct nature, capable of demanding its share of power in the Lebanese regime. Within the context of Hezbollah's emergence, he also made a great contribution to changing the image of Shiʿite clerics, who before he entered the scene were totally detached from the sociopolitical reality of most Shiʿites, especially the youth.

For the young generation, al-Sadr constituted an example of a non-arrogant yet charismatic cleric, whose extensive network of social relations helped him revive the status of clerics among the Shiʿite community. Through Iranian support and internal tribal synergy in the Biqaʿ, the new clerics like al-Sadr succeeded in directing large segments of the Shiʿite community toward a broader project that would challenge and attempt to destroy the sociopolitical regime that had marginalized them for decades.

To understand the ideological roots of these young clerics, one must shed light on the perceptions and innovations originating with such clerics and intellectuals as Musa al-Sadr, Muhammad Baqir al-Sadr, ʿAli Shariʿati, Ayatollah Ruhollah Khomeini, and Muhammad Husayn Fadlallah. A special emphasis should also be placed on the way each of these intellectuals established and promoted the ideological basis on which Hezbollah would later build its own ideological infrastructure. This infrastructure would give to Hezbollah the flexibility that would enable it to move from one political strategy to another.

3

The *Muqawama* Thought

Intellectual Roots of Hezbollah's Resistance

The word *shi'a* in Arabic means "party." "'Ali's *shi'a*" is the party of 'Ali, the fourth caliph of the Muslims, after the death of Prophet Muhammad.[1]

The Shi'ite stream in Islam came into being following the death of Prophet Muhammad in 632 CE and the emergence of the first political question considering the disagreement between his followers about the person who would lead the young Islamic state he left behind. The "Shi'ites" were the group that stood at that time by 'Ali, the Prophet's cousin and the husband of the Prophet's daughter, Fatima. They believed 'Ali was the most suitable candidate, and for support they quoted *ahadith*, or statements, of the Prophet, in which he declared 'Ali the legitimate successor. Even after the election of Abu Bakr al-Siddiq as the first caliph, followed by 'Umar ibn al-Khattab and 'Uthman bin 'Affan, the "Shi'a" of 'Ali felt that these elections were unjust and so cast doubt on their legitimacy, especially that of 'Uthman bin 'Affan, the third caliph. *Al-tashayu'*, meaning "to support the caliphate of 'Ali," started while 'Ali was still alive, but the Shi'a developed and matured following 'Ali's murder in 661 CE.[2]

The Shi'a emerged as a political movement with a political say regarding the identity of the Islamic state. Here, it is worth indicating that the first revolution to erupt in Islam was the first rebellion against the caliph 'Uthman. His rule, during which the Arab Muslim aristocracy matured and class splits worsened in the Muslim Empire, led eventually to the seizure of power by 'Ali, who symbolized the opposite of 'Uthman and was known for his contemplations on class equality.[3] 'Ali's rule lasted only four years, thus enabling Mu'awiyah and the Umayyads to establish their monarchist kingdom, which highlighted the Arab superiority in the Muslim Empire and contributed to drawing additional opposition forces, especially in the remote areas far from the empire's center and in the non-Arab lands, to the central oppositionist stream against the Umayyads—namely, the Shi'ite stream.

Throughout history, many splits occurred within the Shi'a, but the central stream that continued to develop and is currently ruling in Iran, South Iraq, and Lebanon is the Twelver Shi'a, the stream that believes in the twelve imams, the first of whom was 'Ali ibn Abi Talib, and that the twelfth imam, al-Mahdi, is concealed but will return in the future to impose order, peace, and justice in the world.

The historical development of Twelver Shi'ite political thought demonstrates that it was greatly affected by having been created and adopted by a minority group in the Islamic world, giving rise to hostility and aggression among Orthodox Sunni state institutions. The latter have often opined that the Shi'a movement deviated from the true Islam; in certain cases, it was even deemed heretical.

A thorough examination of Shi'ite political thought clearly reveals the psychology of an oppressed minority. In the most prevalent Twelver Shi'ism, this political thought is cloaked in messianism, which commands the believers to wait for the reappearance of the twelfth imam, al-Mahdi, from an occultation that has lasted for more than a millennium to lead the believers and realize a just state on earth. This position of waiting resulted in Shi'ite political life being characterized as negative and passive for hundreds of years.[4] Supporters of this line of thought had determined that those who act differently in any other state or regime, apart from the state of the twelfth imam, severely violate the imam's right and commit a real heresy.

The change in Shi'ite thought started with the opening of the gateways of *ijtihad* (independent reasoning and interpretation) and the suggesting of solutions for the problems that were still facing Muslims many centuries after the twelfth imam's occultation began.[5] The *ijtihad* led to the development of *al-niyaba al-'amma* (literally, "the general representation") theory, which authorizes the *fuqaha'* (Islamic jurists) to judge among people and to collect the *zakat* (tax or obligatory alms), thus providing the *fuqaha'* with an operating space. However, clerics are not allowed to lead the community because this authority is granted exclusively to the imams, who are both *ma'sum* (sinless) and descendants of 'Ali.

In 1501, upon the establishment of the Safavid Empire in Iran by Shah Ismail I, the state's adoption of the Shi'ite "ideology," and its transformation into a Twelver Shi'a Islamic state, the shah sought to develop a new theory that would bypass the *intizar* (waiting) theory (that is, waiting for Imam Mahdi). He claimed to have met the vanished imam and Imam 'Ali, who commanded him to establish the Shi'ite state and to serve as their delegate until the reappearance of the vanished imam. This theory was called *al-niyaba al-malakiyya*, the "royal representation."

Although several clerics legitimized the ruling of the Safavid kings as representatives of the imam, the majority determined that these kings had arbitrarily taken over the rule and the imam's rights. These developments caused a split within Twelver Shi'a Islam into al-Akhbari and al-Usuli. The former continued supporting the passive position of awaiting the imam's return and opposing the *al-niyaba al-'amma* theory, whereas the latter followed the path of the *mujtahidin* (reasoners) and the reformists who opened the gateways of *ijtihad*.

Following the collapse of the Safavid state, Sheikh Ahmad Ben Muhammad Mahdi al-Naraqi (d. 1829) developed the theory of *wilayat al-faqih*, or "guardianship of the Islamic jurist." Through this theory, al-Naraqi granted the *faqih* all the rights that the Shi'ites attributed to the imam at the political level as long as the vanished imam did not reappear and without requiring that the *faqih* be *ma'sum* (sinless) or a descendant of 'Ali. Al-Naraqi called on the *fuqaha'* to run governments in the vast Shi'ite state.[6]

Knowledge of the significant historical turning points in the Shi'ite clerics' activism and their involvement in sociopolitical realms will in turn help us comprehend the historical background of the emergence of the ideologists whom I introduce in this chapter. These historical turning points took place in Iran, the largest Shi'ite state and the main articulator in the development of Shi'ite thought in modern times.

Developments in Iran

The Tobacco Crisis of 1890

The status of the Shi'ite cleric in Qajar Iran was not like the status of his parallel in Safavid Iran. The relationship between the Qajar regime, which did not accentuate its religiosity, and the clerics had weakened to some extent. Moreover, foreign influence, especially by Britain and Russia, on the Iranian state had gradually increased during this period. This influence had irritated the clerics, both in a religious sense because they perceived it as the excessive influence by heretics on the Islamic state and in an economic sense because the European empires opened Iran's gates to European merchants, thus affecting Iranian merchants, who were the clerics' main allies.[7]

In the period preceding the Tobacco Crisis in 1890, the secular opposition in Iran for the first time cooperated with the clerics. Iran's ruler at the time, Shah Nasreddin, had granted the British Imperial Tobacco Company a monopoly over the Iranian tobacco market for fifty years, thus arousing objection and embitterment among the Iranian bazaar (traditional market) merchants, who were the strongest allies of the Shi'ite clerics. This alliance had grown because the clerics had originally belonged to the merchant social segment and because the bazaar's people were the main source of economic support for the clerics. In response to the opposition to the granted tobacco monopoly and concurrently with the activism of the Islamic reformist Jamal al-Din al-Afghani,[8] the supreme *marji'* (legal authority), Mirza Shirazi, who lived in Iraq, away from the shah's regime, issued a fatwa that banned consumption of tobacco all over Iran, resulting in a complete tobacco boycott by all the Iranian people. The shah eventually was obliged to annul his decision regarding the monopoly granted to the British company.[9]

The Constitutional Revolution of 1906

In 1905, Iran was ready for a political revolution because of the unsuccessful economic politics of the new shah, Mozaffar al-Din, and the fast growth of the middle class and its support of democracy, legality, nationalism, and secularism.[10]

The Constitutional Revolution erupted in 1906 against the backdrop of the economic situation, the strong foreign presence in Iran, and Shah Mozaffar's absolute monarchy. Therefore, the revolution was a sort of national democratic revolution.[11] Moreover, the coalition established between the activist clerics and the anti-imperialist secular forces was further enhanced following the failure of Russia—which greatly influenced Iran during those years—in its war with Japan. The Japanese victory was the first Asian triumph over a European nation in modern history, and supporters of constitutions associated this victory with the fact that Japan was the only Asian state with a progressive constitution, whereas Russia was the only European state that lacked a constitution.[12]

Yet this revolution in Iran also witnessed an internal controversy between the clerics regarding their position as either progressives or conservatives. Conservative clerics, such as Sheikh Fazlollah Noori, denied the right to create a new constitution that would replace the divine constitution and the Qur'an, whereas the more progressive clerics, such as Ayatollah Mirza Hossein Na'ini, supported the revolutionaries' demands and praised the advantages of a constitution that would allow the people to express their opinions and choose their ruler.

This controversy had a socioeconomic aspect, too, for many clerics leaned economically on the shah's support, whereas the more independent clerics were freer to resist. The new constitution included an important clause that was later revived following the revolution in 1979. Clause 2 appointed a council of clerics who were granted the power of veto of parliamentary legislation so that the state's laws would not contradict the Shari'a.

In 1921, the rule of Iran moved (under British auspices) into the hands of a senior officer in the Iranian army, Reza Khan, who in 1925 became the shah of Iran with a clear pro-Western orientation.[13] The sixteen-year period of Reza Shah's rule witnessed the growing concentration of wealth in the hands of a small elite group and dire poverty among the vast majority of the Iranian people.[14] In 1941, as a result of the world war, the Allies (the British, the Soviets, and the Americans) decided to dethrone Reza Shah, known for his sympathy toward the Germans, in favor of his son,

Muhammad Reza Shah, who would be the last king in a kingdom that had endured for twenty-five hundred years.

The Mossadegh Government and the Nationalization of the Iranian Oil Industry, 1950–1953

In 1950, Mohammed Mossadegh was elected the prime minister of Iran against the background of the Iranian oil crisis and British companies' exploitation of this oil. Mossadegh had led the National Front coalition, which was composed of nationalist forces, Marxists, secularists, and clerics who had allied together to weaken the foreign interference of Western forces, especially Britain, in Iranian affairs, mainly oil and oil trading.[15]

After the British and American rejection of all compromises, Mossadegh nationalized the Iranian oil industry, causing Britain to lead a global boycott, which was later joined by the United States. This US decision exacerbated Iranian hostility toward the Americans, particularly considering Iran's high expectations of the United States to oppose the British.

Aided by the CIA, the British and the Americans overthrew the government of Mossadegh and returned Mohammad Reza Shah, who had fled Iran for Rome, to power. This egregious interference raised questions regarding the legitimacy of Muhammad Reza Shah's regime.[16]

The Uprising of 1963

In 1963, an uprising erupted as a response to Muhammad Reza Shah's White Revolution, which included the nationalization of forests, the privatization of governmental companies and factories, and the expansion of voting rights for women. Thousands of workers, students, clerics, and unemployed people went to the streets to protest against this "revolution"; meanwhile, a new political figure appeared on the Iranian scene—Ayatollah Ruhollah Khomeini.[17]

In that same year, Khomeini started defaming the monarchist regime, attacking mainly its reliance on the United States and Israel. Later that same year, the Iranian internal security service, SAVAK, attacked a religious assembly being held in memory of the third imam, Husayn. Khomeini was deported to Turkey, and after that he moved to Iraq.[18]

The Revolution of 1979

In his book *Iran between Two Revolutions*, Ervand Abrahamian notes that the common explanations for the Iranian Revolution are the rapid modernization led by the shah, on the one hand, and the extremely slow process of modernization led by the shah, on the other. Abrahamian maintains that neither explanation is correct or incorrect, for each contains a half truth. He argues that the revolution resulted from the extremely rapid modernization process led by the shah at the socioeconomic level, which created new social classes and a growing class-based polarization. However, the shah simultaneously led an infinitesimally slow process of political modernization, which did not adapt itself to the socioeconomic changes occurring at that time.[19] The Iranian Revolution thus included the vast majority of Iranians—middle class, bazaar merchants, workers, clerics, and students.

The first incident thought to have instigated the Iranian Revolution was the suppression of the Writers' Association conference on November 19, 1977, attended by ten thousand students, at which one student was killed and dozens were injured and arrested. This incident was followed by the publication of an article in the newspaper *Ittila'at* (Information) on January 7, 1978, that criticized Khomeini, calling him a British spy and claiming that he was Indian and not Iranian. These two incidents sparked a series of demonstrations that resulted in many casualties and deaths, which in turn led to further demonstrations, especially on the fortieth day marking the fall of the first victims, as well as to further casualties.

These demonstrations and the use of the religious holidays and Friday prayers to mobilize the masses ignited Iran completely. The shah's reaction to the demonstrations was not decisive. On the one hand, he attempted to exhaust the demonstrators; on the other hand, he granted them and their leaders several "rewards." He eventually had to escape from Iran, Khomeini returned to Tehran in February 1979, and the nationalist, Communist, and Islamist revolutionary forces triumphed over the shah and his forces.[20]

Undoubtedly, the regime's oppression of the organized secular opposition during the years leading up to the revolution was more potent than its treatment of the religious opposition. The regime found it easier to oppress the former than the latter, which sought to recruit the masses through well-oiled religious and traditional slogans and propaganda. Moreover, the religious opposition and its activists were loosely organized, making it harder for the regime to respond to their activism and thus to oppress them completely.[21]

The radical guerilla organizations Fadaiyan-e Khalq (the People's Sacrificers, a Marxist-Leninist movement) and Mojahedin-e Khalq (People's Mujahideen, a radical leftist-Islamist organization that espoused the beliefs of 'Ali Shari'ati and others) played a significant role in undermining the security of the shah's regime and in thwarting the suppression of the revolution by the shah's liberal pro-Western forces in the last stages of the revolution.[22]

This historical process, which ultimately led to the establishment of the Islamic Republic of Iran, was buttressed by far-reaching ideas and developments in Shi'ite political thought, particularly in Iran and in the region in general. Modern ideologists and clerics developed renewed perceptions of the role of clerics and Shi'ite doctrine in the present world. Through an interesting interaction among different ideologies and historical developments, these ideologists and intellectuals actively reinterpreted some of the basic concepts and the basis of Shi'ite doctrine in an attempt to restore the activist dimension of the Shi'a and to transform it into a resistive and revolutionary tool that could confront the complex reality in which the Shi'a and the entire region's population lived in the second half of the twentieth century. In fact, this tool was crucial to the development of a new type of Shi'ite cleric—namely, the organic ideologist and intellectual who tied his fate to that of the people, with whom he had a direct and constant interaction.

In the next section, I review five outstanding thinkers in Shi'a revivalism.

Organic Intellectuals in Shi'a Revivalism

Muhammad Baqir al-Sadr

Muhammad Baqir al-Sadr was born in 1933 (or 1935) in al-Kazmiyya, near Baghdad. He was called *sayyid* because he was considered a descendant of the Shi'ite imams, his kinship dating back to Imam Musa al-Kazem. His family was originally from Jabal ʿAmel in southern Lebanon, and his wife was the daughter of his cousin Musa al-Sadr, the founder of the Amal movement in Lebanon.[23]

Baqir al-Sadr started his theological studies in early life and became a *mujtahid* at a young age. He was the disciple of Ayatollah Abu al-Qasim al-Khoe'i and Sheikh ʿAbbas al-Rumaithi. From the very beginning of his journey, Baqir al-Sadr manifested a tendency toward political activism, unlike the general tendency prevalent among Shiʿite clerics in the *hawzat* (religious schools) in Najaf and Karbala' and in the Shiʿa centers of theological study in Iraq and worldwide during those years.

Baqir al-Sadr was unofficially involved in the establishment of the Islamic Daʿwa Party in Iraq in the 1950s and hosted students and young disciples from all Shiʿite regions around the world, in particular Lebanon, as shown in the previous chapter. These youth groups were influenced by the nontraditional activist approach taken by this young and senior cleric, who differed from the other Shiʿite clerics at that time.

Close to the group of Najaf scholars who called for a more active role among the clerics in political and daily life,[24] Baqir al-Sadr was aware of the appeal of radical leftist and secular ideologies such as communism, socialism, and pan-Arabism among young Shiʿites in Iraq. Therefore, he strove to attract these young people back to religion. He realized that to achieve this goal he needed to render religion more relevant to youth, which motivated him to further enhance his activist orientation among the Shiʿa.

Many of the Communist militants in the 1950s belonged to families of Shiʿite clerics from Najaf and other holy cities whose economic situation had worsened during this period, and the Marxist ideology served as a tool for protesting and for analyzing their long-lasting dire economic situation.[25]

Baqir al-Sadr initiated the use of a more "academic" writing, different from the writing style adopted by traditional Shiʿite ʿulama'. Two of his most prominent books are *Falsafatuna* (Our Philosophy, 1959) and *Iqtisaduna* (Our Economy, 1961). In the former, he deliberates on the Western philosophies, mainly Marxism, that served as a magnet to young Shiʿite Iraqis and non-Iraqis. Throughout this book, he attempts to demonstrate the weaknesses of this philosophy and its incompatibility with the Eastern context.

The second book, *Iqtisaduna*, is more developed at the ideological level; there, Baqir al-Sadr provides in-depth Islamist answers to meeting the challenge that Marxist and capitalist economies posed to the Islamic perception and religion in the modern world. The book is dedicated mostly to analyzing and deliberating on Marxism because of its reinforcement by the Communist movement in Iraq and the Middle East in the 1950s and 1960s among minorities in the region, such as the Shi'ites in Iraq, Lebanon, and other places, and especially among the intellectuals within these communities.[26]

The historian Hanna Batatu maintained in the mid-1980s that Baqir al-Sadr's ideas had little originality and that he had borrowed the ideas of other thinkers and Islamized them so that they corresponded with Islamic philosophy.[27] However, there is no doubt that Baqir al-Sadr succeeded in addressing a wide audience and in shattering the "traditionalism" of the Shi'ite clerics, who were at that time distant from believers' daily and political life. Baqir al-Sadr's success was reflected in the massive number of supporters and imitators he garnered among the young.

Islamist activists perceived Baqir al-Sadr as an intellectual figure who evoked pride. Iraqi Shi'ites deemed him, with his serenity and depth of thought, as an adequate Arab and Iraqi Shi'a parallel to the charismatic Iranian cleric Ayatollah Khomeini.[28] Khomeini and Baqir al-Sadr were friends, and many similarities can be drawn between these two exceptional clerics. However, an Iraqi Shi'ite once told Batatu that "in their heart of hearts, Iraqi Shi'is like things to grow from their own soil."[29]

In the 1970s, following the death of the *marji'* Muhsin al-Hakim, three *marji*'s were left in Iraq: Abu al-Qasim al-Khoe'i, Ruhollah Khomeini, and Muhammad Baqir al-Sadr, who was the only Arab among them, the other two Iranian. Therefore, Baqir al-Sadr gained great support from the Shi'ite community in Iraq and was most identified, among all clerics at that time, with the Islamic Da'wa Party. However, Batatu emphasized that, contrary to the prevailing understanding, Baqir al-Sadr was not the founder of this party.[30]

Baqir al-Sadr's nontraditional activist perception had been remarkable since the beginning of his journey and theological studies. What is particularly interesting is the book he wrote in 1955, *Fadak fi al-tarikh* (Fadak in History), in which he describes the incident that took place on the first days that followed the death of Prophet Muhammad and the argument that erupted between the Prophet's daughter, Fatima al-Zahra', wife of the first Shi'ite imam, 'Ali bin Abi Talib, and the first caliph, Abu Bakr al-Siddiq, concerning the Prophet's bequeathing of the village Fadak to his daughter, Fatima, and its nationalization by Abu Bakr, who claimed that prophets cannot bequeath, according to the Prophet Muhammad's own hadith.

Fadak in History, Baqir al-Sadr's first publication, accentuates his nontraditional thinking. It demonstrates the radical change in his perception of the figure of Fatima, which he wished to instill in the believers. Baqir al-Sadr transformed her image from a marginalized woman whose significance merely was in her being daughter of the Prophet Muhammad, wife of 'Ali, and mother of the second and third imams, Hasan and Husayn, into a central figure in her own right because of her revolutionary and resistant challenge to the first caliph, Abu Bakr.

This revolutionary role is not implicit but rather eminent in Baqir al-Sadr's multiple use of the words *thawra* (revolution) and *tha'ira* (female revolutionist) in his book. He uses these two words eighteen times in the first chapter, entitled "'Ala masrah al-thawra" (On the Revolution's Stage).[31] Unlike other Shi'ite and Sunni clerics, Baqir al-Sadr put Fatima through a far-reaching process of alteration, transforming her from a constantly crying, weak woman (a moaner) into a strong and revolutionary woman whose crying had resulted from successive harsh blows—the death of her father and the denial of her husband's right to be the caliph who would represent his cousin, Prophet Muhammad, and to lead the Islamic nation after the Prophet's death.[32]

Baqir al-Sadr's potent portrayal of Fatima grew stronger because his writing was essentially different from the traditionalist writing produced in *al-hawza al-'ilmiyya* (scientific religious schools) in Karbala' and Najaf in the 1950s. The dominant view that prevailed among Shi'ite clerics at that time favored the *intizar* (waiting) theory, passivity, and abstention from taking political positions as long as the twelfth imam remained in occultation.

Not only did this young cleric write about a woman in Islamic history, but he also refrained from portraying Fatima stereotypically as a passive and weak woman and instead depicted her as powerful and rebellious. Baqir al-Sadr portrayed her as taking active steps and confronting authority (Abu Bakr)—an attitude to which Baqir al-Sadr would adhere throughout his life—as well as steadfastly resisting illegitimate or corrupt authority.

Fatima's activism is strongly depicted in terms of independence and leadership, for she confronts the caliphate of the Islamic state and presents her argument in front of the new leadership in the mosque. She bursts into the mosque and does not fear confronting the new authority. Baqir al-Sadr described her outburst as resulting from deep thinking and planning rather than from an emotional breakdown.

Baqir al-Sadr was aware that Fatima's resistance was not fruitful and that she could not regain her inheritance. Yet he emphasized that the revolution that she had started succeeded even if she had failed.[33] Opposition and dialectics of this sort will reappear in the activist perception of Imam Husayn's triumph over Yazid, despite the failure of the third imam's "army" in its battle against Yazid's army in Karbala'. This historical event has accumulated abundant myths and revolutionary operations, which the different forces in Shi'ite history have channeled to propel activist and revolutionary energy within the Shi'ite faith in different periods of history. The same motif of the blood's triumph over the sword (*intisar al-dam 'ala al-sayf*) also exists in Christian mythology, according to which Jesus is the victor despite his crucifixion or probably because of it.

This early writing by Baqir al-Sadr clearly demonstrates the impact of Marxist philosophy on him and his complete awareness that although he wrote about a historical event that had occurred more than a thousand years earlier, he was thinking mainly about the current youths' alienation from religion and clerics in Iraq and about the great impact that communism had on young Iraqis. In fact, his writings even featured certain motifs of socialist philosophy. For example, he described the Islamic Golden Age in which a rich man could not be respected merely for his wealth and a poor man could not be despised merely for his poverty. He differentiated between people based on their individual productivity,[34] citing a verse from Sura al-Baqara that corresponds to the Marxist slogan "from each according to his ability, to each according to his needs": "Allah does not charge a soul except [with that within] its capacity. It will have [the consequence of] what [good] it has gained, and it will bear [the consequence of] what [evil] it has earned" (verse 286).

Baqir al-Sadr, along with his sister Amina (bint al-Huda), was executed by hanging in 1980 by the Ba'th regime in Iraq led by Saddam Hussein after being accused of treason and an attempt to initiate a coup d'état against the Iraqi regime.

Baqir al-Sadr's supporters, whom he recruited from within youth groups and among the masses in Iraq, deemed him the "Khomeini of Iraq."[35] He was indeed much like this nontraditional Iranian cleric who introduced reforms into religious perceptions in Iran, Iraq, and the entire Shi'ite world.

The Iraqi authorities, however, did not tolerate the close relationship between Baqir al-Sadr and Khomeini, who in the year before Baqir al-Sadr was executed had succeeded in overthrowing the shah's regime in Iran with the same rhetoric and actions that Baqir al-Sadr used. The Iraqi regime despised the activism of the new clerics, who drew comparisons to and made references to the ongoing history of oppression of the Shi'a—the activist dimension or the "Husayni dimension," as Khomeini used to define it, rather than the "Hasani dimension."[36]

Ruhollah Khomeini

Ruhollah Khomeini was born in Iran in 1902 in the village Khomeyn, located about 120 kilometers to the southwest of the holy city Qom. Like his future friend Muhammad Baqir al-Sadr, he was also born to a family that genealogically dated back to the seventh Shi'ite imam, Musa al-Kazim. Early in 1918, Khomeini became a disciple of Ayatollah 'Abd al-Karim al-Hae'ri and followed him to Qom in 1922. In the early 1930s, he was a *mujtahid* and a schoolteacher there.[37]

In 1943, Khomeini published his book *Kashf al-asrar* (Unveiling of Secrets), in which he criticized Reza Shah's "secular" regime for being distant from the divine laws. He also criticized the shah's support of Hitler and his admiration for the Third Reich and Nazi racial science.[38] In this book, the young Khomeini sided with the clerics' position expressed in the Constitutional Revolution, which called for allowing a council of religious sages to ratify laws legislated by the Parliament.[39]

Khomeini had gone through a process of radicalization during the regime of Muhammad Reza Shah, especially following the shah's White Revolution, which resulted in severe socioeconomic damage among the clerics and the merchant class in Iran. Moreover, Khomeini and others concluded that the revolution did not ameliorate the status of the marginalized communities in Iran.[40]

During the *'Ashura'* procession on June 3, 1963, commemorating the martyrdom of Imam Husayn, Khomeini gave one of the most foundational speeches of his political life in which he compared the shah to Yazid, the Umayyad caliph whose army killed Imam Husayn. The following day more than one hundred thousand demonstrators took to the streets of Iran, and on the day after that the shah's regime detained Khomeini for nineteen days.[41] Even after his release, though, the demonstrations did not dwindle. On September 4, 1964, Khomeini was deported to Turkey and later to Iraq, where he lived for the next thirteen years as a teacher and a disciple. During these years, he never ceased providing statements on the Iranian political issue, but at a "low dosage," issuing only about fourteen statements and manifestos.[42]

While residing in Iraq, Khomeini developed a new political theory in which he blended the theories of *al-niyaba al-'amma* and *wilayat al-faqih*, representation and guardianship by Islamist jurists. Khomeini rejected Shi'ite political thought that entitled kings to rule on behalf of clerics and the vanished imam and instead advocated direct rule by clerics on behalf of Imam al-Mahdi. He explained the principles of his theory in lectures he gave in Iraq, particularly in 1969, which were published later as *Al-Hukuma al-Islamiyya* (The Islamic Government)[43] and served as the foundation for the regime that he established in Iran ten years later, following the revolution.[44]

Khomeini rejected the theory of *intizar* and the general philosophy that prevailed among traditional Shi'ite clerics, which banned the establishment of an Islamic government or state until the reappearance of the vanished imam. In *Al-Hukuma al-Islamiyya*, Khomeini described such statements as worse than a statement claiming that Islam is totally false.[45] He supported his argument with several rhetorical questions, such as "Are the rulings of the Shari'a and Islam relevant only to the periods in which the Prophet Muhammad and Imam 'Ali lived, or are they constantly applicable in all times and in all places?" He proceeded to argue that law enforcement, protections of Muslims, and the collection of Islamic taxes could not be postponed until the reappearance of the imam, for chaos would prevail otherwise in this world.[46] He warned of the collapse of the state and the social order as well as of regression to a prestate period and to the "war of all against all" in the absence of state authority, although state authority was not as perfect as the rule of the vanished imam would be.

Khomeini's revolutionary statements opposed hundreds of years of tradition that called for the Shi'a to wait—*intizar*—until the reappearance of the vanished imam. This criticism prepared the ground for Muslim Shi'ite activism in Iran and the Islamic world. It is evident that Khomeini's goal at that time was to build a theoretical basis for the rebellion against the shah under the banner of Shi'a Islam.

Furthermore, in *Al-Hukuma al-Islamiyya* Khomeini emphasized that the imamate (*imama*) should exist even during the occultation of the *ma'sum* (sinless) imam. Hence, he argued that social leadership during the occultation of the vanished imam should be handed down to the clerics, for Islam, according to Khomeini, requires that the *faqih* be knowledgeable in the topics of Shari'a law and that they be just ('adil). These two unique qualities, inherent only in the figures of supreme imams, qualify one to lead the society. Khomeini thus bestowed upon the cleric all the political privileges that pertained to the twelfth imam and to the Prophet Muhammad, but without demanding that the cleric be *ma'sum* or a descendant of 'Ali.[47] As Khomeini wrote, "God has given the actual Islamic government that is supposed to be formed in the time of absence the same powers that he gave the prophet and the ruler (*amir*) of the faithful."[48]

In addition to his criticism of the *intizar* theory and his support of the view that clerics are the only and the right people to lead on behalf of the vanished imam, Khomeini added another dimension to the theory of *wilayat al-faqih*. He maintained that supreme clerics' leadership and suitability for governance are absolute and equivalent to those of the imams and the Prophet. The sole difference between the clerics and the other two is that imams and prophets are superior to the rest of the people, including clerics, and enjoy sanctity that clerics can never obtain.

In one of Khomeini's letters, written following the establishment of the Islamic Republic of Iran and addressed to the president at the time, he maintained that "the ruler [i.e., the *faqih*] can destroy the mosques for the good of the religion and the state in the absence of other means capable of rectifying injustice."[49] The question raised here is, "Who determines what is good for the religion and the state?" Khomeini provided an explicit answer, maintaining that the *faqih* has that authority. He thus allowed the cleric to be the absolute governor in a sort of absolute religious dictatorship. Khomeini argued that in Islam there is neither monarchy nor dictatorship, for the cleric rules according to the Shari'a.[50]

Unlike Baqir al-Sadr, Khomeini not only added a theoretical dimension and prepared the theoretical ground for linking Shi'a Islam to a political process but also used this theory and promoted it so that he could implement it within the Islamic Republic of Iran established following the revolution in 1979. In addition to being a religious leader, a *marji' al-taqlid*, who controlled a network of religious organizations and a theoretician, Khomeini was also a charismatic leader with rhetorical skills that could touch the hearts of the masses and motivate them to initiate a revolutionary act.

Various studies have deemed Khomeinism an Iranian version of populism. In his book *Khomeinism: Essays on the Islamic Republic*, Ervand Abrahamian argues that Khomeinism is a populism that meets the definition of populism the way he comprehends it: "By it I mean a movement of the propertied middle class that mobilizes the lower classes, especially the urban poor, with radical rhetoric directed against imperialism, foreign capitalism, and the political establishment. . . . [P]opulist movements use charismatic figures and symbols, imagery, and language that have potent value in the mass culture." He proceeds to argue that "populist movements, thus, inevitably emphasize the importance, not of economic-social revolution, but of cultural, national, and political reconstruction."[51]

Mansoor Moaddel maintains that Khomeinism is a sort of fascist movement that suits the Third World and has a similar ideological dimension, which simultaneously glorifies heroic death, antiliberalism, antimaterialism, anticommunism, terrorism and a secret police regime, as well as the state's independence in the face of social classes.[52]

In fact, one can compare Khomeinism to other movements around the world. Khomeini used popular motifs and myths to mobilize the Iranian masses. George Sorel, one of the major philosophers of revolutionary syndicalism, devoted part of his philosophical work to explaining the significance and centrality of the use of myths to promote revolutions. He maintained that for the myths and symbols to generate revolutions, they must translate thoughts into actions. He attributed great significance to myths as irrational tools used in place of rational ideas for mass mobilization—especially of the proletariat and then of the petite bourgeoisie—and for political activism because the instrument of myth encompasses mythical thought, which, as explained by Zeev Sternhell, Mario Schneider, and Maya Ashri, is "an alternative to the theoretical and discursive ideas; a religious mentality that stands against a rational mentality. However, this system also has an immediate role: recruiting the masses and changing the world." "The myth is completely immune against any possibility of failure; the myth cannot be subject to reasonable and logical criticism; therefore, there are no limits to its power of mobilization and action."[53]

Khomeini, like the other religious leaders and philosophers discussed in this chapter, was aware of the potency of symbols and myths and used them in the most effective and sensitive way in addressing people, such as Shi'ite believers, who were imbued with the emotional impact of these symbols.

The innovation that Khomeini and his contemporaries introduced was the transformation of myths and events, which had served for more than a millennium as religious emblems or as symbolic means for expressing anger over the historical injustice inflicted upon the Shi'ites (such as 'Ashura', the martyrdom [*shahada*] of Husayn at Karbala', and so forth), into inspirational, motivating symbols that would lead to revolutionary action.

The Khomeinist perception and rhetoric divided the world into two main segments: the *mustakbirin* (the tyrants) and the *mustad'afin* (the downtrodden), the latter encompassing the vast majority of Muslims who have been subjected to deprivation and oppression by the tyrants, "Muslim" leaders in name only, and by the imperialists, in particular the United States, which Khomeini called the "Great Satan," and Israel, the "Little Satan." Khomeini successfully used Muslim resentment toward Israel to direct hostility also toward the shah, whom he portrayed as a marionette in the hands of the Israelis and the Americans.[54]

Khomeini interpreted Shi'ism in a revolutionary manner, transforming it into an instrument of rebellion and a mass mobilizer. The Shi'ite philosophy was capable of legitimizing explicit activism as well as absolute passivity in waiting for the vanished imam. Khomeini praised resistive activism. In his book *Al-Hukuma al-Islamiyya*, he addresses disciples and clerics: "If you do not deal with the colonialist policy and if your study of the laws does not go beyond the theological framework, they will not bother you. Pray as you wish. They want your oil, so what do they care about your prayers? They want our minerals, and they want to open our markets for their goods and capital."[55]

This statement is an evident demonstration of Khomeini's view regarding religion as a comprehensive ideology and way of life that cannot be detached from politics. Moreover, he positioned Islam as a revolutionary and resistive instrument that contributes to the confrontation of foreign imperialism.

In addition, Khomeini used populist and semi-Marxist slogans such as *mustad'afin* and *mustakbirin* and talked of himself and of Iran as the avant-garde of all oppressed Third World countries. He used a universal language, calling for the unity of the oppressed people of all races, faiths, and languages, but in this case all under the wing and banner of Shi'a Islam—the true revolutionary ideology and instrument that faithfully represents the *mustad'afin*.

Khomeini's speeches accentuated the linkage between the shah and the detestable monarchist history. The shah himself organized a memorial event for the twenty-five hundred years of monarchy in Iran and associated himself with the Iranian kings who had ruled in the pre-Islamic period, appropriating the title of *shahinshah* (king of kings), which the Prophet Muhammad had deemed the most detestable among all titles. Khomeini constantly emphasized this statement by the Prophet Muhammad.

To further emphasize and deepen the difference between the *mustakbirin* and the *mustad'afin*, Khomeini drew the most loaded comparisons from Shi'ite history. He always referred to the shah as reminiscent of the Umayyad caliph Yazid and compared the majority of the Iranian people to Husayn's family. There is no doubt that Khomeini knew how to make use of the tremendous emotions within tragic events featuring Yazid and Husayn. Further enhancing this analogy was the fact that Khomeini's supporters consciously called him "imam" without claiming that he truly belonged to the holy imams of the Shi'a Muslims. Positioning an imam on one side and a king or shah on the other was the shortest way for the masses to associate Khomeini with Imam Husayn and Muhammad Reza Shah with the detested caliph Yazid.

'Ali Shari'ati

Although Khomeini was the supreme leader of the Islamic Revolution in Iran, Dr. 'Ali Shari'ati was its ideologist. He was born in 1933 in a small village in Khorasan. His father was Muhammad Taghi Shari'ati, founder of the Kanun-e Nashr-e Haqayeq-e Eslami (Center for the Propagation of Islamic Truth), which aimed to disseminate Islam through logic and science. Its goal was to reattract intellectual and modern youth back to Islam and faith,[56] a goal destined to be one of the main objectives in young Shari'ati's philosophy and activism.

Shari'ati was a philologist, a sociologist, and a graduate of Western academia. During his studies in Paris, he was exposed to Western revolutionary movements, Marxism, socialism, and existentialism, and he could foresee the flow of Iranian and Shi'ite youth moving in pursuit of these ideas. Shari'ati maintained that the Shi'ite faith should be renewed and transformed into a comprehensive revolutionary faith. He interpreted the Qur'an and Islam in modern and socialist terms and depicted prophets as leaders of the oppressed populations around the world. Some skeptical clerics and supporters of the shah even deemed him a Marxist hiding behind Islamic terminology.[57]

Shari'ati joined the Jebhe Melli Iran (National Resistance Front), which included observant Muslims, secular nationalists, and Marxists who operated against the dominance of the West over Iran and its natural resources.[58] Together with his father and other clerics, he joined the movement of "God-worshipping socialists" founded by Muhammad Nakhshab,[59] its name taken from the title Shari'ati gave to a translated biography of one of Prophet Muhammad's companions, Abu Dharr al-Ghiffari. The biography portrays Abu Dharr as a prototype of the socialist hero, the revolutionist who is opposed to poverty, capitalism, feudalism, racism, and dictatorship and who can inspire all revolutionaries worldwide, especially in the Middle East.[60]

Shari'ati's main criticism was directed toward clerics who dedicated their vigor to unnecessary details and thus abandoned the core of true Islam, which is, according to Shari'ati, social justice and resistance against oppressive powers. Shari'ati differentiated what he considered pure Shi'a Islam, the revolutionary and authentic Islam of 'Ali, and the passive and inauthentic Shi'a Islam of the Safavids.[61]

Shari'ati maintained that Shi'a Islam had sided with oppressed people for many centuries and sought to liberate them from the different tyrants: "We can see that for more than eight centuries (until the Safavid era), Alavite Shi'ism was more than just a revolutionary movement in history that opposed all the autocratic and class-conscious regimes. . . . Like a revolutionary party, Shi'ism had a well-organized, informed, deep-rooted and well-defined ideology, with clear-cut and definite slogans and a disciplined and well-groomed organization. It led the deprived and oppressed masses in their movements for freedom and for seeking justice."[62]

Shari'ati was less concerned with the confrontation between secularism and Islam. He instead preached about the clash between one religion and another—between the "red Alawid Islam," as he named it, and the "black Safavid Islam."[63] Whereas "red" Islam praised martyrdom and revolutionary activism, the Safavids castrated Islam and transformed the heroic activism of Imam Husayn into an act of contrition, constant self-pity, passivity, and infinite waiting, which prevents believers from acting in a way that changes the status quo.[64] Shariʿati aspired toward a Shiʿism without clerics, or at least without traditional clerics who are concerned mainly with unimportant issues. He sought to render religion an ideology that mobilizes the masses toward a revolutionary act that will establish the empire of justice in this world at the present time instead of making them wait until the end of history and the far distant future for that justice.

Shariʿati was considerably influenced by his sojourn in France. During his studies there, he was in contact with the Algerian resistance movement, the National Liberation Front. He was also influenced by Franz Fanon, the prominent theoretician of revolutionism in the Third World, and by the French philosopher and activist Jean-Paul Sartre.[65] In fact, Shariʿati attempted to bring the revolutionary ideology he acquired in France into a process of Islamization by rendering it more relevant and clear to the masses, who did not necessarily know or comprehend Western worldviews, ideologies, or philosophies but who were strongly attached to Islam and Islamic tradition, which were integral to their lives.

Therefore, Shariʿati adopted a pungent, critical position not only toward traditional clerics and others who glorified passivity and *intizar* but also toward the Westernized intellectuals who attempted to eliminate the clerics, Islam, and Islamic traditions, both progressive and reactionary. Shariʿati denigrated both groups for their inability to struggle against imperialism.[66] In his lecture "Where Shall We Begin?," he emphasized this point: "Our own history and experience have demonstrated that whenever an enlightened person turns his back on religion, which is the dominant spirit of the society, the society turns its back on him."[67]

Shariʿati attempted to delineate the way for intellectuals to become organic intellectuals in Iranian society and in Muslim societies in general, whose activism is driven by society's popular-national faith, not isolated from it.

As previously stated, Shariʿati was deeply influenced by European Marxism and existentialism and tried to Islamicize these philosophies in a way that would be accepted by Muslims and would be based on the Islamic tradition and faith in Iran. As he maintained,

> Adherence to real faith and *tashayu'* [Shi'ism] in our society unites us with the masses and enables us to speak in their language, hence our ability to disseminate conscious and instill a sense of responsibility [among the masses]. . . . [T]his is achieved through interpreting and analyzing the events and the figures in the history of Islam. This adherence rescues us from being alienated from people (*al-nas*) and builds between us—namely, the intellectuals and the masses—a stable bridge. Therefore, the consciousness regarding the *tashayu'* becomes a general conception in the society we live in since it helps us understand genuine and deep truths in our land.[68]

Yet Shari'ati had a twofold purpose. In addition to mobilizing the masses toward revolutionary activism, he still adhered to the objective his father had voiced years earlier—to bring the Westernized Iranian intelligentsia back to Islam. To achieve this, he needed to use one of the central worldviews that prevailed in Europe at that time, Sartre's existentialism,[69] which constituted a common ground, language, and influence shared among the Iranian intellectuals.

In an article on Shari'ati and the *tawhid* theory, Elisheva Machlis emphasizes that Shari'ati succeeded in formulating an authentic theory that linked Islam to existentialism, achieving this mainly through transforming the concept of *tawhid* from an Islamic theological perception into an ideology and worldview of revolutionary activism that seeks to change reality—that is, to position human beings and their future, instead of the divine essence and nature, at the center of concern.[70] In his unique perception of the concept of *tawhid*, Shari'ati merged God, nature, and human, rendering them one essence.

In his lecture on *tawhid*, Shari'ati determined that "there are many people who believe in *tawhid*, but only as a religious-philosophical theory, meaning nothing but 'God is one, not more than one' but I take *tawhid* in the sense of a world-view, and I am convinced that Islam also intends it in this sense." In the previous paragraph, he wrote: "But *tawhid* as a world-view in the sense I intend in my theory means regarding the whole universe as a unity, instead of dividing it into this world and the Hereinafter, the natural and the supernatural, substance and meaning, spirit and body. It means regarding the whole of existence as a single form, a single living and conscious organism, possessing will, intelligence, feeling and purpose."[71]

Shari'ati's theory of *tawhid* was designated to bridge divine authority and human activism and freedom of choice, which ultimately lead to humans' freedom of political activity in this world here and now. This bridging is made possible by virtue of the inherent unity, as suggested by this theory, among God, humans, and nature and in light of Shari'ati's renewed interpretation of the perception of the human being as "God's caliphate"—that is, God's successor on earth. Shari'ati thus concluded that God and man are part of one entity; therefore, man constantly progresses along an infinite path (for God is infinite) toward the comprehension of the universe and of God, which will enable man to choose and act freely in this world and to be responsible for his choices and deeds.[72]

It is evident that Shari'ati's *tawhid* philosophy is not an ideological or intellectual game for its own sake. It was activism intended to achieve justice with "authentic" Islamic instruments, even at the expense of Orientalizing Western ideologies and Westernizing Islam.

Shari'ati was not merely interested in the afterlife; rather, he was imbued with the motivation to change the present world in which people currently live and suffer as human beings, as he argued: "This is the *tashayu'*; it is not about praying in a hope of gaining *hur al-'ein* [heaven's beautiful virgins]. The real *tashayu'* is not about accumulating 'requitals' (*thawab*) in preparation for the life hereafter; it is about gaining requital and all the good in this world. It seeks to achieve salvation, 'divine interceding,' and all the goals that exist on earth. . . . [I]t even builds heaven in this world."[73]

Shari'ati accentuated the goal of achieving social justice and maintained that "Allah" in the Qur'anic references to social issues can be replaced with *al-nas* (the people):

> In the affairs of society, therefore, in all that concerns the social system, but not in creedal matters such as the order of the cosmos, the words *al-nas* and *Allah* belong together. Thus when it is said, "Rule belongs to God" the meaning is that rule belongs to the people, not to those who present themselves as the representatives or the sons of God. . . . When it is said, "property belongs to God," the meaning is that capital belongs

> to the people as whole, not to Croesus. When it is said "religion belongs to God" the meaning is that the entire structure and content of religion belongs to the people; it is not a monopoly held by a certain institution or certain people.[74]

These explanations demonstrate that Shari'ati's perception was radical and humanistic. It was not that of an Orthodox Marxist, but it was influenced by this approach.

In his lecture on the dialectic of sociology, Shari'ati reduced the social structures and regimes of history into two groups, those of Abel and those of Cain. In the first group, he incorporates all just and egalitarian social structures, primitive communism in early history, and the future socialist society. In the second, he incorporates all the social structures based on oppression and exploitation, such as slavery, feudalism, capitalism, and so forth.[75] Shari'ati divided the regimes that existed throughout history into two opposing forces—the exploiters and the exploited. In the former, Shari'ati included kings, wealthy people, aristocrats, and traditional clerics. In the latter, he included the people, *al-nas*, and God. Shari'ati emphasized that in a class-based society "Allah sides with *al-nas* in all the social issues mentioned in the Qur'an. Allah and *al-nas* are actually synonyms, and very often they can replace each other without changing the meaning."[76]

In this way, Shari'ati surpassed other contemporary clerics and philosophers. He tried to match Shi'ite Alawid Islam, as he called it, with revolutionism and to transform it into an ideology and a revolutionary instrument that could change the world and confront Western imperialism without alienating the masses.

Shari'ati ultimately was unable to enjoy the fruits of this linkage because they were manifested in the triumph of the Iranian Revolution two years after his death in London in 1977, apparently through assassination by the shah's secret police, SAVAK.

Musa al-Sadr

Unlike the preceding three thinkers, Musa al-Sadr did not excel in philosophy, nor was he a distinguished cleric among his contemporaries, even though he descended from a family of *asyyad* and outstanding clerics whose roots were in southern Lebanon and its environs and who flourished in Iraq and Iran. Al-Sadr's uniqueness lay in his being a cleric of a new type that developed at that time, especially in the new arena he entered—Lebanon.

The new politics and history of the Shi'a in contemporary Lebanon would be incomprehensible without an understanding of the project developed by the Iranian Lebanese cleric Musa al-Sadr; this fundamental connection is why he was deemed one of the founding fathers (although not directly) of Hezbollah in Lebanon and of the *muqawama* philosophy strongly associated with Shi'ism in Lebanon.

Imam Musa al-Din al-Sadr was born in 1928 in the Iranian holy city of Qom.[77] His father, Ayatollah Sadr al-Din al-Sadr, was a distinguished cleric whose family was originally from a small village in Lebanon. One of his forefathers, Sayyid Saleh Sharaf al-Din, had escaped the tyranny of the Ottoman governor Ahmad Pasha al-Jazzar, who had terrorized the Shi'ite community in the region of Jabal 'Amel (currently southern Lebanon and Upper Galilee). Sharaf al-Din ended up in Isfahan, Iran, where he fathered five sons, all of whom became 'ulama'.[78]

Musa al-Sadr completed primary and secondary education in Qom and pursued higher education at the University of Tehran, where he studied law and political economy. Although he did not aspire to become a cleric, pressured by his father he returned to Qom, where he studied theology in the madrasa. During his theological studies, he was editor of the periodical *Makateb Islami* (Islamic Schools). In 1953, he moved to Najaf and pursued his theological studies under the supervision of the cleric Sayyid Muhsin al-Hakim.

The first time al-Sadr visited Lebanon, the land of his forefathers, he made a very positive impression on his hosts. Therefore, he was invited to succeed the cleric of Tyre, Sayyid Abdul Husayn Sharafeddine, after his death, and become the mufti of Tyre. He accepted the invitation, encouraged by his teacher in Najaf, and moved to Tyre in 1959.[79]

Imam al-Sadr, as he was called later by his supporters, arrived in Lebanon at a momentous time. His arrival coincided with the return of the Shi'ite nouveaux riches and the wealth they had accumulated mainly in West Africa but also in other regions. The nouveaux riches looked for new channels of influencing their community and their homeland, which was ruled under a Maronite–Sunni hegemony that had excluded them and thus caused them to leave Lebanon and seek success in distant countries.[80]

After their return to Lebanon, these nouveaux riches found themselves between a rock and a hard place. On the one hand, they could not relate to the radical leftist parties, which were well established among young and oppressed Shi'ites. These parties sought to radically transform Lebanon with a class-based revolution that would fundamentally alter the position of merchants and bankers, hand the rule of the country over to the oppressed and poor people, and abolish the sectarian division that excluded Shi'ites from centers of power and from having any influence on the state's institutions. On the other hand, the nouveaux riches were not partners in the comprehensive Arab dream that would lead to the "fusion" of all Arabs in the Arab nation, regardless of their religion, race, or faith, and unite all Arab countries, including Lebanon.

The nouveaux riches also disliked the traditional clerics and their absolute reliance on the generosity of the traditional *zu'ama'*, who for their part deemed the nouveaux riches potential competitors.[81] Therefore, amity did not prevail between these two social groups either.

Into this divided social scene, Imam Musa al-Sadr, a cleric of a new type, arrived. As mainly a cleric but also the mufti of Tyre and later head of the supreme council of the Shi'ite community in Lebanon, he could play the role of a traditional cleric. But he was also an organic intellectual who established a broad network of relationships with both the masses and the Shi'ite nouveaux riches, who looked for a leader who would help them claim their place in the centers of power in the Lebanese state.

Al-Sadr faced the challenge of transforming the Shi'ites into one united group. As already stated in the previous chapter, Shi'ites were divided into residents of southern Lebanon and residents of the Lebanese Biqa', and the relationship between these two groups was loose. To render the Lebanese Shi'ites a homogenous community, al-Sadr started a process of bridging gaps between the members of the strong tribes of the Biqa' and the observant residents of southern Lebanon, who were more religious, more educated, and more submissive to their *zu'ama'*. Al-Sadr intensively sought to unite these two communities and initiated a process for building one "homogenous imagined community." In the speeches and protest rallies he organized in the early 1970s, he focused on the connection between the people of the Biqa' and the people of the South.

Al-Sadr transformed the religious rituals, especially 'Ashura', into an instrument for solidarity between the different groups of the Shi'ite community.[82] He sought to disseminate the activist interpretation of the Karbala' story and the murder of Imam Husayn:

> Husayn had three kinds of enemies: those who killed him—and they were tyrants; those who tried to obliterate his memory, like the men who plowed the earth and covered the spot where he was buried or like the Ottomans who prevented any remembrance of him. The third kind of enemies are those who wanted to ossify the example of Hussein, to restrict the meaning of his life and martyrdom to tears and lamentations. The third kind of enemies are the most dangerous, for they threaten to destroy the living roots of Hussein's memory.[83]

By the third kind, al-Sadr meant the Shi'a, the serene and silent tradition of the Shi'a, the tradition of the traditional clerics. He attempted to bridge a centuries-wide gap since the murder of Husayn by drawing a comparison relevant to the contemporary reality of the Shi'ite community in Lebanon.[84] Al-Sadr did not consider Shi'a Islam a religion concerned solely with the end of time. Like the other thinkers surveyed in this chapter, he perceived it as an instrument that could not be detached from daily life.[85]

Al-Sadr was deeply inspired by the Egyptian intellectual and author 'Abbas Mahmud al-'Aqqad's book *Al-Husayn abu al-shuhada'* (Husayn, Father of the Martyrs), which was published in 1944 and depicted the battle between the third Shi'ite imam and the caliph Yazid as a conflict between completely different "moral conceptions." Husayn represented the nobility in the family of Prophet Muhammad, whereas Yazid inherited all the negative attributes of the Umayyads, who were opposed to Prophet Muhammad in early Islam and joined his ranks only after their defeat. According to al-'Aqqad, Yazid represented corruption, and Husayn represented pure Islam, which emphasizes justice and equality. The *shahada* path that Husayn chose was the only means to maintain the spirit of Islam. Despite Husayn's military defeat, al-'Aqqad deemed him triumphant in the judgment of history.[86]

Al-Sadr, like other contemporary Shi'ite modernists, adopted this interpretation of Imam Husayn's heroic story. In his numerous speeches, he reminded Shi'ite believers that the lesson to be learned from 'Ashura' is not lamentation but rather activism and the *shahada* path that Imam Husayn chose to protect the oppressed and realize justice and equality. Al-Sadr succeeded in rendering Karbala' and 'Ashura' a centerpiece in the self-understanding of the Lebanese Shi'ite community and in the collective resemblance of all Shi'ites in Lebanon.

Al-Sadr highlighted the changed self-perception of Lebanese Shi'ites that was manifested in the rejection of the pejorative attributed to them, *matawila*, whose connation was always negative throughout history: a humiliated community whom everyone despises. Al-Sadr instead named the members of his community *rafidun* (refusers), which is also a historical appellation given to the Shi'ites that accentuates their being an opposition throughout most of their history. In one of his famous speeches, al-Sadr stated, "Our name is not *matawila*; our name is 'men of refusal' (*rafidun*), 'men of vengeance,' men who revolt against all tyranny . . . even though this may cost our blood and our lives."[87]

Al-Sadr wanted his community to become unified and proud of its identity, so he chose the word *rafidun* to accentuate that the Shi'a is a resistive group within the Islamic world. He also chose it to remind Lebanese Shi'ites that they are not a minority group on the margins of a small state called Lebanon but rather an integral part of a much larger Shi'ite world, which included communities in influential states such as Iran, Iraq, the Gulf states, Afghanistan, Pakistan, Turkey, Syria, China, parts of the former Soviet Union, and elsewhere.[88]

Al-Sadr based his project on three main components. The first was the activist interpretation of Shi'a Islam and the transformation of the Shi'ite perception into one of pride and identification. The second was the unity between wealthy and intellectual Shi'ites mainly from southern Lebanon who sought a new leader who would help them achieve desirable positions in the Lebanese state. The third component was the establishment of a militia and a military force that could protect the Shi'ites and the new project developed by al-Sadr. This component was dependent in particular on the Shi'ites from the Biqa' Governorate, who were known for their military capacities and force.[89]

However, despite al-Sadr's ability to introduce an activist dimension among the Lebanese Shi'ites and to provide them with an authentic religious context that did not contradict Shi'a Islam—an objective not made possible by leftist parties—his activism was not directed toward creating a radical and revolutionary change within the Lebanese state. In this regard, the scholar Augustus Norton indicates that al-Sadr had a reformist way of thinking that sought to help the Shi'ite community regain the position they were deprived of within the Lebanese state.[90] Al-Sadr called for allowing his community—or, more precisely, the new elite within this community—to have a piece of the Lebanese pie; however, he did not seek to turn the game upside down. It was for this reason that he maintained amicable relationships with the elites of the different Lebanese communities, especially the Maronite community.

The events that took place late in al-Sadr's life did not enhance his efforts, and the Lebanese Civil War posed an obstacle to his project. The Lebanese equation was resolved before al-Sadr could completely develop his project to its fullest, and although he unprecedently succeeded in uniting a large part of the Shi'ites under the wing of his "movement of the oppressed," which included leftists, conservatives, radical Islamists, liberals, and others, the movement's unity did not last for long, particularly following al-Sadr's disappearance during a visit to Libya in 1978. Imam al-Sadr's activist call for "reforming" the Shi'ite tradition, especially the 'Ashura' rituals, gave way to a more radical and revolutionary call in Lebanon, and one of its prominent advocates was Ayatollah Muhammad Husayn Fadlallah.

Muhammad Husayn Fadlallah

The person who indeed prepared the ground for the emergence of Hezbollah's Shi'ite *muqawama* was another cleric, Muhammad Husayn Fadlallah. He was born in Najaf, Iraq, in 1935 to Abdel Ra'uf Fadlallah, a Lebanese cleric. Fadlallah the son acquired his primary theological knowledge from his father and pursued his studies among distinguished Shi'ite *mujtahidin*, especially Abu al-Qasim al-Khoe'i.

Fadlallah arrived in Lebanon, his father's native land, at the invitation of the Shi'ite Jam'iyat 'Usrat al-Ta'akhi (Fraternity Family Association) in Beirut.[91] He became part of *al-hala al-Islamiyya fi Lubnan*, the Islamic atmosphere that developed in Lebanon following the rise in the number of Shi'ite clerics within the state, chiefly in the late 1960s and the early 1970s after the Ba'th regime in Iraq deported many young Lebanese men who had gone to Najaf to study the Shari'a. Among them were future Hezbollah leaders such as Raghib Harb, one of first leaders of the organization; 'Abbas al-Musawi, its second secretary-general; and Hassan Nasrallah, its third (and current) secretary-general.[92]

Fadlallah attracted young believers who were disappointed with traditional Shi'ite clerics,[93] and he became the main ideologist of the resistive and revolutionary Islam to which these youths aspired, especially with respect to the aggravation of war in the mid-1970s. In the shadow of the Shi'ites' expulsion from the eastern part of Beirut by rightist Christian militias, Fadlallah wrote *Al-Islam wa-mantiq al-quwa* (Islam and the Logic of Force), a book that served as a local ideological and religious-legal basis for the resistive philosophy in Lebanon.[94] In it, Fadlallah suggested solid religious foundations for the young Shi'ites who sought a militant and resistive Shi'ism rather than a conciliatory religion based on the *taqiyya* (the attempt to hide the Shi'ite believers' real faith).[95] He denounced the lamentation and self-flagellation that prevailed in the 'Ashura' rituals and instead praised power, force, and control. Fadlallah further proceeded with the resistive and revolutionary interpretive line of 'Ashura'. Like Khomeini, Shari'ati, and others, he maintained that the revolution did not end with the death of Imam Husayn and that Shi'ites would be misinterpreting the legacy of Husayn and the imams if they continued to adhere to their conciliatory and peaceful attitude.[96]

The second development of Fadlallah's philosophy was consolidated in the lectures he gave in a mosque in southwestern Beirut during the Civil War and the Israeli invasion in 1982. In these lectures, later collected and published under the title *Al-Muqawama al-Islamiyya* (The Islamic

Resistance), Fadlallah granted the Shiʿites in Lebanon, in particular the young militants who went through the radicalization process of their community, his approval of their *muqawama* actions against the Israeli conquerors. Fadlallah analyzed at length the resistance activism and the resistors' martyrdom not as the outcome of "brainwashing" but as rational acts because they aimed to push their nation and homeland a step forward toward the major goal of defeating the occupation.[97]

Fadlallah's greatest contribution is his definition of the *muqawama* as a comprehensive project not limited to resisting the Israeli occupation of southern Lebanon. He presented the *muqawama* as an inclusive universal and Islamic project under which all the *mustadʿafin*, both Muslims and non-Muslims, could operate.[98] He said: "We do not want to be only an Islamic *muqawama* that operates only in the South. We strive to be an Islamic *muqawama* in the Islamic world and among the wretched peoples of the Third World."[99]

Fadlallah reemphasized that the *muqawama* sought to liberate both Muslim and non-Muslim people. This perception corresponded with the philosophy of Khomeini and Shariʿati, who also maintained that Islam was the comprehensive and genuine worldview that would liberate all marginalized people. It was this same perception that later enabled Hezbollah to consolidate a national project directed at the different parties within the Lebanese sectarian mosaic, although in this case it developed under the influence of the revolutionary movement of Shiʿa Islam.

Despite Fadlallah's continuous attempts to differentiate himself from Hezbollah and to emphasize that he was not its spiritual leader, it is evident that his influence on Hezbollah was deep and would explain some of the changes that the organization went through given Fadlallah's openness toward the "other." Despite his enthusiasm and support for the Islamic Revolution in Iran, Fadlallah consistently maintained the position that Lebanon would never be Iran because of the complexity and diversification of its demographic and social structure. He did not believe in the possibility of establishing an Islamic state in Lebanon in the foreseeable future. Therefore, he replaced this notion with that of *dawlat al-insan*, "the human state," as a step toward establishing the ideal and anticipated

Islamic state. This state (the human state) would abolish sectarianism and equally respect all human beings, whoever and wherever they are and whatever their different religious perceptions may be.[100]

Fadlallah suggested the idea of the "human state" in the 1980s, determining that Lebanon is not Iran and that the process of establishing an Islamic state in Lebanon would take remarkably longer there and necessitate a long-term conceptual and popular preparation of the ground. He maintained that realizing this long-term goal required the recruitment and mobilization of the Christian and secular parties in Lebanon in order ultimately to abolish the sectarian system in Lebanon.[101] Fadlallah's idea was an explicit reference to the Gramscian perception of the war of position strategy instead of blitzkrieg. In other words, the "war" would be an attempt to slowly and discreetly embed Islamic ideas and perceptions in the different institutions in the Lebanese state and its society rather than to instigate a violent revolution in which Islamists would assume control, as was desired by many young Lebanese radicals who took part in the Civil War and who longed for successive takeover of all positions of power within the complex and heterogeneous Lebanese society.

Fadlallah's views applied both to the moderateness and to the apoliticism of his teacher Ayatollah al-Khoe'i and to the revolutionary and activist radicalism of his political source of inspiration, Ayatollah Khomeini. The combination of these two different and opposing teachers, alongside the dynamics of the development of the Civil War in the Lebanese context in which Fadlallah operated, explain well the contradictions in his views.

Fadlallah's enthusiastic support for the Iranian Revolution did not derive mainly from its contribution to applying Shari'a law but rather from the revolution's ability to free humankind and human will, particularly in Third World countries, from the burden of oppression by draconian and heretical powers. Fadlallah and other thinkers who can be defined as "humanist Islamists" were on an internal quest within Islam and Islamic philosophy for a revolutionary tool that would liberate all the Islamic states and the wretched nations from the historical burden of imperialism and continuous oppression. Fadlallah considered Iran's Islamic Revolution as one way, among many others, to release the internal power of oppressed people (especially in the Islamic world) and to transform it into a constructive rather than destructive force, which would contribute to development and not just to liberation.

Intermediate Conclusion: Islamic Revolutionism

The ideologists reviewed in this chapter were representative of a group within the Shi'ite community in different countries, mainly among radical youth who sought change but were uncertain about how to create far-reaching social transformation that would improve their status and that of their families and community members.

In the agitated world of the national liberation and decolonization movements of the Third World from the 1950s to the 1970s, during which an increasing number of youth followed radical and socialist ideologies and views, religious institutions in general and the Muslim Shi'a in particular seemingly became obsolete and disconnected from the continuously developing lives of the youth. At that time as well as in other historical periods, the Shi'ite clerics were a sort of prototype of the traditional intellectuals to whom Gramsci referred in his prison notebooks in the sense that they were a type of a remnant of the past that adhered to that past and to the very limited knowledge that served as a sedative for the masses. These clerics supported passivity and abstention from the pursuit of any activist initiative to change the reality in which the Shi'ite believers lived or to challenge the injustices they had experienced for centuries.

In this context, a new and different type of clerics and thinkers came on the scene and gained support by looking to the early history of Shi'a Islam, which was much more active, and to the contemplations of the first and third imams, 'Ali and Husayn, respectively. These revolutionary clerics could not come onto the scene until radical, socialist, and patriotic perceptions were deeply instilled in Middle Eastern societies, particularly in the countries that had large Shi'ite and religious minorities, such as Iran, Iraq, and Lebanon.

These clerics were "organic intellectuals" not only in the sense that they were the product of the growth of a specific socioeconomic class but also because they established organic relationships with the populations that supported them and responded to the challenges that other radical movements put in their path. But no less important was the challenge posed by the Shi'ite community itself, which searched for an instrument of rebellion that would change Shi'ites' lives.

More precisely, these clerics can be depicted as religious intellectuals who were "organic through tradition." Their traditionalism, not in the Gramscian sense, derived from their connection to their ancient religion and tradition. They dug into this tradition and extracted the "revolutionary-resistive" parts that characterized early Shi'a history especially. These clerics reconnected the Shi'ite emblems and tradition to the daily lives of believers and transformed them into a powerful political stimulus that enabled Shi'ites to gain life both in this world and in the afterlife. Passivity and abstention from political activism were not needed anymore in the present world; on the contrary, one needed to be active and to lead oppressed people worldwide by using the most authentic and rebellious means. One concurrently needed to believe that social activism in the present world would accelerate the reappearance of the twelfth imam, the Mahdi, who will both bring justice to this world and lead believers toward absolute justice in the afterlife.

The ideologists reviewed here applied three central points that they believed would activate the revolutionary-resistive potential within the Shi'ite perception and benefit it. The first was a renewed and active reinterpretation of the *shahada* of Husayn in Karbala'—namely, a transition from an interpretation that for centuries had focused on lamentation and self-suppression by the Shi'ites, remorse for not standing by their imam in his battle against Yazid's army, to the Christian-like message that "blood triumphs over the sword" (*intisar al-dam 'ala al-sayf*). In other words, they interpreted the martyrdom of Imam Husayn as a historical event that should apply to all times and places, or, as Shari'ati stated, "Every day is 'Ashura', and every land is Karbala'."

The second point was the rereading of *al-ghayba*, the occultation of the twelfth imam, from a passive interpretation that demands that the believers remain idle and refrain from political activism until the imam's reappearance to a more active interpretation in which, according to authentic and true Shi'a, the believers take initiative in the present world to accelerate the return of the Mahdi. The Messianic dimension of the Shi'ite doctrine and the integration of the activist view are reminiscent of the dilemma that Marxists faced in the late nineteenth and early twentieth centuries. Orthodox and economic Marxists believed that the revolution was inevitable, according to their beliefs in historical determinism, which Marx had sublimely interpreted, and according to which conscious political activism was not needed to accelerate the process because, in the end, once the materialist conditions ripened, the revolution would surely erupt. However, modernizers and radicals such as Lenin and others considered this perception as a sort of neutering. They opined that political activism in history should be initiated by the avant-garde, who would lead the proletariat to play an active role in bringing about a revolution in the here and now.

Socialist and Marxist philosophy undoubtedly influenced the philosophy of the Shiʿite revolutionists and ideologists reviewed here. This influence is manifested in particular in the philosophy of Shariʿati and al-Sadr. These ideologists believed that Shiʿism was the rebellious instrument of the avant-garde that could lead the wretched of the earth to justice, freedom, and independence.

The third point is that of the *taqiyya*, the attempt to hide the Shiʿite believers' real faith. The ideologists deemed *taqiyya* a sign of weakness, and the activism that they tried to arouse in the lives of the believers and their supporters attempted to link the *taqiyya* solely to a specific historical period during which the Shiʿites were a defeated and persecuted minority. Nowadays, it is well known (as always highlighted in Musa al-Sadr's speeches) that Shiʿites are estimated to number tens of millions worldwide. This great number further emphasized for the Shiʿites themselves that they are a force majeure, carrying the most "revolutionary" instrument or ideology that can provide an answer not only to all Muslims but also to all the oppressed people around the world. Therefore, they should cease hiding and stand out prominently in the here and now of this world.

4

The *Muqawama* of Hezbollah

Components of the Project

In the late 1990s and particularly at the outset of the twenty-first century, Hezbollah consciously and more concertedly developed its *muqawama* project, adding further layers to it in order to provide the basis for this new hegemonic venture. It is a project that aims to bring Lebanese together with marginalized people more broadly across the region and throughout the world. However, the organization has also sought to give the project a distinctly Islamic emphasis based on Hezbollah's own ideology.

Hezbollah's *muqawama* project was founded on three main pillars: a revolutionary religious interpretation; a new imagined community in which *muqawama* is a central mission; and a populist-economic position. In this regard, Hezbollah has succeeded in articulating the main signifiers of each area of the *muqawama* in order to build a coherent project that links the central arenas of Lebanese society.

The Religious Interpretation

Hezbollah's Shi'a Muslim origins have constituted a challenge to its expansion. However, these origins have also enabled Hezbollah to build and expand its foundation of resistance by using the Karbala' paradigm and applying a revolutionary interpretation to it.

Karbala': Timeless Muqawama

The murder of Imam Husayn, his family members, and associates at Karbala' in 680 CE has shaped Shi'ite history as a tragic history of the marginalized, who raise the banner of justice against the tyrants who wield evil power.[1] The massacre was perpetrated while Imam Husayn, his family members, including his sons and siblings, and seventy-two associates were heading to Kufa in what is now Iraq on the invitation of that city's residents.

Following the death of Mu'awiyah, the first Umayyad caliph, his son Yazid inherited his position. Yazid was known for his lack of adherence to Islamic morality, so a bitter controversy arose among the Islamic community regarding his reign, and the people of Kufa invited Husayn to their city to declare him caliph.[2] Upon their arrival in Karbala', Imam Husayn, his family, and his associates encountered Yazid's army, which was commanded by 'Umar bin Sa'd and consisted of thirty-two thousand soldiers, according to some sources.[3] On 'Ashura', the tenth day of Muharram in the Islamic calendar, Yazid's forces killed Husayn and his companions and took the women and children prisoner.[4]

For centuries, the Shi'ites have read Husayn's tragedy as a founding myth in Shi'ite doctrine. They released the "martyrdom of Husayn" from the time–space chain of that concrete event and transformed it into a symbol: "Every day is 'Ashura', and every land is Karbala'." 'Ashura' and Karbala' have diverged from their historical context and become an integral part of the Shi'ite ideology of resistance.

However, this Shi'ite interpretation of the third imam's martyrdom has developed over the years. As mentioned in the previous chapter, one can refer to two main interpretations of this founding event in the history of the Shi'ite Islam: a passive-conservative interpretation of repentance and an active one of revolution.

For hundreds of years, 'Ashura' rituals, in which the story of the murder of Imam Husayn is retold, have been ceremonies of continuous weeping among Shi'ite believers. This weeping is directed mainly inward to enhance the believers' feelings of guilt, weakness, and fear. It is coupled with the striving to abolish the original sin, which was to disregard Imam Husayn's need for assistance in his confrontation with Yazid's forces and to abandon the Prophet's grandson to his bitter fate.

The 'Ashura' ritual had already been practiced for centuries before the establishment of the Safavid state in Iran in the early sixteenth century CE. However, the Safavids developed it systematically in order to consolidate their rule over Iran and to tighten the Shi'ites' hold over the local population. This ritualism further developed over the subsequent hundreds of years to occupy an even more encompassing status in the community, including believers' need to slash and whip themselves with chains and swords in order to seek pardon from God and Imam Husayn by shedding their own blood.

Such extreme self-flagellation has caused much controversy among the Shi'ite clergy. A debate between two Lebanese clerics on this issue in the early twentieth century clarifies the controversy. Sayyed Muhsin al-Amin sought to free the 'Ashura' rituals in southern Lebanon from all masochistic practices: "The conduct of some people, namely the self-flagellation with swords and the self-inflicted injuries, is a satanic practice."[5] Sheikh 'Abdul Husayn Sadiq, head of the Shi'ite community in Nabatiyya, firmly rejected al-Amin's position, however, emphasizing that all self-inflicted injuries resulting from 'Ashura' rituals were insignificant in comparison to the suffering of Imam Husayn and his family. He maintained that such rituals were the way Shi'ites could identify with that suffering.[6]

The acrimony between these two clerics masked more profound disagreements on social and political issues. Sadiq was associated with the leading aristocratic families that dominated southern Lebanon in the late nineteenth and early twentieth centuries and advocated their hegemonic interests. The aim was to maintain the status quo: these rituals helped release intense emotions bound up with the death of Imam Husayn and directed them back upon the believer himself so that he would remain submissive under the burden of self-blame.[7] Sadiq was also the leader of the Shi'ite community in Nabatiyya, where a substantial tourist industry had developed around the 'Ashura' rituals. His objection to changing such commemorative practices was thus probably driven by the economic interests of the city's merchants and others.

The turn of the nineteenth century was also notably a period in which the Salafi–Wahhabi movement in the Arabian Peninsula launched a comprehensive offensive against the Shi'ites and their rituals and holy sites, claiming that they were pagan. These external attacks inspired firm resistance among Shi'ites to any change to the form or content of these rituals.[8] Al-Amin's position stemmed in part from his social status as a cleric who lived in Damascus and away from Lebanon and who sought Islamic unity and removal of rituals and practices that would exacerbate factionalism within Islam. He was therefore less motivated by the need to serve the interests of local leaders.[9] His fervor for unity also stemmed in part from the fact that Damascus was a stronghold of Arab nationalist revivalism, which sought concord in place of the factionalism and sectarianism fostered by the Ottoman Empire.

This Arab national revival movement that prevailed in the Arab regions of the empire centered on the Levant. Both the act of self-flagellation, which included striking oneself on the head with a kind of sword (*tatbir*) so that one would bleed as much as possible in order mournfully to commemorate Imam Husayn's fate, and the controversy over it continued right into the 1990s. This ritual also later became another arena for competition between Hezbollah and the Amal movement over dominance in the Shiʿite community in Nabatiyya and Lebanon more broadly.

Supreme Leader of Iran Ayatollah ʿAli Hosseini Khamene'i issued a fatwa in 1994 banning believers from practicing *tatbir* and any similar self-flagellation with swords.[10] Hezbollah, both as organization and as imitator (*muqallid*) of Khamene'i, thus ordered its supporters to cease such practices. It inaugurated blood-donation campaigns as an alternative, according to some sources, to better represent the real message of ʿAshura' as it saw that commemoration ritual. Blood donation was also an appeal to the masses that provided a way for them to contribute to the *muqawama*.[11]

Whichever way the ʿAshura' ritual is observed, it is deeply rooted in Shiʿite culture, especially in Lebanon. Other interpretations and practices of intense ritualism have continued to emerge in Lebanon, Iran, and elsewhere in the Shiʿite world.

Clerics and the new activist frameworks that emerged in the mid–twentieth century sought to channel the tremendous energies of the ʿAshura' ritual and the attempts to comprehend the historical and mythical death of Imam Husayn as a model for contemporary sociopolitical activism. The activist interpretation of the events at Karbala' emphasized Imam Husayn's strong will to reach Karbala' and to confront Yazid's army even though he knew that he and his family were destined for martyrdom and inevitable death. The aim was to realize the divine plan that strove for "the triumph of blood over the sword."[12] Husayn became and continues to be a symbolic figure for both the wretched of the earth and all those who resist. Although he and his family were massacred and defeated, commemorating him and the myths that arose around him after his death have preserved the "true faith" and shown the world the importance of resistance and martyrdom as opposed to the evil embodied in various "Yazids" throughout history. Through ritual, the events of 'Ashura' and Karbala' evolved from historical phenomena to an integral part of Shi'ite collective memory. Guy Rocher maintains that

> the collective memory is not necessarily the historians' history, although it would be a source of inspiration. The past should be simplified, summarized, pruned, deformed and transformed into a myth; that is what symbolism is meant for. It suffices to list some names of superheroes surrounded by the halo of the myth; it suffices to refer to dates and places saturated with memories, and to some deformed events.
>
> The collective memory, both tangible and deformed, is the most powerful element that enhances mutual social responsibility; and the symbols it uses are filled with meanings and interpretations.[13]

Karbala' also has become an irrefutable myth. It has provided the resistors and the revolutionists of subsequent generations with revolutionary fuel, as defined by George Sorel. Sorel maintains that the significance of myths lies in the fact that they are irrational means for mass mobilization toward political activism, replacing rational ideas.[14]

Ayatollah Khomeini transformed the interpretation of 'Ashura' from lamentation and repentance to resistance and revolution against oppressive regimes and global imperialism. In his book *Nahdat* 'Ashura' (The Renaissance of 'Ashura'), he writes, "Do not think that these funerals and these convoys aim toward a ceremony of weeping over the Master of Martyrs. The Master of Martyrs does not need this weeping ceremony; and this ceremony does not lead to any activism. The significance of these assemblies lies in mass gatherings and in the target they are all heading to." He adds that "what matters in 'Ashura' is the political dimension, the appeal to Allah and the concentration of the masses on one point and on one goal. This is what mobilizes the people for the Islamic cause. . . . [W]hat matters is the political dimensions that the believers had planned for from the dawn of Islam to guarantee its sustainability. It is about holding the same banner to achieve the same goal."[15]

Khomeini accordingly opines that the aim of 'Ashura' is mass mobilization to resist oppressive forces even if they are stronger or more numerous than the believers: "Imam Husayn (peace be upon him) taught people not to fear the quantity, for it is not the essence. What really matters is the quality and the way one should confront the enemies and fight against them. This is the essence and the path toward achieving the goals."[16]

Khomeini's interpretation of 'Ashura' and Imam Husayn's revolt implies that the believers' victory is inevitable, that they ultimately cannot lose. If they defeat the enemy in the battle, they will be victors both in this world and in the one to come. Yet even if they fail in the current battle, their loss will nevertheless also be a victory because they will be martyrs in heaven and commemorated as advocates of righteousness and justice on earth. Imam Husayn has always been glorified even though he "lost," whereas Yazid is recalled in curses even though he "won."

Khomeini validated the great resistive potential that lies in Shi'a Islam as a resistive and insubordinate religion and supported the interpretations developed by nonreligious Shi'ite intellectuals (for example, 'Ali Shari'ati and his teacher Jalal Al-e-Ahmad, a former Communist who joined forces with religious parties and adopted potent Iranian nationalist positions).[17] As a revered cleric, Khomeini lent to the interpretations of these Shi'ite intellectuals and reformists a religious legitimacy, transforming them into a powerful motivator of revolutionary resistance for an organization such as Hezbollah. Hezbollah has thus acquired religious and resistance credibility from the reformist interpretation of Shi'ite Islam and from one of its founding myths, 'Ashura'.

Hezbollah established its concept of *muqawama* on this resistive interpretation of Shi'a Islam. Therefore, the organization could easily connect its religious roots and its resistance project, which has served simultaneously as both a goal and an identity.[18] This active interpretation of Shi'a Islam especially emphasizes other unifying foundations that prepare the ground for different anti-imperialist forces in the region and that consolidate a common discourse even with Christian parties and other non-Muslim groups that support the liberation theology.

The Dilemma of Shi'ite Activism: The "No" Predicament

Hezbollah's perception of the history of Shi'a, as defined by 'Ali Shari'ati and others, places a special emphasis on the word *no*. Islam in general and Shi'a Islam in particular are held up by a profound resistive supportive pillar.

Hamid Dabashi radicalizes the resistive nature of Shi'a Islam and challenges Shi'ite activists in general and Hezbollah in particular with a difficult dilemma. He demonstrates that Shi'a Islam is a resistive Islam, an Islam of the marginalized versus the tyrants. Thus, he argues, "Shi'ism is a paradox. It dies at the moment of its success. It succeeds at the moment of its failure." Dabashi maintains that since Husayn is *mazlum* (oppressed) and symbolizes all the oppressed people worldwide, he cannot win and establish his state. However, he is capable of and obliged to continue struggling and resisting oppression, and his triumph is actually his murder and "his loss." Dabashi argues that the essence of Shi'a Islam is the attempt to cope with the loss of the charismatic phase in the development of Islam that coincided with the death of Prophet Muhammad. This coping is achieved through the theory of the Imamate and the attempt to preserve and maintain the (unstable) charismatic phase of the Islamic nation through the imams up to the twelfth imam, the hidden imam.[19]

The Shi'ites' ability to seize power and practice Shi'a Islam without losing its essence is nonexistent, according to Dabashi. Upon seizing power, the Shi'a, like any other state, is supposed to expropriate the absolute legitimacy of using power (according to Max Weber's definition of the state). Therefore, by virtue of this definition, Shi'a Islam will lose its resistive essence; it will project its resistance onto others and will consequently lose its Shi'ism (resistance).[20]

Dabashi argues that Shi'ism and resistance were interwoven until the Islamic Revolution in Iran lost its Shi'ite essence once it seized power and moved from being the oppressed to being the oppressive power. The revolution thus lost not only its essence but also the basis of its legitimacy.

Dabashi compares Hezbollah to Iran and maintains that the former is also likely to lose its essence of resistance. Thus, the Ayatollah Mohammad Husayn Fadlallah of today will become the Ayatollah Ruhollah Khomeini of tomorrow.[21] (Fadlallah died in 2010, two years after Dabashi published his book, but Dabashi's argument still applies.)

Yet, according to Dabashi, a pluralist state such as Lebanon, which has multiple ethnic and political groups (unlike Iran, where the vast majority of the population is Shi'ite), has the potential to constitute an interesting synthesis that would preserve the resistive essence of Hezbollah and Shi'ism and pose a serious challenge to Israel (the Jewish state). Thus, the resistive project that Hezbollah originally embarked upon will be continued. "The real threat to Israel and its religious polity is not Shi'ism (or Hezbollah). The real threat to Israel is the Lebanese political cosmopolitism, civil society, economic prosperity, cultural pluralism, in short a deeply rooted civility in character and disposition."[22]

Dabashi does not elaborate on how Hezbollah can further develop this potential. But I would argue that Hezbollah, in its transition from so-called ideological purism to "openness" and "Lebanonization," has already partially attempted to develop this potential by raising the banner of *muqawama* and by building the *muqawama* project as a counterhegemonic project, thus rendering Hezbollah as the leading authority in a historical bloc founded by different players. This potential would be achieved by virtue of the pluralism that Dabashi notes but without the seizure of absolute power, which would (theoretically) undermine Hezbollah's legitimacy as a force for continued resistance.

The process of hegemonic politics in the Lebanese arena is in some ways an "infinite" process that necessitates continuously preserving the essential balance in Lebanese society, and Hezbollah will seek to maintain its status in this arena as *primus inter pares* (first among equals) for a long time to come.

As discussed later in this chapter, Hezbollah has attempted to maintain the built-in tension between its embodiment of the pure resistive Shi'ite project, on the one hand, and its status as a significant player who strives to achieve a certain form of control in the internal Lebanese arena, on the other. It has achieved this by articulating the *muqawama* signifier in both its religious discourse and its economic-national discourse in order to unify the various social and political forces in the pluralist Lebanese arena.

However, before proceeding to a discussion of the national dimension of Hezbollah's *muqawama* project, we must address another facet of its religious perception that presents a serious barrier to its development: *wilayat al-faqih*, guardianship of the Islamic jurist. This prominent concept in Hezbollah's religious perception presents a major challenge to its ability to communicate with other players in the Lebanese arena. It needs to be superseded or at least interpreted more flexibly if the organization is to continue the development of its partnership project.

The Development of Hezbollah's Perception of Wilayat al-Faqih

As shown already, *wilayat al-faqih* is a relatively new concept in Shi'ite political thought. It has its roots in past Shi'ite thinking but reached its zenith in Ayatollah Khomeini's thought. Khomeini maintained that the right to rule a state in the absence of the twelfth imam should be given solely to clerics—and not just to any clerics but to the *marji'* al-taqlid (source of imitation), who is both deeply righteous and deeply knowledgeable in religious matters. Khomeini opined that the *marji'* al-taqlid could establish a regime of which he is the supreme leader to whom all the other sources of imitation are subject: an unprecedented idea in Shi'ite thought.[23]

I do not intend to go back over the historical development of this theory, but it is important to explain how Hezbollah as an organization has related to it, especially since it has declared itself from the very beginning "the party of *wilayat al-faqih* in Lebanon." This theory did not constitute a hindrance to Hezbollah in its early radical phase or during the Lebanese civil "war of all against all" from 1975 to 1990. However, little by little the organization moved into a phase of openness and Lebanonization, or, as I have defined it, a phase of hegemonic politics instead of blitzkrieg. Therefore, it needed to clarify its position regarding this religiopolitical theory that could be said to cast doubt on its loyalty to its operational homeland.

In his essay on the development of Hezbollah's perception of *wilayat al-faqih*, Jason Wimberly points to a transition from a radical and totalitarian view in the organization's early years, as he defines it, to a changed state of openness elaborated mainly by the organization's deputy secretary-general, Sheikh Na'im Qasim.[24] Wimberly points to a book by Hezbollah member Muhammad Zeiter, *Nazra 'ala tarh al-jumhuriyya al-Islamiyya fi Lubnan* (An Insight into the Perception of the Islamic Republic in Lebanon), issued in 1988 at the height of the Civil War and the "War of Brothers" between Hezbollah and Amal. This fact explains the "loud voice" and trenchant discourse that for the most part characterized Hezbollah's literature in those years. Zeiter promoted the combined embodiment of religious and political leadership in the figure of the guardian of Islamic jurisprudence, the *wali al-faqih.* He even accused supporters of the separation of political and religious authority of idolizing colonialism and argued that the *wali al-faqih* is the political reference point for all Muslims regardless of their place of residence.[25]

This strict and all-encompassing view of *wilayat al-faqih* became an obstacle in Hezbollah's path toward openness. Because the concept does not distinguish between the religious and political authority of a supreme leader, it left the organization's patriotic loyalty to Lebanon in doubt. Yet as Hezbollah's secretary-general Hassan Nasrallah stated, "The spinal cord of Hezbollah is *wilayat al-faqih.* Take out *wilayat al-faqih* and Hezbollah becomes a dead body, even a divided one. An Ummah without Ali is an ummah without spirit, an ummah without Husayn is an ummah without soul and an ummah without *wali al-faqih*, who must be obeyed, is a dead, torn ummah."[26]

Hezbollah was therefore obliged to reshape its perception of *wilayat al-faqih* in a way that maintained this philosophy's status as the organization's "spinal cord" while simultaneously enabling flexibility and openness toward other players in the Lebanese and regional arenas. This aim is reflected in the contemplations of Sheikh Na'im Qasim. In his book on Hezbollah, Qasim divides authority into religious and political aspects. The source of authority for believers can exist on two levels: "The first is personal; it is related to rituals, to human interactions, and to whatever concerns the personal and daily life. The second is related to the nation and its interests, to war and peace, and to general regional issues." He goes on to state, "Therefore, the first aspect requires a *marji' al-taqlid* who is familiar with the law and its limitations, while the second aspect requires a leader, namely a *wali al-faqih*, who determines the general policies in the nation's life, and the role of whoever should enforce the holy laws in the nation's life. This guardianship and authority could exist in one figure."[27]

Qasim thus divides authority into personal and religious aspects, wherein every individual can choose a *marji'* to imitate, but for general political authority there can be only one *marji'*—the *wali al-faqih*. To resolve the discrepancy between a religious philosophy that identifies the source of general political authority for the Islamic community as lying outside the Lebanese motherland and the Lebanonization/openness policy that Hezbollah adopted from the 1990s, Qasim further states, "There is no fear of collision between the subordinates in the different states, for the orders of the guardian of Islamic jurisprudence consider two things: first, the *marji'* obeys the Shari'a [the Islamic law] and does not breach its rules; second, the objective and unique context of each group or state affects the circle of the subordinates and the area of interest."[28]

This means that the *wali al-faqih* is not a dictator who can make arbitrary decisions, at least in theory. He is bound by an Islamic Shari'a that is consistent with requirements of the soul, freedom, and justice. The guardian also does not make decisions regarding all states and groups in a unilateralist way but takes into consideration positions, power relations, and context in every state or region. Qasim maintains that

> as activism in a certain state is related to its unique nature and surrounding, Hezbollah's [activism] combines the Islamist methodology and the Lebanese nationality, for Hezbollah is a Lebanese organization in the full sense of the word—its cadres, leaders, and members—and is concerned with whatever happens in the Lebanese arena—at the jihadist, political, social, and cultural levels. It also raises the banner of Islam that embraces Hezbollah and others worldwide. The concern for various issues in the Islamic world and among the most marginalized groups does not contradict the concern for national issues.[29]

Qasim's writings invalidate Zeiter's position, expressed a decade earlier, which unequivocally opposed any division in the authority of the *wali al-faqih*, calling it polytheism, the most egregious form of blasphemy according to Islamic thought. Through his writings, Qasim attempts to preserve Hezbollah's spinal cord, the theory of the guardianship of Islamic jurisprudence, while adapting it for the period that followed the death of Khomeini, the end of the Lebanese Civil War, and the participation of Hezbollah in the Lebanese general elections, with all that this participation implies for the organization's perception of the nation and nationalism. In fact, there has been some flexibilization of the organization's religious perception to match its nationalist spirit.

The moderation of the organization's radical Islamism, the "reform" in the notion of *wilayat al-faqih*, and the organization's adaptation to the new context in Lebanon, along with its emphasis on overtures to other groups in the Lebanese political scene, have helped Hezbollah erect a second supporting pillar in its *muqawama* project: the national perspective.

The National Aspect of the *Muqawama* Project

The second pillar of Hezbollah's hegemonic project is Arab Lebanese nationalism. In this pillar, as in the religious pillar, Hezbollah is attempting to create a new imagined community around *muqawama*. To achieve this, Hezbollah must undergo a process of change and openness, reduce the intensity of its radical religious-Islamic rhetoric and perception, and adopt a comprehensive ideology that brings together the different ideological and religious movements and groups that create Lebanese society. As in how Hezbollah has interwoven Shi'ism with *muqawama*, it has sought to consolidate a new Lebanese nationalism that will disseminate Shi'ism as a central and leading component of the new imagined community. This Lebanese nationalism would be achieved by allocating a central place to the *muqawama* ethos that unites all the Lebanese parties into one entity.

Hezbollah transformed the Islamic term *jihad* into *muqawama*. By emphasizing the resistive-defensive aspect of jihad, especially in the Islamic-Shi'ite tradition, Hezbollah could bridge the narrow and marginalizing perception of jihad and a broader and more comprehensive one, *muqawama*.[30] The main characteristics of this process can be observed in part by examining Hezbollah's two main manifestos outlining its ideological and political basis and reflecting its worldview: "The Open Letter" of

1985, which announced the birth of Hezbollah, and "The Political Document" of 2009.

The Muqawama*: From "The Open Letter" to "The Political Document"*

In the press conference that followed the publication of "Al-Wathiqa al-siyasiyya" (The Political Document) in 2009, Hezbollah's secretary-general Hassan Nasrallah stated that many changes had taken place in the world during the twenty-four years of the organization's overt existence and that Hezbollah wished to be seen as a party that had changed.[31] One of the most prominent manifestations of change observable in this document is quantitative in character: *muqawama* and derived terms occupy a larger part of the more recent document. Although *muqawama* is more frequently used than *jihad* in both documents, it is even more prominent in "The Political Document." In "Al-Risala al-maftuha" (The Open Letter), *muqawama* as well as *muqawim* and the plural form *muqawamun* in reference to Hezbollah's activists and fighters appear eighteen times, while the more traditionally Islamic term *jihad* and its variations appear ten times.[32] In "The Political Document," the term *muqawama* and its derivatives appear fifty-two times, while *jihad* appears only seven times.[33] This disparity is an indication of a definitive change in Hezbollah's narrative, even more remarkable given that the more recent document is shorter.

The reduced presence of the Islamist identity in "Al-Wathiqa" and Hezbollah's openness are reflected in the number of Qur'anic verses quoted in both documents. In "The Open Letter," at least fourteen verses are quoted, but "The Political Document" reduces the number to half, with an explicit tendency to transform Hezbollah into a Lebanese party that targets different populations in the state, not just the Muslim Shi'ite community that served as the first fertile earth for its development.

"The Open Letter" starts with a quote from a very potent verse directed against infidels: "And say, 'The truth is from your Lord, so whoever wills—let him believe; and whoever wills—let him disbelieve.' Indeed, We have prepared for the wrongdoers a fire whose walls will surround them. And if they call for relief, they will be relieved with water like murky oil, which scalds [their] faces. Wretched is the drink, and evil is the resting place" (Surat al-Kahf 29).

"The Open Letter" later presents verses that call for guiding the infidels to the true religion and another directed against Jews in the context of the Israeli occupation of southern Lebanon and the massacre perpetrated in Sabra and Shatila in 1982: "You will surely find the most intense of the people in animosity toward the believers [to be] the Jews and those who associate others with Allah" (Sura al-Ma'ida 82).

"The Political Document," however, begins with two verses from Surat al-'Ankabut 69 and Surat al-Ma'ida 35: "And those who strive for Us—We will surely guide them to Our ways. And indeed, Allah is with the doers of good," and "O you who have believed, fear Allah and seek the means [of nearness] to Him and strive in His cause that you may succeed." Both clearly refer to jihad and consciously aim to link Qur'anic jihad to Hezbollah's *muqawama* project at the beginning of the twenty-first century. The purpose is to achieve a smooth transition from the concept of jihad to that of *muqawama*. Despite the process of openness and Lebanonization, an organization like Hezbollah cannot relinquish its Islamic foundations. The key questions, however, are: Which foundations should be emphasized, and which verses should be quoted? Should they be foundations that serve to isolate the organization or ones that embrace partnership in the homeland and the region more broadly?

The two verses quoted in "The Political Document" are very germane to the general Hezbollah narrative. They form a bridge to the document issued nearly a quarter-century earlier. As also noted in chapter 1, the terms *jihad* and *muqawama* have been used interchangeably by various movements, including secular ones, throughout the history of the Middle East and North Africa.

Hezbollah has succeeded remarkably in moving from the closed discourse of jihad to the more open discourse of *muqawama* by closely linking the defensive sense of the term *jihad* to the secular overtones of the term *muqawama* without detaching the party from Islamist discourse in a way that would be counteractive to its core support. A sudden and extreme departure from this discourse would lead some activists to abandon the organization, as indeed happened when its first secretary-general, Subhi al-Tufayli, exited over Hezbollah's decision to enter the Lebanese parliamentary arena.

One cannot interpret the quantitative and qualitative changes in the organization's discourse in these two documents as completely detaching it from its Islamist tradition. Rather, there is a new formulation of its Islamist perception that renders it more open to partnership locally, nationally, and internationally, while allowing it to remain insistent in its opposition to US imperialism and its "metastases," as "Al-Wathiqa" calls them.

Muqawama *as a Comprehensive National Project: The Example of "Al-Wathiqa al-Siyasiyya"*

Na'im Qasim defines the Hezbollah *muqawama* project as a "social worldview in every dimension" and argues that it is "a military, cultural, political, and communicative *muqawama*. . . . That is why we have always called for building a *muqawama* society and have never been satisfied with being a *muqawama* group. *Muqawama* society incorporates its own continuity, whereas the activism of a *muqawama* group is temporary."[34]

Qasim contrasts two notions of *muqawama* that he deems completely distinct. He asserts that Hezbollah's project is to build a sustainable social formation in which *muqawama* shapes organizational culture as opposed to a narrative based on an elite, a vanguard, or a self-contained militia: a "*muqawama* group."

Qasim refers to the Lebanon War of 2006 and demonstrates that all the factions of Lebanese society took an active part in it harmoniously to defend the nation. He adds, "The warrior [of the *muqawama*] was protected by the woman who endures the hardships of being a refugee, by the child who aspires for a better future, by the elderly . . . by the proud Lebanese people who proved to the entire world that every grain of this land, every soul, and every drop of blood are *muqawama* in all the Lebanese regions and not just one."[35]

Qasim, backed by Hezbollah, thus prepares the ground for a project entwined with Lebanese society that will stave off the possibility of Hezbollah being isolated.

In the introduction to "The Political Document," one explicitly observes Hezbollah's attempt to prepare the grounds for integrating the Left, the father of resistance in Lebanon, in the new *muqawama* project through a semi-Marxist analysis of the global economic crisis of the capitalist system and its impact on the United States and Israel.

> What deepens even more the international hegemony system crisis are the collapses in the international and US financial markets and the fall of the US economy in a situation of failure. This gives a clear expression of the peak of the structural crisis of the arrogant capitalist sample. Therefore, it's possible to say that we are amid historical transformations that signal the retreat of the US role as a predominant power and the fall of the arrogant uniloparism and the beginning of hastening historic demise of the Zionist entity. The resistance movements stand at the heart of these international transformations and emerge as a strategic factor in the international scene after performing a central role in producing or promoting these transformations in our region.

It is further argued that "savage capitalist forces—embodied mainly in international monopoly networks of companies that cross the nations and continents, networks of various international establishments, especially the financial ones backed by superior military force—have led to more contradictions and conflicts, of which not less important are the conflicts of identities, cultures, [and] civilizations in addition to the conflicts of poverty and wealth."

In "The Political Document," Hezbollah points out the role of the different movements united in their resistance to US imperialist hegemony and domination. Therefore, the organization defines itself not only as an Islamic or patriotic movement but also as an integral part of the global resistive movements representing the most marginalized forces (rather than the tyrants, headed by Israel and the United States).

Hezbollah's reference to Lebanon's foreign relations is important in this regard. Hezbollah sees the European countries as a source of legitimacy for its *Lubnan al-muqawama*, "Lebanon of resistance," project: "Europe holds responsibility for the damage it has caused from the colonial 'inheritance' it has left behind—of which our people still suffer from the consequences and results. Because some European people have a history in resisting the occupier, Europe's ethical and humanitarian duty—before its political duty—is to acknowledge the right of the people to resist the occupier on the bases of distinguishing between resistance and terrorism."

In "The Political Document," Hezbollah also sketches a map of potential cooperative relationships between liberation and resistance forces worldwide, especially those in Latin America:

> We look at the experience of independence and liberation that rejects hegemony in the countries of Latin America with a lot of respect, attention, and appreciation. We see vast intersection platforms between their project and the project of resistance movements in our region, which lead to constructing a more just and balanced international system. Such an experience—that of Latin America—brings hope on the international level in the light of a common humane identity and a common political and moral background. In this context, the slogan "unity of the wretched" remains a major and basic pillar of our political intellect in building our relations, assents, and comprehension in international issues.

Although Hezbollah's renewed identity reflected in "The Political Document" is not totally new—the new manifesto is based largely on the earlier "Open Letter"[36]—the later document prominently features the organization's ideological institutionalization and its transformation from a small organization focused on military activism to a large one that now enjoys considerable status at the local and regional levels.

In "The Open Letter," Hezbollah addressed those states opposing American hegemony and called them to join the religion of truth (*din al-haq*), Islam. However, in "The Political Document" issued twenty-four years later Hezbollah abstains from such an appeal. It rather calls those opposing American hegemony to act on the basis of common interests and mutual respect for the ideology and unique nature of each group.

"The Political Document" introduces Hezbollah's new perception of its priorities and improvements at different levels. Opening with a chapter entitled "Hegemony and Revival," it analyzes the current global power relations and the dominant American hegemony. The discourse is explicitly revolutionary, pertaining to the Third World, in which the resistance to American hegemony and its metastasis, Israel, is justified not only by religious sayings and beliefs but also especially by a "materialistic analysis" of this hegemony's motives.

In the second chapter, the organization refers to *muqawama* in an "expanding manner." It proceeds from a specific (and more significant) reference to the newly built project to a broader one. The opening paragraph concerns the homeland:

> The Homeland Lebanon is our homeland and the homeland of our fathers and ancestors. It is also the homeland of our children, grandchildren, and the future generations. It is the country to which we have given our most precious sacrifices for its independence and pride, dignity, and freedom. We want a unified Lebanon for all Lebanese alike. We oppose any kind of partition or federalism, whether apparent or disguised. We want Lebanon to be sovereign, free, independent, strong, and competent. We also want it to be powerful, active, and present in the geopolitics of the region. We want it also to be an influential provider in making the present and the future as it was always present in making the history. One of the most important conditions for the establishment of a home of this type and its persistence is having a strong, capable, and just state, in addition to a political system that truly represents the will of the people and their aspirations for justice and freedom, security and stability, well-being and dignity. This is what all the Lebanese people seek and work to achieve, and we are a part of them.

This text is a radical development in the organization's perception as well as a disconnect from the discourse of "The Open Letter," which totally disregarded the Lebanese homeland and always referred to the Nation of Islam, "whose pioneers gained victory in Iran, with the Help of God." In contrast, "The Political Document" refers to the *muqawama* as being interwoven in the homeland and as gaining legitimacy from its being national-Arab-Lebanese rather than religious-Islamic-Shi'ite.

The third section of the second chapter discusses the state and the regime that should govern it, not mentioning an Islamic regime at all. But this does not mean that Hezbollah has banished the "dream" of an Islamic regime from the distant horizon.

The fourth section of the second chapter deals with the Lebanese-Palestinian relation, especially the issue of Palestinian refugees in Lebanon. The organization's analysis and discourse are, again, not religious in character here. Rather, they are founded on the rationale of human rights, the Arabism of both the Lebanese and the Palestinian people, and the people's pertinence to the *muqawama* camp.

The fifth section defines Hezbollah's attitude to the other Arab countries, but it first alludes to the precedence of pan-Arabism over pan-Islamism. Hezbollah provides nationalist justifications for Lebanon's integration with the Arab environment and its active involvement in the national Israeli–Arab conflict as defined by the organization. This attitude is completely different from the condemnatory discourse of "The Open Letter," wherein the organization referred to the "so-called Israeli–Arab conflict" because at that time it deemed the conflict a religious rather than a national one.

In the sixth section, Hezbollah defines the organizing principles of Lebanon's attitude toward the Islamic world, unlike the narrative in "The Open Letter," which is completely bound up in Lebanon's being an integral part of an "Islamic nationhood" that does not recognize divisive national borders. Hezbollah also refers in the sixth section to the need to maintain pluralism in the "Arab Orient" (al-Mashriq al-'Arabi) and to stop the continual emigration or "bleeding" of Christians to the West. It emphasizes in the more recent document that it sees this minority as an integral part of the Arab Orient in Lebanon, Syria, Iraq, and Palestine.

One of the significant points in the discussion of the Islamic world is Hezbollah's reference to Iran. The high tone in "The Open Letter" and the then new organization's enthusiasm for the Islamic Republic barely distinguished between Lebanon and Iran and saw them as being merely two regions in the broader Islamic nation and integral parts of the true Islam. A quarter century later, the organization's reference to Iran in "The Political Document" is not religiously framed. Iran is instead considered a partner in the resistance movement against imperialist hegemony, a position that can be adopted by any Lebanese citizen and one unlikely to arouse essentialist religious or sectarian objections.

The end of the second chapter addresses Lebanon's international relations, which Hezbollah refers to in terms of distance, and different countries' positions toward US hegemony.

The third chapter deals with Palestine and the negotiations being held at that time (2009) between Israel and the Palestinian Authority, with special emphasis placed on the organization's support for the Palestinian *muqawama*.

Following the line of thought introduced in "The Political Document" and the *muqawama* banner raised as a cultural and political project that consolidates Hezbollah's legitimacy and simultaneously widens the circle of its supporters and allies, Hezbollah has invested maximum effort in building a "*muqawama* society," as defined by Na'im Qasim, and in developing an alternative culture, a *muqawama* culture.

The Attitude toward Christians in Lebanon: The Transition from Religious to Nationalist Discourse

"The Political Document" also reflects Hezbollah's changed attitude toward the Christian Lebanese, transitioning from the discourse of *ahl al-dhimma*, "protected peoples," to that of citizenship.[37] Furthermore, Hezbollah has intensified its efforts to ally with the Christian Lebanese, in particular the Maronites, as reflected in its meeting with the Maronite patriarch in the 1990s, its election of Christian candidates to the party list running for the Lebanese Parliament,[38] and ultimately its signing of a memorandum of understanding with Michel 'Aoun's al-Tayyar al-Watani al-Hur (Free Patriotic Movement).

The move to this greater closeness is reflected in the transition from a special chapter dedicated to the Christians in "The Open Letter" to the later document's presentation of the Lebanese people of all factions as an integral part of the Lebanese homeland and the construction of a renewed Lebanese nationalism. In spite of this redefinition, however, when Hezbollah criticizes the long-running Maronite hegemony in Lebanon in "The Political Document," it still describes that hegemony as political sectarianism. "The Political Document" states that all Lebanese are victims of this sectarian setup:

> The major problem in the Lebanese political system that thwarts its reform, development, and regular updating is political sectarianism. The fact that the Lebanese political system was founded on a sectarian basis represents in itself a strong restriction to the achievement of true democracy, where an elected majority can rule and an elected minority can oppose, opening the door for a proper exchange of power between the loyalty and the opposition of the various political coalitions. Thus, abrogating sectarianism is a basic condition for the execution of the majority–minority rule. Yet until the Lebanese can achieve through their national dialogue this historic and sensitive accomplishment, which is the abrogation of political sectarianism, and as the political system in Lebanon is established on sectarian foundations, the consensual democracy remains the fundamental basis for governance in Lebanon because it is the actual quintessence of the spirit of the Constitution and the core of the charter of the coexistence.

Elsewhere in the document, it is stated that "the consensual democracy represents a proper political formula to assure true partnership and contributes to opening the doors for everyone to join the phase of building the reassuring state."

Hezbollah's perception of the Christian Lebanese has evidently changed from viewing them predominantly as a religious minority to seeing them and the other groups in Lebanese society as equal citizens in one state. Until the ideal of a state for all citizens is achieved, the organization will accept a state for all its "sects."

Based on the thought of Shi'ite intellectuals and scholars such as Muhammad Husayn Fadlallah and their ability to enrich Islam with renewed interpretations that Shi'ites, unlike Sunnis, facilitate, Hezbollah's view of Christians in Lebanon has developed from their being *ahl al-dhimma* to their having *muwatana* (citizenship).[39] This evolution in perception has been influenced largely by the concept of the "human state" that Fadlallah proposed in the late 1980s and that pervaded the organization subsequently.[40] Fadlallah attempted through this concept to map out an Islamic ideological infrastructure for establishing the "human state" within Lebanon. The vision is of a state that treats all citizens respectfully regardless of their religious affiliation or, more precisely, their essentialist religious affiliation. For Fadlallah, the goal of respecting human beings simply as such is the same for both Christianity and Islam.[41]

Hezbollah's position, embodying the pluralistic spirit of the Lebanese identity, has been reinforced in its literature and public statements by the organization's leaders, particularly since the eruption of civil war in Syria in 2011 and even more so since Hezbollah became a protagonist in that war in May 2013.[42] This position is set against a background of threat to the pluralist spirit prevailing in the region, particularly in Lebanon.

Ironically enough, Hezbollah has appropriated one of the pillars of the preceding hegemony of merchants and bankers. One of the hegemony's main ideological planks—as I showed in chapter 2—is the fact that Lebanon is the center of pluralism in the region, the "Switzerland of the East." Hezbollah has appropriated and refashioned that popular-national belief by adding a dimension of "heroic" resistance to it. Hezbollah argues that it, the organization, not only preserves the Lebanese homeland but also protects the pluralist homeland from the new live danger that seeks to destroy it through the Syrian conflict. This is how the organization now chooses to present itself, not through a narrative of inflexibility and sectarian radicalism counterposed to the practice of *takfir* (deeming fellow Muslims to be nonbelievers) that sectarian Sunni organizations have adopted.

The organization has justified its intervention in Syria by deeming itself the protector of Lebanon and of all groups that sustain the country's unique character. Hassan Nasrallah put it this way in an interview on October 18, 2015: "The *muqawama* protects all the nations of this region—the Christians, the Sunnis, the Shi'ites, and the minorities—on the right of partnership and freedom of opinion."[43]

This realignment of the resistance dimension rests on the premise that Hezbollah has become the guardian of the pluralist and culturally rich "Lebanese essence" not only against Israel and Western imperialism but also against fundamentalist movements such as al-Qa'ida and the Islamic State, which seek to combat the Lebanese and Syrian spirit of identity. It is evident that Hezbollah was unlikely to proffer this argument in the early months of the Syrian crisis in 2011. However, as events developed into all-out civil war involving not only Syrians but also external forces, Hezbollah could put this argument forward, and the argument won the acceptance of significant factional players in Lebanon.

That being the case, the legitimacy that Hezbollah has sought in its recent activism in Lebanon is not just religious. It is also pluralist and national, revolving around the notion of Lebanese uniqueness based on full civil equality among the different factions inside and outside Lebanon and with a special emphasis on the resistance character of this nationalism.

The Economic-Distributive Aspect of the *Muqawama* Project

Hezbollah in particular and the different Islamist groups in general do not have one coherent and consolidated economic theory. Although Hezbollah's literature introduced the division between the "downtrodden" and the "tyrants," the distinction between them is not necessarily economic or manifested through dominance over the means of production, relations of production, or infrastructure, as defined by Marxism.

In that sense, Hezbollah and the populist movements worldwide have several common denominators. These movements do not seek to provide a rooted alternative to the dominant economic regime in the countries in which they operate. They instead attempt to introduce a reformed distribution of resources in a way that benefits the "people" or the less-favored communities that have not received their relative share of the local economic pie.

Is Hezbollah a Populist Organization?

The concept of populism is interpreted in many ways in the literature, and there is no consensus on it among researchers. Various movements in different countries and periods have been dubbed "populist": the populist movement in the United States in the nineteenth century, Peronism in mid-twentieth-century Argentina, and like movements elsewhere in Latin America, among others.

The theorist Ernesto Laclau calls for a detailed account of the research on populism. He divides the approaches to populism into four types: the investigation of each historical case separately, populism as an ideology, populism as a political expression of a certain social status, and populism as the false consciousness of the proletariat. In discussing approaches to populism, Laclau acknowledges an additional approach in which populism can be defined as a movement acting on the popular-democratic axis—that is to say, on the axis of the people's confrontation with the hegemonic bloc ruling a certain state. He prioritizes the class struggle; therefore, he maintains that the social struggle is actually a process of articulation of different components around the class essence. He argues, however, that the dominant conflict in the modern state is not necessarily the class conflict but rather a conflict between the dominant group and the other marginalized groups or those alienated from the government. Laclau perceives the populist movement in its essence as a movement that broadens the scope of political participation of the masses and helps them become a political subject.[44]

Rudiger Dornbusch and Sebastian Edwards propose an analytical approach to the economic perspective of populist movements. They argue that these movements highlight economic growth and renewed distribution of resources in a way that benefits the "people"—that is, the impoverished and marginalized communities. Dornbusch and Edwards summarize the main features of economic populism:

> 1. The movement leaders, together with the wider public influenced by the movement, are not satisfied with the economic performance of the state. They strongly believe that one can achieve better performance on the economic level. This perception is hostile towards world trade organizations and international financial institutions.
>
> 2. [The populist movements] disregard the external limitations and the macroeconomic conditions.
>
> Based on the two precedent points, the populist movements emphasize three elements: reactivation, renewed distribution of capital and rebuilding of the economy.[45]

Hezbollah bases its economic position on the views of thinkers such as ʿAli Shariʿati, Muhammad Baqir al-Sadr, Ayatollah Ruhollah Khomeini, and others. According to Hezbollah, the economic division shall be made between those who own the resources and the vast majority of the people regardless of their religious, national, or ethnic background. Alternatively, as maintained by one of Hezbollah's leaders, Ibrahim Amin al-Sayyid,

"Hezbollah's friends are the Muslims and the Christians who confront the tyrants."[46]

Hezbollah's parliamentary electoral platforms have not especially emphasized economic matters. In the parliamentary polls in 1992, in which Hezbollah participated for the first time, its platform did not address the economy except for a reference to "the aspect of growth." That platform placed special emphasis on the regions that were still under Israeli occupation in southern Lebanon and the western Biqa' Valley. It also highlighted the need for agricultural and industrial investment and the development of marginalized areas, especially Shi'ite-dominated regions.[47]

The party's platform in 1996 included a separate economic chapter. In addition to the previous emphasis on the investment in the Occupied Territories, it asserted, "The state's role in the economic process is to coordinate between the activation of the private sector, its growth and flourishing investments, and the need to hinder the state's attempts to evade responsibility toward the citizens and the public affairs; it is also the state's role to enhance steadfastness [of the citizens] (*sumud*) in the conflict zones against the Zionist colonizer."[48]

The thread connecting these perspectives, as manifested in various platform statements between 1992 and 1996, is the extent to which the economy serves the *muqawama* and the *muqawama* society's ability to remain strong in the face of the long war against Israel. The organization's positions were still too general and not cohered around deep and cohesive economic perception, despite the fact that its slogans expressed solidarity with the most marginalized communities and its adherents in southern Lebanon, the western Biqa', and the southern suburbs of Beirut.

In the parliamentary elections of 2009, the party platform provided further detail on Hezbollah's understanding of economic matters. For the first time, the organization explicitly attacked the "service economy" that in its view had harmed the productive sectors of the Lebanese economy:

> Lebanon has suffered since independence from a lack of a comprehensive perception and a well-organized growth plan based on potential income, national needs, and adjustment to the region's economy. For all these reasons, the process of developing and ameliorating the economic performance was encumbered and random, thus leading to a withdrawal

> among productive sectors, strangulation of certain sectors, and illogical inflation among others. In this manner, the service economy took over Lebanon . . . thus landing a harsh blow to the productive economy that employs workers, such as agriculture, industry, and other different professions. To be able to introduce a genuine economic reform, we should first assign the state a new role and move forward from a reality in which the state is a neutral institution with limited social and economic contributions to a reality in which the state is responsible for achieving growth and justice.[49]

The different features of populism mentioned by Dornbusch and Edwards characterize Hezbollah—the harsh criticism of the national economy's dire situation and the sense of urgent need for a radical change (at least at the rhetorical level). Hezbollah accordingly attempts to reactivate the Lebanese masses through contemporary economic demands and reforms that benefit the "people." It calls for rebuilding the Lebanese economy so that the investments benefit the productive sectors, especially the agricultural sector, the historical economic basis for the residents of southern Lebanon and the Biqa'.[50]

In the years following the Lebanese Civil War, Hezbollah opposed the neoliberal policies of the Lebanese government headed by Rafiq Hariri, which the organization perceived as continuing the economic policies of the former Lebanese regime by prioritizing certain geographical areas, in particular Beirut, over the peripheries.[51]

Hezbollah's consistent opposition to neoliberal policies and to the reestablishment of the prewar regime was remarkable in its antagonism to Hariri's various administrations. Over the years, Hezbollah has abstained from lending its confidence to various Lebanese governments, mainly because of their economic policies. Between 1992 and 1996, three votes of confidence were held in Lebanon, and in all of them al-Wafa' lil-Muqawama (Loyalty to Resistance, the Hezbollah-linked parliamentary bloc) voted no.[52]

In 1998 for the first time, Hezbollah abstained from taking part in a vote of confidence on the new government headed by Selim Hoss, who was closely associated with Syria and who introduced policies that generally matched Hezbollah's economic and political positions. Despite its agreement with Hoss, Hezbollah abstained, claiming that the organization should first see the Hoss government in action.[53] It adopted the same approach in the votes of confidence on the two subsequent governments: Hariri's from October 2000 to April 2003 and Omar Karami's from October 2004 to April 2005.[54]

The change in Hezbollah's attitude from opposition toward governments (especially in the early period of Hariri's administration) to abstention from 1998 until 2004 was deemed slight progress in its occupation of a more central political position in Lebanon and the region. But the organization's priority from the very beginning has been to preserve and enhance the *muqawama*, as Nasrallah stated after the elections in 1992: "If asked to choose between the *muqawama* and the parliamentary representation, we will definitely renounce the latter."[55]

Based on this view and during the years that immediately preceded the Israeli withdrawal from southern Lebanon, the organization was obliged to set aside some economic priorities in order to gain different governments' acquiescence to its being an armed organization, especially in light of the increased pressures exerted at both the local and international levels on the organization to lay down those arms.

Abstention later became a form of support in the 2005 and 2009 elections following the Syrian withdrawal from Lebanon and the organization's need to penetrate all aspects of the political life in Lebanon and form part of the Lebanese government. It was used as a way to maintain the *muqawama* even after the withdrawal of the Syrian regime.

Hezbollah's populist economic stances were more insistent in its early years. The organization did not renounce these positions later, but the *muqawama* was the priority and led to some changes in the organization's positions on the economy. The organization had to navigate between its deeply rooted opposition to the Lebanese regime and the preservation of its arms and the *muqawama*. It chose the latter, aiming also at damage control.

In any event, Hezbollah's economic-populist position enabled it to articulate the *muqawama* discourse with the idea of protecting all the marginalized and impoverished citizens of Lebanon, regardless of their background, but especially the Shi'ite community, whose members were the most disadvantaged. This common foundation enabled the organization to engage in dialogue with leftist and nationalist forces in the Lebanese arena without absolutely committing to a purely essentialist, socialist, or liberal position. Hezbollah's general stance connected with those who did not benefit from the present economic system and with those who were positioned on the margins of the hegemonic project that had prevailed in Lebanon for decades.

Hezbollah: The Representative of Popular Shiʿite Communities versus the Bourgeois Amal Movement

Musa al-Sadr first established the Amal movement to enable the Shiʿite nouveaux riches who emerged in or returned to Lebanon in the late 1960s and early 1970s to claim what they considered to be their share of the pie. This social group consisted largely of those who had begun returning home after building up their wealth in West Africa, the Arabian Gulf, and the Americas.

This social group wanted neither to be confined by the patron–client system of the traditional Shiʿite leaders nor to be aligned with the leftist and radical movements that had gained influence among the Shiʿite population in Lebanon. Moreover, these Shiʿite nouveaux riches were not sufficiently mature as a group to take the reins of leadership. They considered the charismatic cleric al-Sadr their bridge to influence in the Lebanese arena, and so they constituted the main constituency backing him and his newly established movement.[56]

Roschanack Shaery-Eisenlohr characterizes Amal as the party of the Shiʿite bourgeoisie trying to imitate political Maronism by representing the Shiʿite community through existing Lebanese methods. She also maintains that Lebanese nationalism operates through sectarian affiliation.[57]

Amal channeled the early support it gained in bringing the Lebanese Republic and its sectional system back into the Shiʿite areas in southern Lebanon and the Biqaʿ and in backing the Lebanese armed forces' efforts to prevent Palestinian organizations from making the South a base for their activism against Israel.[58] Amal acted as a conservative force that sought to reestablish the old sectarian Lebanese system—with slight cosmetic changes that would benefit the Shiʿite bourgeoisie—within the framework of the contemporary regime.[59]

As opposed to Amal, Hezbollah has from its beginning defined itself as the representative of the most disadvantaged community in the most oppressed factions in Lebanon—the Shi'ites. Upon inception, Hezbollah adopted a radical Islamist position detached from the reformist discourse that prevailed in the existing Lebanese regime, the one promoted by Amal. Hezbollah opposed receiving the Shi'ite community's "share" in Lebanon's existing sectarian system;[60] it instead called for major changes to the Lebanese regime based on the pillars of an Islamic state, an end to sectarianism, and a lifting of all disadvantaged communities, chief of which were the Shi'ites.

Although Hezbollah's position corresponded to the radical discourse of the leftist organizations with respect to the need essentially to transform the Lebanese regime, that shared philosophy did not at this time serve as a basis for its rapprochement with these leftist forces. This was mainly because the organization's radical position was founded on a radical Islamist discourse that marginalized other groups and caused the leftist organizations, which could have been "natural" allies in terms of class ideology, to distance themselves from Hezbollah and even to confront it when they disagreed with it. For example, an article in Hezbollah's journal *al-'Ahd* (The Promise) described clashes that erupted between Lebanese Communist Party members and Hezbollah members over Communists' murder of a Hezbollah activist in Beirut.[61]

On June 13, 1986, *al-'Ahd* also reported the assassination of Nassar Nassar, an Islamic *muqawama* leader, by the Syrian National Party in the Biqa' following a confrontation between armed partisans of both groups.[62] Clashes of this kind were common throughout the Civil War and into the 1990s.

When Hezbollah set up its civil society foundations in the late 1980s and the early 1990s and decided to stand in the parliamentary elections of 1992, entrepreneurs who had already returned from countries in West Africa began to join Hezbollah and donate to its projects. Hezbollah thus incorporated an increasing number of middle-class people and professionals such as doctors, engineers, and merchants, especially from the southern Beirut suburbs. This inclusion provoked a certain change in the organization's economic rhetoric, though it has not fundamentally altered the perception of the organization as the representative of the ordinary Shiʿite communities in southern Beirut, southern Lebanon, and the Biqaʿ.[63]

Hezbollah faced another serious dilemma in 1997 when Subhi al-Tufayli, its first secretary-general, who had exited the party over its decision to stand in the parliamentary elections, organized the "revolt of the hungry" in the Biqaʿ, including demonstrations and boycotts of tax payments to Hariri's government, an administration that Hezbollah opposed. More than thirty thousand Biqaʿ residents participated, and Hezbollah feared losing ground regionally to al-Tufayli.[64] Its disquiet increased when al-Tufayli used the same slogans Hezbollah had advanced in its early years—slogans advocating the cause of the marginalized and railing against the corrupt Lebanese regime and against Hezbollah's bitter rival, Rafiq Hariri.

Hezbollah supported the protestors' demands rhetorically while in practice siding with the government that suppressed al-Tufayli's organization, an operation during which one of al-Tufayli's men and a Lebanese soldier were killed.[65] Hezbollah justified its support for the security forces against al-Tufayli as prevention of crisis and *fitna* (sedition) that would lead Lebanon into a civil war again, in which Hezbollah would not take part.

Despite these events, Hezbollah continued to present itself and to be perceived by its supporters as the organization of the Shiʿite popular masses. In a survey conducted in June 2006, out of four hundred respondents who defined themselves as supporters of Hezbollah, 81 percent belonged to a low socioeconomic status, with a monthly income lower than $1,000; 36.8 percent were uneducated or had not completed primary education; 45.6 percent had completed secondary education; and only 15.8 percent had attended university or received higher education.[66]

Hezbollah has continued to occupy this position in the Shiʿite community in part because of its ability to articulate between its resistive and anti-imperialist activism and slogans and the Islamic rhetoric that it embraces and with which it recruits the masses, in particular the most economically marginalized populations. However, the organization has also had the ability to establish an "Islamic socialism," as defined by Ahmad Hamzeh,[67] which is based not on the conflict between the different social classes but rather on mutual responsibilities and a broad network of civil society and economic organizations that support the masses to help them continue and persevere in the face of Israeli attacks and the government's disregard for their needs.

Independent Economy: Civil Society as the Realization of the Muqawama Project

From the beginning, Hezbollah has developed its own social institutions but also its own economic independence that has allowed it to help its supporters, perceived as the most marginalized population in Lebanon. Researchers have contrasted nonfunctioning state institutions with Hezbollah's more successful establishment of social, cultural, and welfare organizations and institutions. The party's creation of such institutions was a step in preparing for the future revolution and in replacing the state's existing institutions. This activism is described as a "state within a state."[68] Hezbollah perceives these institutions as integral to the *muqawama* society that would enable its members to continue supporting the resistance against the Israeli occupation in southern Lebanon and to push this struggle forward after the Israeli withdrawal, according to the ethos of the continuous *muqawama*.[69]

Hezbollah's social and economic institutions have played a major role in establishing and expanding the *muqawama* project. Hezbollah has been always proud of the fact that its institutions provide services to all the Lebanese people in all regions without discriminating, especially in the remote suburbs.[70] In this regard, these institutions have greatly contributed to consolidating and expanding the *muqawama* project and have increased the organization's exposure to other communities in Lebanon. In this context, the organization constantly fears the possibility of interpreting the provision of support to non-Shi'ite communities as an attempt to take over the regions located beyond Hezbollah's "natural" areas.[71]

These concerns have gradually diminished, especially in mixed-community regions, including those located on the front line with Israel, such as Shib'a and Kafarshuba. Although most of the residents of these areas are Sunni, Hezbollah's foundations operate there as well to support the residents' steadfastness in the face of the Israeli threat.[72] The services that these foundations provide include, inter alia, schools and educational systems; hospitals and clinics that often provide better-quality health care at cheaper prices than public hospitals; scholarships for university students, with an emphasis on natural sciences and advanced technology; water supply to many peripheral areas that do not receive this service from the state; professional guidance and assistance; support for the martyrs' families; support for the disabled and their families; reconstruction of houses that were destroyed in the ongoing confrontations with and wars against Israel. The organization also provides services in other domains that I discuss in chapter 5.[73] Its foundations include the following:

- Jihad al-Bina' (Effort for Construction) aims to reconstruct and maintain houses destroyed during Israeli military operations. It rebuilt approximately five thousand houses following the armed confrontation between Israel and Hezbollah in 1996 (Qasim maintains that the actual number is 6,714[74]). After the Lebanon War in 2006, it also played a major role in reconstructing destroyed houses, donating $12,000 to every family to rent an apartment until the work was completed.[75]
- The Shahid (Martyr) Foundation supports the families of Hezbollah fighters and others killed during the *muqawama* against Israel. According to Hezbollah's deputy secretary-general Na'im Qasim, the organization supports more than one thousand families and meets their educational, health, and housing needs.[76] This number has presumably increased following the mass involvement of Hezbollah in the Syrian Civil War.
- The Qard al-Hasan (Charitable Loan) Foundation was established in 1982 to provide Hezbollah's supporters and others with interest-free loans on nonprofit terms in accordance with Shari'a law and aids the most marginalized communities in Lebanon.
- The Hay'a al-Sihhiyya al-Islamiyya (Islamic Health Organization) provides health-care services to the *muqawama* society. It encompasses three hospitals, twelve medical centers, twenty clinics, dental clinics, public-health programs, and other facilities with forty-seven branches throughout Lebanon.[77]
- The Jam'iyat al-Imdad al-Khayriya al-Islamiyya (Islamic Relief Association) was established to support downtrodden families and orphans

in all areas of life, such as education, health, and professional training, and claims that it provides support to thousands.[78] The roots of this association, like those of many others, are in parent associations operating in Iran, such as Lajnat Imdad al-Imam Khomeini (Relief Committee of Imam Khomeini), whose first branch in Lebanon was established in West Beirut in 1983. Over the years, Jam'iyat al-Imdad al-Khayriya al-Islamiyya has further developed its activities and established additional branches in southern Lebanon and the Biqa'.[79] The association has also helped train workers in basic professions and technical jobs throughout Lebanon.[80] Like other associations established by Hezbollah, it has gone through a process of Lebanonization in that it tries to be an income generator, at least in the domain of civil society organizations. As the anthropologist Lara Deeb states, only 90 out of 440 workers in the association receive salaries, and the rest are volunteers, with some paid employees also serving as volunteers in other aspects of the organization's work.[81]

Hezbollah has also developed its educational unit, including the al-Mahdi and al-Mustapha schools, which serve approximately fourteen thousand students.[82] It has also distributed millions of dollars in scholarships to students from disadvantaged communities, especially for technological, engineering, and theological studies.[83]

The organization has established numerous colleges and higher-education institutes to serve the increasing numbers of ambitious young supporters willing to pursue higher education and step out of the cycles of poverty and backwardness in which their families have suffered. Examples include Rasul al-A'zam Technical Institute, Sayid 'Abbas Musawi Institute, Sayyida al-Zahra' Institute, Sheikh Raghib Harb Institute, and Shari'a al-Islamiyya Institute.[84]

Education is crucial for the members of the disadvantaged communities, especially Shi'ites, particularly considering that their presence in private schools in other regions has been extremely limited. Moreover, state-provided education is of poor quality. Hezbollah has therefore set up a broad-based educational system vitally needed by a very large section of Lebanese society. The organization has thus achieved two goals: empowering the most disadvantaged communities that it claims to represent and in this way ensuring the long-term support of these communities for the organization, instilling the *muqawama* perception among supportive communities, and broadening its impact beyond its "natural" Shi'ite constituency.

Summary: A Religious, National, and Economic *Muqawama*

This chapter has surveyed the three supporting pillars of Hezbollah's counterhegemonic *muqawama* project, its roots, and the forces that have molded the organization's character.

In the religious sphere, Hezbollah has recruited all the *muqawama* resources within Shi'ite Islam to support its interpretations. But it has not needed to invest much effort in reinterpreting Shi'ism as a sect based on resistance, for thinkers had already performed this task before the establishment of the organization. According to this interpretation, Karbala' as the foundation of Shi'ite Islam plays a major role in connecting it to the modern world.

Throughout Hezbollah's existence, its leadership has sought to forge a chain of equivalences among key concepts, players, and events such as Karbala', 'Ashura', Husayn, and *istishhad* (martyrdom), on the one hand, and its resistance toward Israel in particular and toward colonialism in general, on the other. This stance against Israel and colonialism had previously been adopted by secular leftist organizations in Lebanon and the region, but now the Hezbollah version added religious and social dimensions.

The fact that Hezbollah's starting point is religious has been a serious obstacle to constructive dialogue with other players in Lebanon, especially given Hezbollah's unique perception of the *wilayat al-faqih*. To overcome this obstacle, Hezbollah has gradually changed its conception of this principle and has tried to deconstruct it into separate religious and political components, while simultaneously emphasizing that this principle is primarily religious and pertains to the believer's faith. The organization has furthermore asserted that the political aspect does not extend into the minute details of political life distant from the strongholds of the *wilayat al-faqih*. It also maintains that the local leadership is quite capable of making decisions based on national and local evaluations.

The religious aspect of Hezbollah's project of resistance is centrally important but insufficient in a pluralist, multisectional country such as Lebanon. The party has therefore gone through a process of national empowerment or Lebanonization. This process has placed less emphasis on the divisively religious aspects of the organization without renouncing them completely and thus alienating its long-term hardcore support. Hezbollah has had to express very explicitly and unambiguously its loyalty to the homeland and started raising the Lebanese flag and playing the national anthem at all of its events. Hezbollah's leaders have also contended that Hezbollah's supporters are the real patriots in Lebanon because it is they who defend the homeland from Israeli occupation and from whoever attempts to impose on Lebanon and the region a certain version of Islam that disregards their pluralism and openness. In this sense, Hezbollah has appropriated elements of the Lebanese national ethos that once constituted part of the hegemonic project of the merchants and bankers' republic and that highlighted the uniqueness and pluralism of Lebanese society. Yet Hezbollah has adapted this perception also to fit the *muqawama* ethos, depicting the *muqawama* as enabling Lebanon to maintain openness and pluralism. Its view is of a homeland "whose strength lies not in its weakness but rather in its pluralism." This conception is deemed authentic and corresponding with Hezbollah's sociohistorical heritage, derived from being a minority in a region with a long history of persecution of Shi'ites.

The third supporting pillar of Hezbollah's project, through which it attempts to develop its own hegemonic project, is the economic dimension. The organization's perception of this aspect of its project has evolved somewhat over the years in an attempt to walk a fine line between seeming too revolutionary and seeming too reformist. Like other Islamist movements, Hezbollah does not have a settled economic doctrine, but it has adopted an approach similar to that of other populist organizations around the world, especially those in developing countries. The dominant contentions of that approach revolve around the most disadvantaged, the poor, the proletariat, the oppressed minorities, and the marginalized majority deprived of its just deserts. This group also includes all those seen as exploited by imperialist forces (especially the United States and Israel) and by inimical tyrants of all kinds. The marginalized are not necessarily laborers or the poor but may also be engineers, merchants, or doctors who do not enjoy their full rights. They may also be part of a marginalized nation confronting imperialist attacks, such as Palestinians, Latin Americans, and the Lebanese themselves.

Although dichotomous, this approach provides a recipe for widening the scope of support for the *muqawama* project that could connect a greater and greater number of groups belonging to the "wretched of the earth." Hezbollah has started integrating with influential Christian forces from Lebanon and the region, such as the Free Patriotic Movement led by Michel ʻAoun, because they are jointly facing brutal attacks from takfirist forces such as the Islamic State and other radical Sunni fundamentalists.

At the socioeconomic level, Hezbollah has identified weaknesses in the services provided by the Lebanese state, especially for the most impoverished and those most remote from the political center. Hezbollah has occupied this vacuum with its welfare, educational, and health institutions, covering the whole community of its supporters. This provision, seen by opponents as an attempt to establish a state within a state, has nonetheless contributed to increased support for Hezbollah. Significant Iranian aid, the proceeds from Islamic taxes such as *al-zakat* and *al-khums*, and the channeling of these resources toward the network of Hezbollah's civil society organizations, in cooperation with a large community of volunteers, have enabled Hezbollah to provide a significant alternative to state institutions. In many cases, this alternative has proved to be more successful and is beginning to realize the dream of a *muqawama* society for a *muqawama* state.

These are the elements on which Hezbollah bases its *muqawama* project. The interaction between these elements and outcomes realized are identifiable in the arenas of representation and construction of this counterhegemonic project—the communicative and cultural arenas that constitute the "laboratory" conditions for consolidating the project.

5

The *Muqawama* as a Counterhegemonic Project

As demonstrated in the introduction, hegemony according to Gramsci and post-Gramscian philosophers is not static. It is a continuous process but also one capable at a certain point of prevailing over the life of a society and imposing itself through the "soft" power of common sense on the social perceptions and behaviors prevalent in a certain social formation. Hegemony can be imagined as a fluid that seeps through the interstices of society and saturates its culture, institutions, economics, and politics. According to Gramsci, hegemony is integral to every layer of society, and he especially emphasizes the need for both political and cultural leadership to attain a position of hegemony.[1] The Gramscian conception of hegemony includes the dimension of compulsion yet also the process of subordinate groups' acceptance of moral and intellectual leadership, given that any project attempts in part to address their interests. Hegemony has cultural, political, and economic dimensions that bring into relief the synthesis of different forces that build the hegemonic project and their willingness to compromise and forgo narrow sectional interests to promote the common will and interests.[2] Hegemony includes the articulation of different social, cultural, and economic forms of leadership aligning into a comprehensive political project.[3] Gramsci furthermore describes the different spaces and "hegemonic mechanisms" through which hegemony operates, such as the press, publishing houses, educational institutions, social organizations, and cultural networks.[4] Any historical bloc that seeks to promote its hegemonic project has to present its unique cultural profile to the masses through practices and institutions in order to attain hegemony over society and the state. This process involves both voluntary and enforced compliance on the part of other social groups with an equilibrium required between coercion and consent.[5]

In this chapter, I attempt to show how and to what extent Hezbollah, as the leader of the *muqawama* project, has gradually succeeded in developing and instilling its perceptions of resistance in civil society, schools, public discourse, and even leisure activities. This thoroughgoing social penetration has been coupled with a certain openness toward other players in the Lebanese political arena. Hence, Hezbollah has been able to further refine its *muqawama* narrative according to its own perceptions and beliefs and to open up this narrative in order to integrate other forces with its "natural" Lebanese Shi'ite constituency.

Books: Teaching the *Muqawama*

For Hezbollah to instill its *muqawama* culture in the Shi'ite community in particular but also more broadly across Lebanon, it has developed the genre of "resistance books" that illustrate the way Hezbollah and its potential allies in the *muqawama* project perceive this term. A prominent example in this genre is *Qiyam al-muqawama: Khayar al-shahada wal-haya* (The Values of the *Muqawama*: The Choice of Martyrdom and of Life). This anthology of twenty essays written by various thinkers, authors, and Shi'ite, Sunni, and Christian clerics in preparation for the Mu'tamar al-Muqawama al-Da'ima (Permanent Resistance Conference) discusses "the perceptions, culture, development, and implications of the *muqawama* revival on the nation's life and inner feelings."[6] This conference, like many others held by Hezbollah, demonstrates the organization's attempts to establish a philosophical and academic infrastructure for *muqawama* culture and its project as a comprehensive one across the three main arenas within which Hezbollah operates: the local, the regional, and the international. Volume editor Na'im Qasim's foreword to the volume encapsulates his argument that *muqawama* for Hezbollah "is not a thoughtless or emotional reaction; it is rather a project of liberation and *muman'a* [passive resistance and steadfastness against pressure]." He does not hide the fact that this project was founded on previous phases of resistance from which it drew the components of its cultural and intellectual foundations. He states that "we refuse to detach our Islamic *muqawama* from a context of resistance activism both regionally and globally."[7] These and many other statements show that the organization's leaders do not perceive their *muqawama* process as an isolated one-off but rather as part of a broader culture that this volume, like many others by Hezbollah, seeks to promote within *muqawama* society.

The first part of *The Values of the* Muqawama incorporates five essays that seek to establish the philosophical foundations of the *muqawama*. Hassan Jonny's essay, "Mashru'iyyat al-muqawama fi daw' al-qanun" (The Legitimacy of the *Muqawama* in Light of the Law), seeks to demonstrate that Hezbollah's *muqawama* is compatible with international law. Jonny depicts it as embedded within a broader historical context of resistance movements not only in the Middle East but also in Vietnam in the resistance to the United States in the 1960s and 1970s and in France in the resistance to German occupation during World War II.[8] Broadening the context of the Lebanese *muqawama* to encompass the whole world is also the purpose of other essays in the collection, such as "Al-muqawama ma ba'd intiha' al-harb al-barida" (The *Muqawama* Following the End of the Cold War) by Munir Shafiq. Shafiq maintains that the end of the Cold War does not mean that the United States became the dominant world power. For Shafiq, contemporary resistance movements worldwide and notably in those countries not under US control are an increasingly potent force against America's imperialist project.[9] A particular theme in this collection is the legitimacy of the *muqawama* in a pluralistic society, with several essays addressing this issue from different perspectives. 'Adnan al-Sayed Husayn's essay "Marji'iyyat thaqafat al-muqawama fi mujtama' t'adodi" (The Source of Authority of the *Muqawama* Culture in a Pluralistic Society) emphasizes that the Lebanese *muqawama* began during the Civil War but has also had continual significance in maintaining national unity. Husayn promotes a concept of Lebanese citizenship whereby the *muqawama* may further enhance such national unity.[10] The Christian cleric Georges Massouh's essay "Ma'na al-hayat fi al-ro'ya al-masihiyya" (The Meaning of Life in the Christian Perception) argues that the *muqawama* not only is a military endeavor but also encompasses nonviolent action that seeks to curb exploitation. Massouh contends that despite the advantages of nonviolent resistance, Christianity does not reject all forms of violent struggle against injustice and occupation. In some cases, it is a necessity, he argues, as in the case of the Lebanese resistance to Israeli occupation and aggression.[11] This book, like many others, highlights the interplay and common thinking within the different constituents of Hezbollah's *muqawama* project, where the religious dimension takes the lead yet also gives space to the national, thus enabling integration with Christian, leftist, and Arab nationalist perspectives.

Another collection, this time of twenty-nine essays, that discusses Hezbollah's *muqawama* and its "victory" over Israel in the Lebanon War of 2006, is *Al-Intisar al-muqawim: Hawiyyat al-intisar wtda'iyatoh al-istratijiyya* (The Resistance Triumph: The Essence of Victory and Its Political Implications).[12] This multidisciplinary book provides an intellectual platform for a *muqawama* culture that continues to take shape in daily culture and events promoted by Hezbollah. Several essays contain the terms *muqawama* and *intisar* (victory), which have great significance for Hezbollah in such a work published immediately after the Lebanon War. Yet this pairing of *muqawama* and *intisar* is also significant for Arab regimes in general, which, according to Hezbollah, embody the culture of *inhizam* (defeat[ism]). The Arabic lexical root ق.و.م underlying the noun *muqawama* appears in the titles of nine of the twenty-nine essays in this anthology, and the word *intisar* appears in thirteen.

The twelve-volume *Mawsu'at al-muqawama al-Lubnaniyya* (Encyclopedia of the Lebanese Resistance) published in 2006 discusses the history of the Israeli–Lebanese conflict, referring to the concept *al-muqawama al-wataniyya*, "national(ist) resistance," as a major inspiration for Hezbollah's *muqawama* project. The organizations mentioned as being resistance movements include the Communist Party, the Hizb al-Suri al-Qawmi al-'Ijtima'i (Syrian Social-Nationalist Party), the Communist Action Organization in Lebanon, the Ba'th Party, the Arab Socialist Movement, and the Amal movement.[13]

Mawsu'at Nasrallah: Al-Rajul allthi yakhtasir umma (Encyclopedia of Nasrallah: The Man Who Embodies a Nation) comprises a three-volume autobiography of the resistance leader Hassan Nasrallah. It emphasizes the character of *muqawama* as both a movement and a culture that led to the first victory of the Arab and Islamic nation, embodied in Nasrallah, over Israel.[14]

Two works by leading figure Hassan Fadlallah published by Hezbollah's publisher Dar al-Hadi are also significant. *Harb al-Iradat: Sira' al-muqawama wal-ihtilal al-Israili* (A War of Wills: The Battle between the *Muqawama* and the Israeli Occupier in Lebanon) was published in 1998, two years before the Israeli withdrawal from southern Lebanon. Fadlallah gives an elaborate presentation of the history of Hezbollah as a religious *muqawama* movement and part of a broader movement of resistance.[15] *Suqut al-wahm: Hazimat al-ihtialal w-intisar al-muqawama fi Lubnan* (The Fall of Illusion: The Defeat of the Occupation and the Victory of the *Muqawama* in Lebanon), published in 2001, includes, in addition to a historical review of Hezbollah and the military operations against Israel, a full chapter examining the future of the *muqawama*, arguing that it is a culture that should be promoted among both the Lebanese people and other Arab and Muslims regionally.[16]

There is also the "*muqawama* novel," discussed in depth by Abir Hamdar, which tells the history of Hezbollah and the Lebanese *muqawama* through fiction. Hamdar suggests that the genre has only recently taken off and calculates that about a hundred works of this type were in circulation in 2014, half of which were published in the previous two years.[17] Hamdar, like others, discusses the process of openness and Lebanonization through which Hezbollah has passed. However, there is much more to the process than this. It constitutes a transition toward a counterhegemonic project in cooperation with other forces and movements at the national, regional, and international levels. The most notable autobiographical work Hamdar discusses is De Gaulle Abu Tas's *Bila qayd* (Without Handcuffs, 2002), in which a South Lebanese Christian tells the story of his joining Hezbollah and the Islamic *muqawama* and how it affected him. Abu Tas writes at one point, "They [members of Hezbollah][. . .]turned their face outward toward an enemy who was responsible for our suffering and misery. . . . [This enemy] has occupied a land that both Christians and Muslims inhabit,[. . .]and for this reason we should be proud of Hizbullah and should embrace and follow in its footsteps."[18]

The main character emphasizes the fact that he is a Christian integrated into the ranks of Hezbollah's *muqawama* and that being a member of an Islamic and national *muqawama* that protects everyone's land has enhanced his sense of dignity and self-respect: "I am honored to be a member of Hizbullah and, as a Christian, I am proud to be part of the Islamic resistance in a nation whose land is the property of everyone . . . for the difference in religious belonging is not reason for separation . . . the nation belongs to everyone." He refers elsewhere to declarations made by his comrades in Hezbollah on their shared interests and beliefs as peers and sons of the same homeland and of this homeland affiliation being much stronger than their religious affiliation, an idea that brings the national dimension of the organization's *muqawama* project to the fore once again.[19]

Other novels, such as the Moroccan author 'Abd-el-Ilah Belkziz's *Halat al-hisar* (The State of Siege, 2008), about the Lebanon War of 2006, blur the division between the whole Arab nation and the *muqawama* fighters and associate nationalist, socialist, and anti-imperialist movements with the warriors of the Islamic resistance· Belkziz writes that "Nasrallah is a historic hero[;] . . . leftists, nationalists, democrats, and liberals wish he was one of them."[20] The author, who witnessed the war, points to the closeness of all of these movements to Hezbollah's *muqawama* and to its development from a small military organization and defined religious group into an organization that stands for a broader Lebanese nationalism, for pan-Arabism, and for the anti-imperialist struggle worldwide. These novels are only two examples of literature that seeks to promote the *muqawama* to a wider public beyond the organization's "natural" constituency.

The Educational System

Most children in Lebanon attend private or religious schools, a United Nations report indicating that about 70 percent do so.[21] Hezbollah has therefore not surprisingly developed its own educational network to instill the movement's values in the younger generation from a very young age. Its education program has three main strands, the most important and recent of which is the al-Mahdi institutions that began in 1993.[22] The first three schools established were, according to Hezbollah's newspaper *al-'Ahd*, "an alternative to the state's unsuccessful policies in the field of education, as in other fields, and as an alternative to the private educational system, which is unattainable for disadvantaged communities due to high fees."[23]

With additional schools, Hezbollah could eventually meet the needs of approximately fourteen thousand students of various ages and in different Lebanese localities, but especially in Dahiya, Biqa' Governorate, and southern Lebanon.[24]

Another educational strand directly associated with Hezbollah and contributing to the promotion of the organization's project is al-Mustafa school chain, first established in 1983. In the academic year 2001–2, this chain had a little more than eight thousand male and female students.[25]

A third chain, relatively independent of Hezbollah but still influenced by it and contributing to instilling the *muqawama* ideal, is al-Mabarat al-Khayriyya, under the supervision of Muhammad Husayn Fadlallah (d. 2010), who was considered for many years Hezbollah's religious authority. The first school was established in 1997 to serve as an orphanage for the Shi'ite community in Lebanon. Six such establishments operate now with around three thousand students based in two schools in Beirut, two in Biqa' Governorate, and two in southern Lebanon. The chain has also established twelve other schools in other areas for all students from the Shi'ite community in Lebanon.

To get the schools that follow Hezbollah's curriculum to adapt to the *muqawama* project, a special emphasis is placed on Islam according to the revolutionary Shi'ite perception that Hezbollah advocates, though not to the exclusion of subjects such as the natural sciences and technical studies that prepare students for a future in the organization's life and activities.

Nasrallah's speech at the inauguration of the al-Mahdi chain of schools in 1993 addressed in detail the need for the mental and cultural preparation of the students for future integration into the organization and *muqawama* activism. At that early stage, however, this activism was still largely religious in character, without reference to the project's nationalist aspects.[26]

A change in emphasis could be detected in Nasrallah's speech at a graduation ceremony at the Lebanese University in 1997. Nasrallah quoted

Jesus saying, "For God's sake, bestir yourself," and interpreted this to mean that students should not use their studies solely for their own benefit but for the sake of the whole nation and of the *muqawama* project. Nasrallah drew a parallel between the progress achieved by each student and that achieved by the resistance fighters against the Israeli army, and he urged the students to conquer summits, like their counterparts in the resistance against the occupation.[27]

Periodicals and Contests for Disseminating *Muqawama* Culture among Students

The *muqawama* ideas elaborated by Hezbollah have been diffused through various means, including a periodical titled *Ajyal al-Mustafa* (Generations of the Chosen One). It was initiated in 1995 by the Jam'iyyat al-Ta'lim al-Dini al-Islami (Islamic Religious Teachings Organization), founded and principally led by Hezbollah clerics and activists, including the organization's deputy secretary-general, Na'im Qasim.[28] Although this organization was established to promote religiosity among the young, its periodical emphasizes *muqawama* values generally, and most of the illustrations that the students publish in it are greatly influenced by these values. The cover of one edition, published after the liberation of the South, features a map of Lebanon painted in the colors of the Lebanese flag beneath the Hezbollah flag, where a sword is stuck in a Star of David, signifying triumph over the Israeli occupation. The image is captioned "Kull-na lil-watan" (We all are for the homeland) and "Kull-na muqawama" (We all are the resistance), a pairing of lyrics from the Lebanese anthem and the resistance anthem, respectively.[29] This proximation of *watan* and *muqawama* is part of presenting a new form of Lebanese "*muqawama* nationalism." It is evident that a comparison of this kind was inconceivable during Hezbollah's prehegemonic period, when its main aim was to overthrow the state and when the very idea of a state, along with the concept of nationalism, was not even acknowledged. As Hezbollah's leading figure, Ibrahim al-Amin, stated in a speech in 1988, "Our project is the project of Islam, not only in Lebanon but worldwide."[30]

Similar motifs appeared in a Hezbollah children's drawing contest, the results of which were announced in *al-'Ahd* on March 5, 1999. The winning picture was of a sword in the shape of the country and painted in the colors of the Lebanese flag. The sword again was stuck in the Star of David, denoting the resistance to Israeli occupation. The runner-up's drawing contained images of Hezbollah's fighters waving to civilians in southern Lebanon, including an old man, a woman, and a child, denotating the close relationship between the people in the occupied South and the organization's activists who fought for their dignity. It also featured a cedar tree, the Lebanese national emblem. Another image that won approval was a drawing of a bird outside a cage alongside the statement "Al-hurriya li-kull makhluq" (Freedom for every creature). The organization's struggle is thus depicted as not just a fight for freedom but as humanitarian advocacy of freedom for all.[31]

The dissemination of Hezbollah's message among the young is not limited to images. *Ajyal al-Mustafa* has also featured poetry written by schoolchildren, such as one written in English, "My Beirut":

> You have your Beirut and I have my Beirut
> Your Beirut is high buildings smeared with black, and pocked with
> Snipers and bombers where warplanes shatter the sky's silence.
> Your Beirut is alleys in which fire is exchanged and shops blown up.
> And my Beirut is a small brick house on whose walls children draw
> Pictures under the shadow of what they feel and what they think.
> And my Beirut is an angel crowned a queen by the whole universe.
> Your Beirut is an old portrait hung on the walls of each house.
> And my Beirut is a young girl who doesn't know but the silver touch of
> Moon and golden glim of the sun.
> Your Beirut is a repeated poem by a very known poet who speaks to
> Himself in a mirror.
> And my Beirut is a poem that is every day changing read by the sky and
> Written on the golden rocks of the seas.
> Your Beirut is dinner parties full of most delicious food and my Beirut is
> A piece of bread in a hand of hungry kid and a doll in the hand of a
> poor girl.
> Your Beirut is sandcastles against the storms.
> And my Beirut is a tough rock that waves could not and will never
> erode.[32]

The poem makes an explicit contrast between the Beirut of the marginalized *mustad'afin* and the Beirut of the rich and arrogant *mustakbirin*, between the *muqawama*'s downtrodden yet resilient supporters and the sons and daughters of the "merchants and bankers" living in fancy houses and owning luxurious buildings. It furthermore contrasts a Lebanon that gains strength through resistance to the old slogan "Lebanon's strength lies in its weakness."

Websites and Television: The Media of the *Muqawama*

Electronic media play a major role in contemporary hegemonic projects, and the internet is an additional arena that all forces seeking to promote their own aims must invest in. Indeed, it provides a further mechanism for resistance and for the dissemination of an alternative that competes with traditional official media channels—television, radio, and print—all of which require greater investment and are generally controlled by the ruling elite.

Tal Pavel has surveyed twenty-three Hezbollah-associated websites and several no longer under the organization's direct control.[33] Many of these websites pertain to civil society organizations and institutions operating under Hezbollah auspices, such as Jihad al-Bina' (Effort for Construction), al-Jarha (Wounded), and the Shahid Foundation. Other sites belong to the organization's periodicals, newspapers, and television and radio outlets. I focus here on Hezbollah's main website at www.moqawama.org.

The home page is loaded with various *muqawama*-related statements linked to the war between Hezbollah and Israel in 2006 and is entitled "Yawmiyat al-wa'd al-sadiq" (Diary of the Honest Promise). "Honest Promise" is the name Hezbollah gave to this war, a promise of the *muqawama*'s true and credible victory as opposed to the vain promises of Arab defeatism. A section entitled "Muqawama wa-ihtilal" (Resistance and Occupation) also concentrates on the *muqawama* conflict with Israel.[34] To remind us that the ultimate aim of *muqawama* is the liberation of Palestine, a special section surveys events in those territories. The website contains a plentiful supply of images, video, and audio of *muqawama* leaders and the martyrs of the resistance as well as of songs. Two notable sections strongly foreground the *muqawama* project.

"Ma'lam siyahi 'an al-muqawama" (A Tourist Landmark on the *Muqawama*) includes articles on such a site built in the village of Mleeta in the Iqlim al-Tufah district of southern Lebanon. This tourist page documents, through various means, the history of Hezbollah's resistance in particular and the *muqawama* in general, with reconstructions of the battles with the Israelis.[35] Another notable section is "*Muqawama* Games," apparently directed to the younger generation and giving a brief overview of the military resistance to Israeli occupation in southern Lebanon. A computer battle game pits the web surfer against the last remaining soldiers of the Israeli occupation. To win, the player must shoot ten Israeli soldiers to open the gate of *intisar*, victory, and liberate the area.[36] The website also features a portal called "Il'ab wa-qawim!" (Play and Resist!), which contains a collection of downloadable games related to the *muqawama* and the war against the Israeli enemy.[37] The organization wastes no opportunity to preface every game with a discourse on the operations of the armed Islamic resistance both during and after the Israeli occupation. One of the games is called *Silsilat al'ab al-tahrir* (A Series of Liberation Games) and has six levels, each highlighting a special event in the *muqawama* from 1982 to 2000: the confrontations at Khaldi in 1982; the occupation of Sujd in 1986; the Israeli Operation Grapes of Wrath in 1996; the assassination of Israeli brigadier-general Erez Gerstein, the commander of the Israel Defense Forces Lebanon-Liaison Unit, in 1999; and the 'Aziyya offensive in southern Lebanon in 2000. The level for each event is accompanied by detailed explanation of each operation, including dates, press releases, and extracts of interviews with those who took part in the operation. To further accentuate the achievements and the credibility of the reporting, there are testimonies from Israeli soldiers who witnessed the operations. Another game called *'Ayn al-sahab* (The Cloud's Eye) is a drone-flight simulator in Israeli airspace, with detailed information on "targets," such as the northern city of Kiryat Shmona, Ben Gurion Airport, the ports at Haifa and Eilat, Ramat David Airbase, Khadira power station, and the Dimona nuclear reactor. The game provides the coordinates and strategic importance of these sites to Israel in order to acquaint children and other players with Hezbollah's reconnaissance and other abilities in pursuing the *muqawama*'s goals. The dimension of psychological warfare against Israel is also highlighted, something that relates very closely to the dissemination of the *muqawama* culture and narrative, accentuating the need for constant readiness and vaunting the organization's status as a serious enemy of Israel.

The 'Eid al-Muqawama wal-Tahrir (Feast of Resistance and Liberation) on May 25, 2000, is also given its own section on the Hezbollah website. The section addresses not only the activities of Hezbollah and subordinate organizations to commemorate the liberation, something pertaining solely to the Lubnan al-Muqawama (Lebanon of the Resistance), but also the activities of other movements such as the Syrian Social-Nationalist Party, Michel 'Aoun's al-Taghyir wal-Islah (Change and Reform) Party, and the Communist Party. The main goal is to differentiate between the *muqawama*'s adherents and its dissenters.

The TV network al-Manar (the Beacon) began local terrestrial broadcasting in 1991 and transnational satellite broadcasting in 2000. In 2014, the channel united its satellite and local broadcasting, branding itself the channel of "Arabs and Muslims" and thus addressing the nationalist and pan-Arab dimension as a priority over the Islamic in response to Hezbollah adversaries' accusation that the organization is solely an instrument of Iran. The channel seeks to address issues of the *mustad'afin* in the cause of national revival, confrontation with tyranny and Zionism, and the takfirist-jihadist movements against which the organization fights in both Syria and Lebanon.[38] The channel also aims to cover all *muqawama*-related events in furtherance of the "victory" narrative. Publicity emphasizes "the *muqawama*'s victories since the 1990s, through to the liberation in 2000 and the victory of July 2006."[39] At the same time, it emphasizes a discourse of openness as opposed to sectarian-religious introversion.

Remarkable progress can be observed throughout the channel's near three-decade development, both technically and thematically. In the early years, the religious content was dominant, but with time there has been a gradual opening out to new elements and broader content, including reality shows and Arab TV series featuring unveiled women, something unthinkable in the channel's early years. It is the "home channel" of the *muqawama*, hosting supporting movements of all kinds—Islamist, leftist, and nationalist. The channel's openness to different movements allied in the *muqawama* project is also reflected in documentary films about leading figures. One covers ʿImad Mughniyya, a Hezbollah military leader whom the organization claims was assassinated by American and Israeli forces in Syria. Another looks at Yasser Arafat, who had a complex relationship with the organization because of his role in the Oslo Peace Accord with Israel and because of his death in doubtful circumstances under an Israeli siege in Ramallah. International resistance figures—even Communists such as Che Guevara, Fidel Castro, Ho Chi Minh, and Mao Zedong—are also documentary subjects. This is a highly significant overture toward a putatively universal resistance culture against US and Israeli hegemony, which contrasts with the organization's early years, which included assassinations of leading Communists associated with the organization or with its entourage.

Anne Marie Baylouny, who has surveyed the development of al-Manar's content, especially for the period 2005–10, highlights the channel's latter-day policy of openness and characterizes the channel as having become a medium for ideological exchange between affiliates of different religions, movements, and parties in Lebanon and in the Arab world more broadly.[40]

This perception is not necessarily pluralist in the "Western liberal" sense but rather in the sense of recognizing the existence of partners within a state that Hezbollah claims to be defending. One should therefore pursue openness toward the others and to accept them not only as passive partners in the Lebanese state but also as forces entitled to express their opinion through the channel Hezbollah itself uses to promote its integrationist project. As already stated, Hezbollah's openness toward others also derives in part from the flexibility of Shiʿite *fiqh* (jurisprudence) and *ijtihad*. Baylouny also emphasizes al-Manar's openness toward women, unlike other Islamic channels:

> Programs with progressive and gender-liberating views coexist with religious programs on personal and family life (*ila al-qalb*, 2008–present), which, while not depicting an oppressive view of women's roles, present

> the issue more narrowly, from the perspective of religion and Hezbollah's traditional constituency. It is not a simple switch. This spectrum of multiple views is playing out on Hezbollah's television, and the audience has become similarly diverse. The varied programming attracts different and new constituencies, and it appears that space is being provided for new perspectives in certain forums.[41]

Thirteen of al-Manar's twenty-four program hosts are women. In some programs, most women are unveiled. This suggests that the channel does not adopt a coercive approach on religious matters, even with regard to dress codes. This is part of the message that the organization seeks to transmit: one of flexibility and a readiness to assimilate with a variety of forces from within Lebanon and the Arab world beyond, too. Al-Manar has provided a platform for figures of both sexes and from a variety of religious and political movements, including long interviews with leaders from the Communist Party, the Syrian Social-Nationalist Party, the Arab Socialist Ba'th Party, the Amal movement, and the Free Patriotic Movement. It also broadcasts serials promoting ecumenicalism, especially between Christians and Muslims in Lebanon, such as the widely viewed series on the life of the Virgin Mary.[42]

Muqawama culture is not left out of the Ramadan TV serials. *Al-Ghalibun* (The Victors), for example, concentrates on the history of the resistance. The title also alludes to the Qur'anic verse included in the Hezbollah slogan featured on its flag: "Fa-inna hizba allahi hum al-ghalibun" (Indeed, the party of God prevails [Surat al-Ma'ida 5:56]). The serial brings together actors from different religious backgrounds around the concept of the *muqawama*.[43]

A review of al-Manar's programs reveals content relating fully to the three dimensions of Hezbollah's *muqawama* project outlined in the previous chapter.

The *religious dimension* is a feature of programming but not in an overbearing way. It mainly promotes unity between sects and religions and places a special emphasis on the Ramadan and 'Ashura' religious festivals, with content also on the resistance character of Islam and the revolutionary implications of 'Ashura'.

The *national dimension* is projected via breadth and openness, as reflected in the interviews with figures who have various religious and political affiliations. The network thus attempts to increase its Arab world audience and reach beyond the Shi'ite community. Broadcasting Syrian, Lebanese, and Egyptian TV serials is also a clear demonstration of this openness. Unlike other religious channels, al-Manar does not attempt to doctor these series by applying rigid religious codes. The channel also frequently broadcasts Arab nationalist songs and video clips from the Gamal Abdel Nasser era, promoting Hezbollah's claim that it is the inheritor of the pan-Arab and anticolonial movement symbolized in the figure of Egypt's leader in the 1950s and the 1960s.

The *economic dimension* is evinced in the special emphasis the network gives to coverage of marginalized groups within the Lebanese society. For example, the program *Ya'ishun baynana* (They Live among Us) concentrates on poor families from all religious backgrounds and the need for viewer, citizen, and government alike to ameliorate their living conditions.

Hezbollah, like other religiously based fundamentalist organizations in the Middle East and beyond, also has a remarkable facility for adapting rapidly to emerging media, and the use that it and these other groups make of internet technology and media is key to their emergence and sustainability. In its early years, starting in the early 1980s, Hezbollah fruitfully identified the great potential of film and television in its psychological warfare with Israel and other enemies. It regularly deployed teams of cameramen with military operations against the Israeli army in southern Lebanon, broadcast video content on al-Manar, and passed such footage on to other networks regionally and internationally. This approach was later enhanced by the development of satellite broadcasting in the Arab world in the early 1990s. Hezbollah was also one of the first organizations to identify the great "resistance" potential of the internet as a channel for propaganda and for communication with millions in Lebanon, the Arab world, and the non-Arab world.

Despite Hezbollah's commonalities with fundamentalist movements, especially the Sunni jihadist movement, the nature of its messaging through this modern medium is significantly different with respect to the extent of its organizational openness toward the "other." Both Hezbollah and its message have undergone significant change since the organization's early years. As the organization began developing its hegemonic project, it also adapted its means of dispersing that message.

There has been very significant exploitation of video and flash clips on al-Manar and various websites, and interest in them grew tremendously during critical periods, such as the years before and just after Israeli withdrawal from southern Lebanon, the Lebanon or July War of 2006, the events on May 2008, and the current and ongoing Syrian Civil War. The volume of clips has grown over time, with Hezbollah producing them via al-Manar, the party's information department, and other means. Those produced during the July War and after that notably incorporated the three main dimensions of the Hezbollah *muqawama* project: the religious resistance dimension, with a special emphasis on 'Ashura' and the link between Husayn's rebellion and the contemporary *muqawama*; the national dimension, which aims to unite not only different religions behind Hezbollah's putative guardianship of Lebanese national unity and dignity in particular but also the Arab and Islamic worlds more broadly; and the economic dimension, with a socioeconomic focus on peasants and the poor that aligns with Hezbollah's self-perception of itself as the representative of Lebanon's marginalized communities. In media content, special emphasis is placed on terms such as *intisar*, *muqawama*, *watan* (homeland or nation), *sha'b* (people/nation), and others that associate resistance with victory, nationhood, and the Lebanese people. For example, the music video *Akbar nasr inkatab* (The Greatest Victory Documented) begins with quotes from Nasrallah's speech to the "victory conference" on September 22, 2006.[44] The song begins with the lyrics "the greatest victory documented in the homeland's book, and a strong nation supporting the *muqawama*." The "people" are mentioned as an image is shown of an old veiled woman and buildings destroyed by Israeli bombardment in the background. A second image features an unveiled younger woman and Christian symbols, thus placing a special emphasis on national unity and attribution of victory to all the Lebanese people, not just to the Shi'ites. Most of the video clips reviewed for this study feature a variety of clerics and religious symbols from Shi'ite, Sunni, Druze, and

Christian traditions. *The Greatest Victory Documented* and many other videos such as *Nasrak hazz al-dunya* (Your Victory Shook the World) feature the flags of Lebanon, Hezbollah, and other allies in the *muqawama* project, such as the Amal movement, the Syrian Social-Nationalist Party, the Free Patriotic Movement, and the Communist Party.[45]

In addition to the *muqawama*'s military dimension, very evident in such video clips, the dimension of reconstruction and revival from the ruins of war and the work done by Hezbollah's civil society organizations are featured as integral to the *muqawama* and complementary to its military operations. The motif of national unity and the portrayal of the *muqawama* as a project for all Lebanese people, not just for Hezbollah, are also displayed upfront. One very striking video, *Kulluna muqawama kulluna lil-watan* (We All Are the Resistance, We All Are for the Homeland), combines the Lebanese national anthem with the resistance theme.[46] In addition to showing footage of national flags and images of national and historical landmarks, such as the one at Ba'labak, it culminates with the Lebanese flag along with the screen captions "We all are for the homeland" at the top and "Together we will be triumphant" at the bottom. In such videos, Hezbollah activists appear alongside the national armed forces, suggesting a continuum between the *muqawama* and the Lebanese state—for example, in the video *Ya watani! Ya watan al-nur!* (My Homeland! The Land of Light!).[47] In addition to these dimensions, a special emphasis is placed on the issue of social class. *Your Victory Shook the World* features a young shepherd calmly playing the flute somewhere in southern Lebanon. Hezbollah militants appear in the fields to the applause of the peasants, and then resisters appear just as a man and a woman sow wheat seeds, the seeds interspersed in the air with the bullets of the resistance. This metaphor is not new, having already appeared in Hezbollah posters published in *al-'Ahd* prior to the conference in 1997 on "the unity between the people and the *muqawama*" that was part of the annual commemoration of the July War or what the Israelis called Operation Grapes of Wrath.[48] The deliberate foregrounding of peasants, the poor, and (less frequently) the working class recurs in these videos to remind us that the *muqawama* project belongs to the marginalized and is protecting them, their lands, and their homeland.

These aspects are complemented by a potent Shi'ite dimension. One of the most evocative comparisons between the Lebanese resistance and revolutionary Shi'ite Islam's 'Ashura' imagery is made in a music video titled *Hayhat ya muhttal* (We Will Not Be Subjugated by the Occupier).[49] The title is a famous statement made by Husayn, the third Shi'ite imam, during his battle with Yazid's army in Karbala' when he was given the option of death or surrender to Yazid's legitimacy as caliph: "Hayhat mina al-dhillah." Hezbollah has frequently applied this statement to Shi'ite political Islam, referring to this founding historical event in order to make timeless comparisons based on the famous motto "Every day is 'Ashura', every land is Karbala'." The organization thus assigns to itself the task of upholding Husayn's legacy, while Israel is likened to Yazid. Bidding to gain the solidarity of all Lebanese, the video also features an image of 'Ali 'Abbas Musawi, son of former Hezbollah secretary-general 'Abbas Mussawi. Father and son are declared martyrs, and allusion is also made to the martyrdom of Hassan Nasrallah's son, Hadi, in a battle with Israeli forces. The aim is to elevate the organization's status within the *muqawama* and as a vital national leader ready to offer itself in sacrifice. This presentation is contrasted with the traditional Arab regimes' and sectarian organizations' concern only for themselves and for their leaders.

The music for these videos is normally provided by Hezbollah's band al-Wilaya (Spiritual Guidance) to further serve the direct dissemination of *muqawama* culture. Other videos feature Arab patriotic songs dating back to the Nasserite period, accompanied by images that glorify Hezbollah's leaders and warriors.[50] One song featured often, especially in videos produced during and after the war in July 2006, is Egyptian singer Abdel Halim Hafiz's "Khali al-silah sahi" (Keep the Weapons Ready), which dates from the 1960s.[51] Another is the *Allahu akbar* song made famous during the Suez crisis of 1956. A direct link is made between the Hezbollah of the twenty-first century and the Arab nationalist, anticolonial movement of Nasserism, and an implicit link is also made between the twentieth century's foremost Arab nationalist leader and the contemporary spearhead of the Lebanese *muqawama* who is Nasser's "legitimate" heir, Hassan Nasrallah. Another major campaign song promoting the *muqawama* beyond Lebanese borders is "Nasr al-'Arab" (The Victory of the Arabs).[52] It has been recorded and performed by a great number of artists from various Arab countries, in particular Lebanon, Syria, and Egypt. The title features wordplay focused on the term *nasr*, alluding to both the *muqawama* victory over Israel, attributed to all Arabs, and the surname of Hezbollah secretary-general Nasrallah (which literally means "God's Victory"). This wordplay implicitly positions him as the leader of the entire Arab nation, a status underlined when a video featuring this song was played at a rally during the Lebanon War in 2006 when Nasrallah promised victory.

The extent of the *muqawama* project's penetration beyond Hezbollah's domestic environment is in part reflected in the great support the organization has from many Arab thinkers and influencers for its position as the leader of the resistance. Julia Boutros, the Christian-leftist Lebanese singer linked with both the Communist Party and the Syrian Social-Nationalist Party, donated her revenue from the song "Ahibba'i" (My Loved Ones) to the cause.[53] The lyrics are the words Nasrallah addressed live to his fighters at the height of the July War. Boutros sings to the guardians and liberators of the homeland and the *muqawama* activists rebuilding its civilization. Left-wing patriotic poets such as Syria's Omar al-Farra and Egypt's Ahmad Fou'ad Najm have published pieces praising Hassan Nasrallah and Hezbollah's leadership of the *muqawama*. Communist musician Ziad Rahbani has also expressed his support of Hezbollah as the leader of the resistance. (I discuss Ziad Rahbani and his views further in the section on the periodical *al-Akhbar* later in this chapter.) Rahbani's statement that his mother, iconic Lebanese singer Fairuz, "loves Hassan Nasrallah"[54] provoked a controversy highly indicative of the degree of Nasrallah's and Hezbollah's status and of the both deep and controversial reach of the *muqawama* project within Lebanon and beyond.

The various videos analyzed here illustrate the multidimensional development of Hezbollah's *muqawama* project and the way in which the parallels between its various symbols reinforce the idea of their complementarity. The various video clips feature the chain of equivalences that the *muqawama* project has gradually established. At the first level, the religious, Hezbollah reaches back more than one thousand years to 'Ashura' and Imam Husayn to take hold of these traditions, import them into the present time, and apply an interpretation of continual resistance to an historical event turned into a timeless myth. Hezbollah marginalizes other long-enduring interpretations of Shi'ite Islam that insist on the necessity of *intizar* and silence, and it instead links all references to the Shi'a with the myth of Karbala' in its resistance aspects. In the process of associating Shi'ism with resistance, Hezbollah has crowned itself the definitive representative of the Shi'ite community in Lebanon and worldwide.

The *muqawama* concept has expanded to encompass the Lebanese people and the Lebanese state with its different ethnic, religious, and political groups. Yet it is not an equal *muqawama* for all parties; rather, it is a "*muqawama–people–homeland*" of the peasants, the simple people who rise early to work the soil and guard the homeland, the poor but proud.

As the leader of the *muqawama* project, Hezbollah broadens the scope of the term *people* through special rhetorical devices, referring to the Shi'ite community—the environment from which Hezbollah emerged—outward to the Lebanese people as a whole, specifically those who have identified with the struggle. Taken a step further, it becomes a reference to all of the Arab people as a whole. The signifier that allows for this expansion of the term *people* is the *muqawama*, along with the attitudes toward it. The message of these video clips and of the structuring of the new hegemonic project is that the "people" as a political subject will reach ultimate self-realization once this subject fulfills the aim of the *muqawama*.

Through the *muqawama*, Hezbollah builds and leads a historical bloc that brings together all the parties that follow the *muqawama*. The developing historical bloc is based on the mass of the Shi'ite community, especially its lower and lower-middle classes, which make up its majority, and integrates supporters of parties close to Hezbollah, such as leftist ones that comprise mainly Shi'ite Lebanese but also Orthodox Christians, Sunnis, Druze, and others. The organization has also sought to integrate Maronite Christians into its project through the Free Patriotic Movement of General Michel 'Aoun.

This attempt to gather everyone under one umbrella has not entirely nullified the pre–Civil War hegemonic project of "the republic of merchants and bankers," at least symbolically and ideologically. It has, however, made some conceptual adjustments to that project and has reformulated its various signifiers. This reformulation can be seen, for example, in the successful inclusion of Lebanese multiculturalism and pluralism in the *muqawama*, reframing a "new–old" interpretation of Lebanon as a land of multiple historically rooted religious minorities, resistance to orthodox Islamic hegemony, and struggle against colonialism. Thus, the *muqawama* project becomes the natural heir, in the way Hezbollah presents it, to Lebanese popular traditions.

The *Muqawama*'s Dissemination through the Design of Space: Khiyam and Mleeta

The hegemonic project relies on more than propaganda, media, and education. It is also promoted through maintaining and developing the physical space in which the project operates and either exercises control or at least seeks to. Following the liberation of southern Lebanon and even more so after the Lebanon War of 2006, Hezbollah's activists made special efforts to build memorials to "consolidate popular consciousness" about the *muqawama*. As one of the initiators of al-Jam'iyya al-Lubnaniyya lil Funun (Lebanese Organization for Arts), established by Hezbollah in 2004, put it, "You can control people by narrating a specific heritage and memory. This is what the Israelis do. We are fighting their culture by providing a counter-culture. We want to fix our memory through architectural and design language. Few people read books, but many people come to visit a building, a museum or a heritage website."[55]

The geographer Mona Harb and the anthropologist Lara Deeb maintain that the establishment of such memorial sites bids in fact to establish a culture both through and within space. These sites have become part of Lebanon's flourishing "*muqawama* tourism" or, as Harb and Deeb call it, "religious and political tourism." Hezbollah has built several sites for such purposes—for example, Khiyam, Mleeta, Maroun al-Ras Park, the 'Abbas al-Musawi Museum in Biqa' Governorate, and the *muqawama* museum and memorial in Dahiya-Beirut.[56] These sites are currently administered by the Jam'iyyat Ihya' Turath al-Muqawama (Muqawama Heritage Revival Organization).

The Israeli army had used the Mu'taqal al-Khiyam (Khiyam Center) in southern Lebanon as a detention camp under the direct control of its ally, the South Lebanon Army, from 1984 until the South's liberation in

May 2000. The detention center held five thousand Lebanese who resisted the occupation or aided the resistance.[57] A committee of local volunteers, mostly former prisoners of Khiyam, was established to host guided tours between 2000 and 2006, relating their experience there to visitors, including the various torture methods practiced in the camp. The volunteers' intention was to reveal what happened under the occupation and the hardships endured by detainees as well as to transmit the message of resistance and patriotism to youth.[58] Many of the volunteers have been affiliated with Hezbollah, though the organization barely invested in the site in its early years. After 2006, though, Hezbollah committed itself to further investment there, and an expansion plan was prepared in 2009 to memorialize not just the torture inflicted on the Lebanese resistance fighters in southern Lebanon but also the detention and torture practices of occupiers worldwide. Harb and Deeb attribute this change to a desire to align with other movements resisting injustice and imperialism.[59]

Mleeta is a southern Lebanese village located on a mountain bearing the same name. Its topography lent it to serving as a significant military base for the *muqawama* operating against the Israeli military and the South Lebanon Army from 1985 until the Israeli withdrawal in 2000 and then later in the July War in 2006.[60] A memorial site was officially opened in May 2010 to mark a decade since Israel's withdrawal from Southern Lebanon. It has become a key *muqawama* attraction, with about a half million visitors in its first three months and a weekly average of forty-seven thousand.[61] There is a grand square at the site entrance, with a pool at its center. Next to the entrance is a 150-seat venue screening videos about the site and the *muqawama*'s history there. The site also hosts an exhibition of spoils gathered by resistance fighters from 1982 to 2006 and is replete with symbols elaborated over the years that aim to enhance the visitor's sense of inclusion in and identification with the *muqawama*. An example of the effort invested in the site is a 3,500-square-meter area called "al-Hawiya" (the Abyss) that exhibits Israeli military equipment, such as a partially buried Merkava-4 battle tank. The Abyss is on the western side of the site, evoking the "sunset" of the Israeli occupation. On the eastern side is Sahat al-Tahrir (Liberation Square), displaying various types of weapons used by resistance warriors over the years as well as a glass noticeboard featuring quotes from the Hezbollah secretary-general's speeches during the Lebanon War of 2006. An observatory also overlooks the villages of Iqlim al-Tufah and a 1,060-meter-high hill symbolizing the ascension of the *muqawama* martyrs to heaven. The eastern location of the exhibits here symbolizes the "sunrise" of resistance and liberation.[62] The site's design helps it merge with the landscape, implying that the *muqawama* is an integral part of the topography: according to Harb and Deeb, "Mleeta's buildings are low-rise concrete structures that are well integrated within the natural environment and do not seek to dominate it."[63]

Ali Tahir, a former president of the Lebanese Organization or the Arts, emphasizes the symbolism of such merging with the natural southern Lebanon landscape: "The resistance sites used to be the cradles of the soldiers. They know them inside out: they know the position of each tree, each rock, each flower, each pebble; they recognize their smells, their sounds, their textures; they know the animals who live there; these sites hold very precious memories. . . . We would like to conceive of projects that will narrate these memories, that would tell future generations about the occupation, its injustice, the wounds it inflicted. We would like a place to narrate this jihad, a place for everyone."[64]

The main idea promoted here is of being an "authentic" descendant of this land, a significant message conveyed through the organization of physical space. The description vaunts the popular-national perception of the natural beauty of Lebanon, the "Switzerland of the Middle East." Hezbollah's warriors are depicted as an integral part of the landscape, the true representatives of the people, the homeland, and the natural environment that is directly related to the *muqawama*.

The *Muqawama* Press: *Al-Akhbar*

A very important and relatively cheap to produce media format in Hezbollah's extensive portfolio is the newspaper. The organization's weekly *al-'Ahd* (The Promise) was first published in 1984. Its name was changed in 2001 to *al-'Ahd wal-intiqad* (the Promise and the Critique).[65] However, the emergence of the Lebanese paper *al-Akhbar* (The News) was far more significant in that it was not officially a Hezbollah newspaper. It was first published on August 14, 2006, the last day of the Second Lebanese War. Although some US newspapers have deemed it a Hezbollah outlet, there is no proof of this as such.[66] Moreover, in mid-2012 *al-Akhbar*'s publisher, Hassan Khalil, printed an article on various organizations', including Hezbollah's, discomfort with the freedom of expression manifested in his newspaper. Khalil asserted the independence of his newspaper from all the various forces inside and outside Lebanon, including Syria, which has periodically banned it.[67] Nonetheless, *al-Akhbar* acts as a laboratory for the multidimensional *muqawama* project, bringing together journalists, authors, artists, and thinkers from various movements that share a like belief in the resistance. Khalil, a Lebanese Shiʿite, established the newspaper in cooperation with the Christian journalist Joseph Samaha, who had previously worked for the established independent, nationalist, leftist daily *al-Safir* (the Ambassador). Samaha had also worked for the paper *al-Yawm al-sabiʿ* (the Seventh Day), which is linked to the Palestinian resistance movement. Samaha was formerly a member of the Communist Action Organization in Lebanon, which joined forces with the Lebanese Communist Party to form the Lebanese National Resistance Front. This front served as an umbrella organization for Lebanese resistance movements, including the Islamist one that established Hezbollah later. The left-wing and resistance orientation of *al-Akhbar* is evinced in the newspaper's website profile, which describes it as "a left-oriented newspaper, affiliated with the camp that opposes the hegemony emerging from the heart of the United States and reaching the Far East, Africa, South America, and Europe."[68] Samaha has never hidden the newspaper's support for the *muqawama* and its opposition to capitalism and US imperialism. In his inaugural article in August 2006, "Tawqit sa 'ib" (The Right Time), he stated:

> We declare our belonging to the camp that is opposed to hegemony emerging from the heart of the United States and reaching the Far East, Africa, South America, and Europe. We also declare that we professionally belong to the camp of pluralism, democracy, objectivity, modernity, and creative culturalism. *Al-Akhbar* refuses another Lebanese setback to the pre-July period,[69] for it was a dependent land or farm meaninglessly

> called a state. One should prevent the restoration of this farm, to advance toward the construction of a civil state that is capable, through its justice, competences, and independent thinking, of internalizing the outstanding readiness [of its citizens] to overcome all challenges and to perceive the *muqawama*, any *muqawama*, as the nerve supporting and enhancing the national unity, protecting its Arabism, and preventing its deterioration toward the great destruction that raises the banner of "neutrality" and hinders the brilliant Lebanese contribution.[70]

Al-Akhbar thus empowers the *muqawama*, under Hezbollah's leadership, to communicate with a diverse audience, not necessarily just the Shi'ite or even the religious. It provides a refuge for secularists, revolutionists, and Arab leftist intellectuals vaunting revolutionary statements and seeking alliances against US hegemony and global neoliberalism as well as against local capitalism. *Al-Akhbar* also boasts articles written by the renowned Lebanese Communist musician Ziad Rahbani. Hezbollah is not exactly enamored of Rahbani, however, given his vocal atheism. The musicals he composed during the Civil War were bitingly critical of sectarianism, clericalism, and religion in general. He argues that religion was one of the reasons for the blood-soaked Civil War and the terrible suffering inflicted on the Lebanese people. Nonetheless, his articles side with the *muqawama* and call Hezbollah activists "comrades," as in the Communist tradition.[71] He means that they are comrades in the joint *muqawama* project and that there is a consensus regarding certain parts of the project but disagreement regarding others.

Rahbani has also consistently attended Hezbollah conferences, especially after the July War, and has shown respect for both Hezbollah and Hassan Nasrallah's resistance. Rahbani's piquant language in a sense aids the *muqawama* project not only against the Lebanese right wing, including the Phalanges Party and Samir Ja'ja''s al-Quwwat al-Lubnaniyya (Lebanese Forces Party), but also against former prime minister Sa'd Hariri's al-Mustaqbal (Future Movement). Rahbani has also criticized former members of the Lebanese Communist Party who split to establish the Harkat al-Yasar al-Dimuqrati (Democratic Left Movement) aligned with Hariri's Tahalof 14 Athar (March 14 Alliance). *Al-Akhbar* has also been a platform for debates on the character of the new Lebanon and of the *muqawama* project through the writings of various intellectuals, politicians, journalists, and artists such as Rahbani, Ibrahim al-Amin (a former Communist, now Hezbollah ally), Pierre Abi-Saʿb, Nahid Hittir (a leftist Arab nationalist assassinated by Islamic State in Jordan in 2016), Saʿdallah Mazrʿani (a former vice secretary-general of the Lebanese Communist Party), and others. *Al-Akhbar* has promoted *muqawama* in its nonreligious dimensions of class on the one hand and its pluralist nationalism on the other.

This support is particularly evident in *al-Akhbar*'s coverage of July War anniversaries. The edition produced on the sixth anniversary on July 12, 2012, featured a series of articles devoted to the resistance operations during the war. One piece revolved around resistance fighter ʿAli Saleh, whom the headline called "the terminator of the Merkava myth." According to *al-Akhbar*, Saleh destroyed fifteen Israeli Merkava battle tanks during the war.[72] He is the epitome of the kind of resister the newspaper likes to promote—from a poor family and lacking an academic education yet also an intelligent protagonist against the Israeli occupation and a soldier able to share a joke with his comrades. The article portrays him as the destroyer of the Merkava myth (that it is indestructible) and the builder of the *muqawim* (resistor) legend. *Al-Akhbar*'s anniversary edition of a year earlier featured an article by then editor in chief Ibrahim al-Amin. In it he revealed details of a meeting in southern Lebanon in 2006 between Samaha and ʿImad Mughniyya, the leader of Hezbollah's military branch, a month before the eruption of the war and two months before *al-Akhbar*'s first edition. Allowing Samaha to meet Mughniyya, a clandestine activist sought by various intelligence agencies, demonstrated Hezbollah's great confidence in Samaha. The edition also praised the southern localities that many *muqawama* fighters originate from and criticized the state's inability or unwillingness to meet the local residents' needs five years after the end of the war and seventy years after the declaration of Lebanon's independence. The same edition also paid tribute to the "American martyr," a Lebanese from the South holding US citizenship who came to Lebanon to take part in the resistance to Israel. "This young American did not fight in Iraq or Afghanistan; he rather protected his homeland and died next to Berket al-Hafour in a battle that the local population deems heroic. He fought in Maroun next to his village, Yaroun, and not in Chicago. He did not take part in the occupation of Baghdad."[73] Once again we encounter the recurring contrast between the colonizer and the *muqawim*, the young man who returns to his homeland despite all the privileges he enjoyed as a US citizen.

Al-Akhbar has a number of functions: it serves as a bridge between the different constituents of the Lebanese *muqawama*; it is a test laboratory for coexistence; and it is an arena for each party to bid for influence over the resistance movement.

All in all, Hezbollah's exploitation of the various media to advance its *muqawama* culture is quite varied as it seeks to transform the idea of resistance into a culture that draws in other forces and gains mass support. Books, websites, TV, radio, newspapers, and periodicals are all part of the ideological arsenal Hezbollah uses to further *muqawama* culture in Lebanon as a stage toward a global culture of resistance.

The Development of the *Muqawama* Project in Nasrallah's Discourse

Hezbollah's third and current secretary-general, Hassan Nasrallah, best exemplifies the development of the organization and its political strategy from blitzkrieg to trench warfare, from a closed organization to a more flexibly open one capable of reaching out into the Lebanese pluralist arena. Nasrallah embodies the advance of a whole generation toward a radical Shi'ism that attempts to provide an "authentic" solution to the unique problems facing Shi'ite youth on the margins of Lebanese society. The aim is to "get back to the future" in Shi'ite activists' and intellectuals' references to religious sources as well as to provide an innovative and active interpretation of those sources as a "progressive" perspective on history and contemporary advocacy of an egalitarian and just society. In other words, Nasrallah could be considered one of Gramsci's "organic intellectuals," who sought leadership of the social group in which he grew up and guides this group toward the consolidation and establishment of a project of its own.

This section is based on numerous interviews with and speeches given by Nasrallah before he was appointed secretary-general up until the notable speech he gave against US regional hegemony on 'Ashura' in 2015. This speech was a summation of Nasrallah's and Hezbollah's ideological development over more than three decades.

Hezbollah's position in its first few years, as I have shown, was that of a classical fundamentalist movement unwilling to negotiate or compromise with other forces in a state afflicted by civil war. Nasrallah's position during those years aligned with the organization's. In a speech given at a Hezbollah conference in 1985, as reported in *al-'Ahd*, Nasrallah stated:

> This resistance originated in the land of Jabal 'Amel,[74] the homeland of Abu Dhar al-Ghafari, the friend of Imam 'Ali, peace be upon him. This resistance could not have been achieved had it be not directly associated with our history, tradition, Islam, and religion. . . . [T]he resistance emerged because the history of the South and of Jabal 'Amel's people includes 'Ashura', Husayn, and Karbala'. . . . If there had not been a link between the residents and Karbala', *the muqawama* would not have existed.
>
> This resistance is an Islamic resistance; we should emphasize this fact because this is the *muqawama* of Muhammad, 'Ali, and Husayn. This is the resistance of Islam and the Muslim, the resistance of all those who belong to the religion of Allah.

The young Nasrallah also referred to the national resistance:

> The believers who initiated the struggle did not fight for their Lebanonism or Phoenicianism but rather for the Islamic tradition and thought and for the Islamic Husayni blood flowing in their veins, resisting injustice and occupation. Some think that we reduce the value of the *muqawama* by considering it Islamic, but in fact when we consider it "national"; we delimit it to 10,452 kilometers [the area of Lebanon]. By naming it "Islamic," we call on all Muslims worldwide; we call one billion Muslims to take responsibility.[75]

Themes of this kind can also be found in Nasrallah's speeches through the late 1990s. However, the speeches of the young Nasrallah highlight a monopoly and control over the resistance and a sharply explicit sectarian discourse that does not align itself with other religions or movements. Quite the contrary, it is a discourse of division and defiance. The young Nasrallah did not conceal the Islamic totalization of Hezbollah's perception. In a Friday sermon in the early 1990s, he preached, "The meaning of the Islamic choice included faith, devoutness, and respect for all the divine Shari'a limits in all of life's domains: politics, economy, security, society, culture, and militarism."[76]

Inclusion is interpreted according to Hezbollah's foundational perception, and people of other religions, such as Christians, are not full partners in the homeland and the state. In general, the term *homeland* is not part of the early Hezbollah's and the young Nasrallah's perception. At that time, the homeland was the whole Islamic world, not just Lebanon or even the Arab world.

Secular forces were not spared the young Nasrallah's invective. At a special conference in September 1986 commemorating the disappearance of Imam Musa al-Sadr, Nasrallah attacked secularists, comparing them to the Zionists: "The others wanted the Qur'anic Islam to turn into secular Islam, but God said His word, and the Qur'anic Islam did not change."

He proceeded to argue, "By commemorating the eighth anniversary of [Imam al-Sadr's] disappearance, we stand up for his ideas, . . . and his war against secularism was an explicitly declared war. He sharply contended that secularists are like the Israelis and that we should follow this path and beware of secularization because secularity for the imam is Zionism."[77]

In this same speech, Nasrallah linked secularism to al-Sadr's reference to dialogue with Christians: "As for dialogue, Musa al-Sadr was in favor of dialogue with *al-nasara* [Christians], but not with the Israelis. Amin Jumayyil is an Israeli, and Samir Ja'ja' is an Israeli."[78] The word *nasara* has the connotation of "protégés" in Islamic discourse. He did not call the Christians *masihiyyin*, as the Christians call themselves in Arabic. This reductively guardian-like dimension to Nasrallah's discourse was salient in the Hezbollah narrative at that time.

Hezbollah's early activism as a radical religious movement that considered itself of a piece with the Islamic Revolution in Iran was clear in its rhetoric. Its principal aim was to fight against everyone who didn't follow its interpretation of Islam: Christians, secularists, dissenting Muslims, and even other Shi'ites with a different line of thought.

By the early 1990s and by the end of the Civil War, however, Hezbollah started to moderate its orientation both rhetorically and ideologically from a revolutionary, fundamentalist religious project aiming to impose Islamic ideology forcibly on Lebanon to a gradualist counterhegemonic project open to collaboration. This was not a sudden change but rather a gradual process. One could characterize the development of Hezbollah's perception from the 1990s to the early 2000s as transitional, preparing the ground for a profound change in its discourse.

The new orientation toward openness was noticeable in Nasrallah's first interview as secretary-general on February 28, 1992: "In the very first years, we were occupied with the establishment of our infrastructure, and this is normal for a project underway . . . for it cannot be directed toward others to develop relationships and alliances." Nasrallah went on to emphasize that Hezbollah's past criticism of Christians was directed toward the small percentage said to have a close relationship with Israel. He added that Hezbollah had never declared that it would forcibly establish an Islamic state in Lebanon unless there were "an objectively broad public basis for accepting this project that will protect it. . . . Historically, the nature of the Islamic state renders it unactualizable if it does not have a wide popular basis. Therefore, we have the right, like all the Lebanese people, to dream of and aspire to the idea of reaching the zenith of a just society and of security and peace."[79]

This statement represents a change in Hezbollah's approach from one of a priori absolutes to one of a Lebanese "market of thoughts." Hezbollah changed its view of the political framework called "Lebanon" from something that needs to be transfigured or destroyed to something that is real and independent. There is no degrading disregard of the independent existence of Lebanon and no declaration that it should exist only as a part of a broader Islamic state.

In a second interview later the same year, Nasrallah outlined the "openness" of Hezbollah toward Christians, especially those outside the Christian hierarchy Hezbollah claimed is biased in favor of Israel. "We deem openness toward Christians as vital and normal, and openness toward the popular classes would be more effective and positive. I do not believe that these people are naturally biased in favor of Israel; their leadership that has certain political dreams and aspirations has manipulated them to make peace with Israel."[80]

This flexible attitude developed further to include overtures to other political parties and organizations, not just to religious groups. Hezbollah started organizing or participating in conferences hosting secular parties and governments that had become integral to the alliances opposing the Zionist discourse that prevailed in the 1980s. In an important speech Nasrallah gave at the Second National Islamic Conference in Beirut in 1997, progress in Hezbollah's attitude toward "a historical reconciliation between two prominent movements against the enemy's project" is discernible. Nasrallah stressed that nationalism is not detached from Islam and that Islam supports nationalism if it is not "racist." He further emphasized that *muqawama* is a deeper and broader common denominator, serving as a basis to enhance collaboration between the national and the Islamic. He asserted that Hezbollah, in addition to its crucial military resistance, aims to revive the Arab nation and establish a state based on social justice and fair distribution of resources.[81]

One week after this conference, Hezbollah announced the establishment of the al-Saraya al-Lubnaniyya Limuqawamat al-Ihtilal (Lebanese Occupation Resistance Brigades), a parallel organization to al-Muqawama al-Islamiyya (Islamic Resistance), Hezbollah's military arm, enabling any willing person to join the military resistance operations, even those who did not follow Hezbollah's line of thought. The relevant main headline in *al-'Ahd* was "Itar watani shamil li-muwajhat al-'adow" (An Inclusive National Cadre toward a Confrontation with the Enemy). Nationalism ceased to be a marginal issue and was presented as a comprehensive framework that could absorb a variety of movements and religious groups to build the *muqawama* against Israeli occupation. The editorial on the establishment of the Lebanese Occupation Resistance Brigades characterized them as part "of the context of establishing national unity and the construction of the resistance society."[82] It was the first time that the whole Lebanese people, not just the Shi'ite community, were mentioned in this context.

Nasrallah's openness and nationalist stance came further to the fore after the Israeli withdrawal from southern Lebanon. Hezbollah marked the day, May 25, 2000, by holding a ceremony for all Lebanese, not just Hezbollah. Nasrallah's speech at Bint Jbeil the following day attributed the victory to the entire Lebanese people: "I would like all the Lebanese people to attribute this victory to themselves. It is not the victory of a specific party, movement, or organization. It is not the victory of a certain religious group or a defeat for another. He who believes so must be ignorant. This is a Lebanese victory, and the *muqawama* is the eternal power of this homeland."

This historic speech urged the building of a "new Lebanon" that would replace the old mantra of "strength in its weakness" with the new mantra "strength through its power." Nasrallah continued, "Lebanon is inherently strong and steadfast. . . . [T]he new Lebanon is a land of real shared life. From now on, no Muslim or Christian will allow the Zionists to manipulate us. . . . [T]he new Lebanon is a land strong against invaders and a tolerant one when it comes to unity between its different factions."

Despite Nasrallah's references to Iran, Syria, Khomeini, and Khamenei, the speech did not seek confrontation with other indigenous forces and religious groups. He thanked all the various *muqawama* organizations twice, while also specifically mentioning the Islamic resistance, the Lebanese Occupation Resistance Brigades, the Amal movement, and the Lebanese National Resistance Front.[83]

The expanding character of Nasrallah's discourse was further revealed after the Lebanon War. The war was a step change in Hezbollah's transition from a tightly closed Shi'ite radical organization of Islamist purism into one vaunting an Arab consensus. In a speech on September 22, 2006, Nasrallah moved even further toward a "resistance internationalism" by referring to then Venezuelan president Hugo Chávez:

> Your [referring to the masses who were celebrating the "divine victory"] strong *muqawama* and steadfastness have revealed the true face of US politics, . . . which call for [but do not reinforce] democracy, freedoms, and dignity. Your strong *muqawama* and steadfastness have raised the level of consciousness and enmity not only in the Arab and Islamic worlds but worldwide. Your endurance and *muqawama* have enabled a great man like [Hugo] Chávez to say these words in the United Nations General Assembly. The Lebanese *muqawama* nowadays constitutes a source of inspiration for all resistors worldwide, for all freedom advocates worldwide, for all the decent souls worldwide, and for all those who refuse to surrender to the Americans worldwide.[84]

Nasrallah associated the Islamic *muqawama*—which by this point had in Hezbollah's discourse become a national Christian-Islamic project—with a global resistance to US hegemony and imperialism. In so doing, Nasrallah further paved a wider path for Hezbollah away from narrow localism and factionalism and toward Arab nationalism and even internationalism. This speech would not have been possible without the openness already demonstrated by Hezbollah even before the war in its signing of a historic accord with 'Aoun's Free Patriotic Movement that garnered two-thirds of Lebanese Christian votes in the elections in 2005 and that formed the basis for a pact that remains in place.

The "Divine Victory" speech further signaled Hezbollah's detachment from fundamentalist rhetoric and the will to demolish the Lebanese state. Nasrallah instead urged joint efforts by both Muslims and Christians to build a "steadfast and just" state, one of social justice and protection of the rights of all Lebanese people, regardless of their affiliations.[85] Shi'ite motifs remain in Nasrallah's and other Hezbollah leaders' speeches, but the discourse also promotes the inclusion of the "other" and the search for common denominators in the resistance to imperialist hegemony.

Nasrallah has stated that Hezbollah does not seek total control over Lebanon but rather to fortify its position through its own hegemonic project and the absorption of its ideas into the "common sense" of the Lebanese. He made this goal explicit in the Hezbollah press conference on May 8, 2008, held when it and allied forces gained control over large areas in Beirut after attacking the forces controlled by Sa'd Hariri and Walid Jumblatt. This battle had followed the Lebanese government's decision to destroy Hezbollah's communication network and to dismiss General Wafiq Shuqayr, a close Hezbollah associate, from his position as security officer at Beirut International Airport.[86] In the press conference, Nasrallah stated:

> There are two outstretched hands. One offers dialogue based on the cancellation of unjust decisions and [on] sitting around the dialogue table, as suggested by Nabih Berri, the Speaker of the Parliament of Lebanon. The other holds a weapon. This weapon will not serve to harm others or perpetrate a coup. We in Hezbollah have come to believe that if the

> Lebanese people, the Arabs, the Muslims, and the international community tell us that we are good, that we function well, that we do not steal the people's money, and they beseech us to rule Lebanon, we would say that we are not willing to take this responsibility because Lebanon should be saved by joint efforts.

Nasrallah expressed absolute rejection of sectarian division, stating that there were currently only two projects in Lebanon:

> That is why we are not concerned with the eruption of Shi'ite–Sunni *fitna* [sedition]. . . . [T]oday's battle is not between the Shi'ites and the Sunnis, for there are a pure resistance project (*watani muqawim sharif*) and an American project fighting against each other. . . . [W]hoever wants to go there can do so, and whoever chooses to remain here can do so, regardless of what he is wearing . . . even if he is wearing the garments of Muslim clerics, Christian clerics, or politicians. This is the nature of the battle taking place in this land.[87]

At those critical moments, Nasrallah did not mention the sectarian issue. Instead, he considered his project, first, a national one that should recruit the greatest number of supporters from different factions and, second, a resistive *muqawama* project around which allies and positions should be consolidated.

However, there is no doubt that in May 2008 sectarian tension reached a new peak. This tension created division in Hezbollah's *muqawama* project following the organization's use of weapons against internal Lebanese forces. This was probably the main reason why Nasrallah further emphasized the organization's strategy to establish alliances beyond the existing sectarian division. In this critical situation, Hezbollah had to prevent a scenario of sectarian tension, which would undermine its aspirations to lead a comprehensive project.

Hence, Hezbollah's "Political Document" in November 2009 accepts the changes the party had undergone over the years since the publication of "The Open Letter" in 1985. In Nasrallah's related press conference, he stated that the lack of consensus around the *muqawama* project was not problematic as such, for no nation in history had ever obtained full consensus on the organization of resistance:

> Some have collaborated with the occupation, and some have sat aside and watched silently; even among those who resisted, some have followed the political path of resistance, while others have followed the military. . . . [T]his is not problem as long as we can talk and hold dialogue with each other. . . . I can also tell you that consensus around the *muqawama* is a prerequisite for its perfection and not for its existence. . . . [T]his does not mean that we do not seek to gain consensus around the *muqawama*; this is what we want most.[88]

Nasrallah sought not only to lower the flames of the clashes in the aftermath of May 2008 but also to demonstrate openness and readiness to negotiate with both those non-Hezbollah elements supporting the *muqawama* project and factions skeptical about it. This shows an even higher degree of flexibility than previously. Nevertheless, Nasrallah was at that point neither ready to renounce the *muqawama* nor to agree with the journalist who argued that the prioritization of the *muqawama* project had been downgraded below the establishment of a strong, just Lebanese state. Nasrallah argued that these aims are interwoven: "No, what I said is that the *muqawama* is still our main mission. I do not think that we are moving it to a lower level; the *muqawama* comes first. . . . In fact, to establish a state and its institutions and to enhance peace, stability, and security in Lebanon, our homeland should be first safe and able to resist the ongoing Israeli dangers. Therefore, I believe that a real *muqawama* is a key prerequisite to enable the Lebanese people to establish the state that they long for."[89]

This statement features a great number of adjustments and concessions, discussed in relation to the project's previous phases. The current period is depicted as a phase for achieving the national credibility of the *muqawama* project as well as the recognition of Lebanon as the homeland. It is the time to work toward the establishment of a just state in the foreseeable future and in partnership with others, not in some distant era when the Mahdi will reappear, as held in classical Shiʿism. This is a realizable revolution in Hezbollah's perception, albeit one more than two decades in the making.

The gradual momentum toward a project that goes beyond Lebanese borders gained considerable traction through Hezbollah's involvement in the Syrian Civil War. It was the first time that Hezbollah had openly used its weapons outside Lebanon and, moreover, in an Arab and predominantly Muslim country. Even more significant was that it supported a secular regime fighting Islamist organizations such as the Nusra Front affiliate of al-Qa'ida and Islamic State. In joining the Syrian Civil War, Hezbollah's narrative took a further turn in light of the region's new reality. This is not the place for a lengthy disquisition on the dramatic change in Hezbollah's discourse in the all-out war on jihadist organizations in Syria. Yet special attention should be drawn here to certain key points on how that discourse has been refined toward a clearer definition of *muqawama* partnership, both ideologically and practically. This is not an analysis of Hezbollah's involvement in Syria but rather of the way Hezbollah has chosen to portray that involvement. The path that Hezbollah has chosen could not have been predicted, for whereas other Islamist movements chose all-out sectarianism, which stoked the conflict, Hezbollah did not.

The Jordanian Marxist journalist Nahid Hittir maintains that Nasrallah borders on historical materialist analysis in his 'Ashura' speech in 2015. He contends that Nasrallah's speech demonstrates a total detachment from political Islam, both Shi'ite and Sunni, and that Nasrallah does not differentiate between the two camps on the degree of belief each side has but rather on the basis of the conflict between imperialism and national liberation.[90]

I think, however, that Hittir goes beyond the bounds of reason in his evaluation of Nasrallah's speech. There is also no doubt that this speech is an especially important one that elaborates a new level of development in Hezbollah's discourse, promoting, as already noted, a historical bloc open to alliances with actors beyond the organization's "natural" religious environment, an openness to the discourse of leftist and Marxist movements in the Arab world, and the revolutionary discourse in the developing world. The speech acquires heightened significance from its being held during a religious ceremony. Nasrallah starts by portraying the United States as the successor to the old imperialist countries, standing alongside Britain and France, whose main objective is to gain "hegemony at all levels, so that the regions become subject to its political, security, economic, and even cultural control." He proceeds to argue that "what America wants requires complete submission, and whoever refuses to submit should be prepared for an intelligent and multifaceted war with the United States, a military war, and an economic, security, and media war as well as sieges and sanctions. This is the price of freedom nowadays, not only in the Arab and Islamic world but for all those who want to be independent and make decisions according to the interests of their homeland, people, and nation. This is not acceptable for the United States." He continues, "They [the Americans] want to take over the crude oil, the gas, and all the natural resources. . . . The United States is not dominated by human rights organizations, but by the owners of giant petroleum and weapons companies."[91]

In other words, Nasrallah explicitly asserts that the motives behind US actions are not based on its "crusader" views and not about being either Christian or anti-Muslim. The United States is driven mainly by its economic interests and in particular by its elites' interests. Nasrallah's discourse here is similar to that of Arab leftist movements and the revolutionary currents in the developing world. Nasrallah further argues that "they want to control, so that we become their markets."

> In this context and according to the logic of the American hegemony in the region, there should not be a strong state; there should not be a strong Arab or Islamic state, a strong state in the sense of an independent state, which makes its decisions independently. A state that takes into consideration the interests of its people, a state that invests in its economy and makes achievements at the scientific, technological, cultural and administrative levels and in all life domains. In the American hegemony project, this cannot happen . . . it does not matter if you are a Shiʿite, a Sunni, or a Christian.[92]

He proceeds to analyze the situation prevailing in the Arab world as one of a war of attrition against those who do not submit or who actively resist the dominance of the imperialist states over the region and its resources. Once again he dismisses the slogans of democracy and human rights that the Americans raise in the region, saying, "I am not talking about theories; I am presenting facts. How many dictatorships are being supported by the United States in the region? The United States supports regimes that do not have constitutions, elections, or even a sparkle of freedom of expression on the internet. . . . For this reason, we should not be deceived by the American lies. Unfortunately, some peoples of the region are misled by these slogans."[93]

Nasrallah makes Israel his second target for attack. He considers it an "instrument" of the United States and the other imperialist countries, not the other way around. In other words, it is not the "Jews" and the Jewish lobby that dominate the United States; rather, Israel is merely a tool that serves the economic interests of the US imperialist hegemonic project in the region. This analysis is close to the one provided by the Arab leftist movements that object to using anti-Jewish themes in the Islamist rhetoric of the religious movements in the regions that do not differentiate between Judaism, Zionism, and Israel.

In an interview on the Russian RT Arabic-language network on April 18, 2012, Nasrallah explicitly disassociated Hezbollah from its long anti-Jewish history. In response to a question regarding Hezbollah's perspectives on the future resolution of the Israeli–Palestinian conflict, he stated:

> Israel is an illegal state; it was established on the occupied lands of other people . . . and on the massacres and displacement of the Muslim and Christian Palestinians. Therefore, the rights should be regiven to the original owner, even after decades. . . . However, taking into consideration the ideological and legal positions and the political facts, we would say that the only solution is just that. . . . We do not want to kill anyone, and we do not want to abuse anyone. We simply want the rights to be returned to those who are entitled to them. . . . [T]he only solution is the establishment of a state on the Palestinian land on which Muslims, Jews, and Christians can live peacefully in a democratic state. No other solution would be durable.[94]

Nasrallah demonstrates a great deal of openness of perception relative to a highly ideological organization such as Hezbollah. There is a distinct transition away from anti-Jewish rhetoric that conceptualized the Jews as a nation of a special and timeless character from the dawn of history until present times to a narrative that differentiates between Jews and Judaism, on the one hand, and Zionism as an imperialist project, on the other. Again, this transition bears comparison with the discourse of Arab leftist movements over decades, facilitating dialogue and foregrounding commonalities between these forces. In the reviewed samples of the speeches by Nasrallah, one of Hezbollah's most significant founders and leaders, the gradualist change in the organization's perception is quite evident. I have also shown how the organization's ideological development has enabled the establishment of a common front with various factions and forces both locally and regionally.

This survey of Hezbollah's development shows that it began as a classic fundamentalist organization that sought forceful imposition of the Shari'a in Lebanon. It then proceeded to identify the unique potential of Lebanon, understanding that it was not Iran but had its own special admixture that deserved to be taken into account. After the liberation of most of southern Lebanon, thanks to the Hezbollah resistance, the organization accelerated its process of openness based on its new self-confidence, defining itself as the "authentic representative of the Lebanese nationalism" and of the Lebanese people.

Following the "divine victory" and the organization's even further enhanced self-confidence, Hezbollah began presenting itself not only as the leader of the counterhegemonic project at the Lebanese nationalist-patriotic level but also as the leader of a comprehensive Arab national project. That great leap forward was made during the organization's most difficult period and during its war alongside the Syrian regime against jihadist Islamist groups in both Syria and Lebanon. The *muqawama* project adopted an internationalist dimension of confrontation with global imperialism, represented by the United States and its satellite states (from Hezbollah's perspective), principally Israel, the Arab Gulf states, Turkey, and the jihadist movements. In this critical period, Hezbollah demonstrated a great deal of sensitivity to the differences in two battlefronts: the fraught and blood-soaked front in the East and the relatively calm front in the South on the Israeli border. Hezbollah has succeeded in promoting the *muqawama* project because it perceives itself as the guardian of the Lebanese homeland and the spirit of the land of the "minorities" in the face of an existential threat to Lebanon and the rest of the Levant. According to Hezbollah, this danger is currently embodied in Islamic State and other jihadist movements that refuse to accept change, even if such change is suggested by other Sunnis. Hezbollah thus revives and appropriates part of the culture of the hegemonic project prevalent in the first thirty years of the Lebanese state: multiculturalism and religious pluralism. The organization justifies its involvement in the Syrian war by asserting the protection of that multidimensional culture.

Conclusion

This chapter has provided a detailed overview of the organizations, processes, and arenas through which Hezbollah has built its unique *muqawama* project in Lebanon. It has examined the hegemonic mechanisms used for the dissemination of the hegemonic project: the media (al-Manar, *al-ʿAhd*, *al-Akhbar*, and other outlets); educational programs; and youth and leisure culture (websites, computer games, digital applications, and so forth). Books have also been an integral part of the *muqawama* project. The implications of the physical space are equally part of the organization's strategic plans, and it has made extensive efforts to visualize the *muqawama* project in a way that promotes the developing *muqawama* tourism in Lebanon (the "Switzerland of the Middle East"). To show the main features of Hezbollah's *muqawama* project, I analyzed numerous videos and songs partially associated with popular-national perspectives in Lebanon and the Arab world, demonstrating the extent to which the *muqawama* project has permeated the region as an "authentic" component and "natural" representative of a diverse Lebanese society and of the Arab world beyond. The development of the *muqawama* project is also reflected in Secretary-General Hassan Nasrallah's speeches, which over the past three decades have evolved from fostering isolation to reaching for national, religious, and human commonalities.

The chapter has clearly demonstrated that the *muqawama* is still a project in progress. It simultaneously operates in various political, social, educational, and communicative arenas, while seeking additional spaces to penetrate. Evidence of the project's ability to break out of its "natural" limitations can be found in the interaction Hezbollah has established with other organizations and intellectual groups. This chapter demonstrates that Hezbollah, with its advanced communicative, organizational, and economic abilities, is capable of leading a hegemonic project that seeks to integrate other forces and organizations (if not always entirely successfully). This process is still in play, and the degree of its success will be determined by the organization's ability to detach itself from its fundamentalist past and establish a more flexible and egalitarian posture toward potential allies. This is not an easy mission for an organization that was first established to represent a specific religious community and that is still categorized as a Shi'ite organization, despite its current openness.

Conclusion

At a Crossroads

Hezbollah has developed impressively over the past three decades from a small radical organization into a major player in the Lebanese, regional, and even international arenas. One of the main reasons for the change in the organization's status is its ability to carry the torch of resistance in the region and to articulate the *muqawama* project in an effective way, with Shi'ite history as well as other forces of resistance, be they nationalist, leftist, or Islamist, serving as sources of inspiration.

This book has presented an innovative interpretation of Lebanese politics as one of competing and indeed combative hegemonic projects comparable to others in the Middle East. This interpretation sheds light on the potentialities within the Lebanese political arena, one of the most unstable in the region for many years, at least until the eruption of the Arab Spring.

Examination of the Lebanese system through a Gramscian lens would not have been possible were it not a distinctive system in the Middle Eastern context. The Gramscian perspective seeks new ways to address the politics chiefly of strong, industrialized countries with developed civil societies rather than security and power mechanisms. However, as we have seen, the Lebanese state, considered for many years the weakest (in the Weberian sense) in the Middle East, has enabled different political forces to engage in hegemonic struggle and form alliances promoting hegemonic projects capable of ruling through "soft power" rather than coercion. This process was made possible because of the state's very weakness, the diffuse character of its power relations resulting from the complex sectarian system, relatively broad democratic space (in Middle Eastern terms), and religious and ethnic pluralism.

Soft power has won the Lebanese people's obedience to authority, acceptance of Lebanese nationalism's dominance, and the internalization of its founding narratives, which in turn have spared the country the need for the drastic assertions of power practiced in other countries in the region. This does not mean that there were no pockets of resistance or clashes between the different forces within the Lebanese state, but they did not pose a threat to the state's existence or to the regime governing it until the early 1970s and then the outbreak of the Civil War in 1975. The descent into a "war of all against all" put an end to the hegemonic project that had ruled the country for three decades. The internal struggle ended with a new equilibrium that some observers considered a somewhat unsuccessful reconstruction of the previous regime, with only cosmetic changes made through some advances in the internal distribution of power among the various sects.

The historical development of the Lebanese state provided a better platform for the Maronite elite and for the Sunnis, to a certain extent, that formed the basic constituency for the merchants and bankers' project that controlled Lebanon for more than three decades after independence in 1943, at least until the outbreak of the Civil War in the mid-1970s. This project was based economically on a dependency on the service sector that tied the Lebanese economy into global forces, in particular Western countries, at first France and then the United States and allied nations.

This economic structure, allied to the way the Lebanese political system worked, marginalized the Shi'ites, the third-largest community in Lebanon at the time of independence and now the largest, according to recent figures. The Shi'ite community was not granted a significant role in Lebanese political structures and thus became fertile ground for radical and revolutionary movements. The first of them were left-wing parties, such as the Communist and Ba'th Parties, that developed within the Shi'ite community, won over the sympathies of young Shi'ites, and sought to build a united platform to express their discontent in the Lebanese system and the injustice that relegated them to the bottom of the socioeconomic pile.

Later, *al-hala al-Islamiyya*, the Islamic atmosphere, emerged, and Musa al-Sadr became the spiritual leader of the Shi'ite community in Lebanon, trying to organize the Shi'ites so that they could claim their place at the Lebanese political table. Activist clerics such as Muhammad Husayn Fadlallah and young clerics schooled in *hawzat* in Iraq but expelled by its Ba'thist regime returned to Lebanon full of revolutionary Shi'ite fervor inspired by thinkers such as Muhammad Baqir al-Sadr, 'Ali Shari'ati, and others. All of this led the community to an activist Shi'ism that made a bid for its share of the Lebanese pie, all within the context of a raging civil war and increasing religious and sociopolitical conflict between Lebanon's various sects.

The young clerics, who thrived mainly in the Biqa' region and did not belong to the families of traditional Islamic scholars, returned to a Lebanon torn apart and burned out by the Civil War. They became the organic intellectuals of a new Shi'ite social stratum imbued with the sense of momentum within radical Shi'ite Islam regionally. Musa al-Sadr's al-Mahrumin movement initiated them into an understanding that they did not belong to a small community on the margins but were rather part of a wider current of tens of millions of believers. These young clerics' success was built on dual intellectual foundations.

The first was the preparation of the ideological ground through the co-optation of activist and revolutionary standpoints developed by radical left-wing organizations mainly within the Shi'ite community. This co-optation enhanced the activism of young Shi'ites and distanced them from traditional leaders, again paving the way for subsequent radical Shi'ite activist stances. By the late 1970s, the Shi'ite community was open to radical and revolutionary ideas with regard to its socioeconomic and political position in Lebanon.

The second was the young clerics' adherence to activist principles established by Shi'ite clerics such as Khomeini, Baqir al-Sadr, and Fadlallah as well as by revolutionary Shi'ite thinkers such as Shari'ati. This approach was distanced from the centuries-old passivism of mainstream Shi'ism and instead tapped into the roots of resistance deep within Shi'ite history, reactivating its founding myths and relating them to the contemporary revolutionary demands for social justice, the elimination of oppression, and the struggle against occupation in the present, not just in the afterlife.

From the very outset, the movement established by these young clerics was one of religious fundamentalism following the "supreme leader" of activist Shi'ism at the time, Ruhollah Khomeini. The ayatollah had succeeded, only a few years before Hezbollah emerged, in leading a popular revolution against a tyrannical Iranian regime that was a loyal ally of Israel and the United States. This success had an immense impact on these young Shi'ites, and their original plan was to copy the Iranian model within the Lebanese arena. The conditions that prevailed in Lebanon at that time—the "war of all against all" that shattered the entire system—helped their cause and enhanced the credibility of their youthful radicalism that sought the abolition of the Lebanese state in favor of a global Islamic state under the leadership of the Iranian supreme leader.

However, with the passage of time and following the end of the Lebanese Civil War, Khomeini's death, and the transition to a more pragmatic stream in Iran, alongside the fall of the Soviet Union and other events domestically and internationally, the Lebanese regime reestablished the sectarian system underwritten by a wide-ranging Syrian intervention in the country's affairs. This led Hezbollah gradually to change its strategy to a more pragmatic approach domestically, though it continued to maintain its radical positions toward Lebanon's external enemies. This more pragmatic position was first reflected in the election of 'Abbas Musawi as the movement's secretary-general in place of Subhi al-Tufayli. Then it could be seen in the organization's decision to stand for the first time in the parliamentary elections in 1992, which came after the Ta'if Agreement and the end of the Civil War. Earlier in that same year, Israel's assassination of Musawi (and his family while they were in a car that was bombed) led to the election of Hassan Nasrallah as the organization's third secretary-general.

Under Nasrallah's leadership, the organization moved toward "openness," "Lebanization," and "pragmatism," as various accounts have described it. As shown here, it went in the direction of a "hegemonic policy," establishing alliances and developing joint projects with various currents within Lebanon and in the broader region. This policy was a natural reaction to external events that imposed such coping mechanisms upon it. However, from the mid-1990s and particularly after the liberation of southern Lebanon in May 2000, this policy became a conscious and planned strategy, albeit influenced, too, by the party's practical and psychological war with Israel, the United States, and the Gulf countries.

The organization faced many domestic challenges following the Syrian withdrawal from Lebanon beginning in 2005 and the division of the Lebanese political arena into two major camps. The first camp was the March 14 Alliance, which included the Future Movement led by Sa'd Hariri, the Lebanese Phalanges Party, Samir Ja'ja''s Lebanese Forces Party, Walid Jumblatt's al-Hizb al-Taqadumi al-Ishtiraki (Progressive Socialist Party), Michel 'Aoun's Free Patriotic Movement (which subsequently left the March 14 Alliance in favor of an alliance with Hezbollah), and other smaller organizations. The second was the March 8 Alliance, which included Hezbollah, the Amal movement, the Lebanese Ba'th Party, the Syrian Social-Nationalist Party, and some smaller Druze parties.

Given these challenges, Hezbollah started to "take an interest in every single detail of intra-Lebanese politics," as Nasrallah put it in a speech following the withdrawal of the last Syrian troops from Lebanon and the intensity of polarization in the Lebanese political arena.[1] Hezbollah's move toward hegemonic politics was based on the development of a hegemonic project capable of articulating the platforms of different forces and parties that would grant Hezbollah legitimacy and status in both domestic and international politics. For Hezbollah to do so, though, it had to downplay its Islamic essentialism, given the pluralistic arena in which it was now operating alongside many other religiously aligned groups. So it instead highlighted the national and populist dimensions and developed its *muqawama* project from a purely military goal to a central mechanism of its broad hegemonic scheme of building alliances. By these means, Hezbollah connected its religious outlook with a nationalist perspective, making its calls for social justice for ordinary people a central motif.

This new Hezbollah-led *muqawama* project replaced commerce and banking as a project, while the manufacturing economy replaced the service economy as a policy priority. The motto that "Lebanon's strength lies in its weakness" was replaced by "Lebanon's strength lies in its power and resistance." Yet these changes did not mean that the new project had entirely ditched all dimensions of the one it sought to replace. In fact, the originally fundamentalist and radical Hezbollah had already appropriated one aspect of the former regime: Lebanese pluralism as an integral part of an essentially populist-national outlook. Hezbollah thus maintains that with the project it seeks to promote, it is the singular force that can protect this pluralism from Israeli attacks, on the one hand, and, no less importantly, from the threat to Lebanon and the region from the fundamentalism of Islamic State, al-Qa'ida, and other radical organizations.

As indicated earlier, the success of a counterhegemonic project is measurable by its ability to permeate and gain control over a multiplicity of domains within any particular state or region. The *muqawama* project still faces serious challenges, such as the essentially sectarian character of Lebanese society, the strength of the long-standing elites both in Lebanon and in the Arab world generally, and the Arab Spring developments in Syria and elsewhere. However, it is nourished by the international division of new versus old, the *mustad'afin* (oppressed) versus the *mustakbirin* (tyrants). The organization counts in the latter camp not only Israel and the United States but also (and more recently) Saudi Arabia, other Gulf states, and various radical organizations fighting in Syria.

The *muqawama* project is by definition a counterhegemonic project. Its ability to become hegemonic in a country such as Lebanon is a possibility as long as the conflict with Israel, the United States, and jihadist movements continues. For the *muqawama* project to be sustainable, it needs an opposing camp, and all external attempts to combat it will only enhance it and increase its relevance.

I have also described the way Hezbollah continues to develop the conceptual, psychological, cultural, and physical infrastructure of its project via different hegemonic mechanisms either that controls directly or that exist in its surrounding. This infrastructure sustains the relevance of the project even if a cease-fire or "cold peace" exists between it and the forces it opposes. To survive, Hezbollah needs to be in a perpetual state of struggle or at least "cold war" with the major foreign powers and their domestic and regional "metastases." It is this perpetual struggle that keeps the hegemonic project alive and resolves, for Hezbollah, the dilemma of Shi'ism being a resistance faith that would lose its philosophical sustainability the moment it gains absolute state power.

Hezbollah has gained much of its power and prestige from its military struggle against Israel in southern Lebanon. Within the framework of the *muqawama*, Hezbollah attributes great importance to the armed struggle against external military enemies, especially Israel. Yet this counterhegemonic project has been developed largely without the need to resort to armed force to impose domination. The use of armed force by a hegemonic force locally would actually demonstrate that hegemony's weakness.

In May 2008, when Hezbollah used armed force against its Lebanese domestic enemies, some cracks appeared in the hegemonic project that the organization had been building and promoting over the previous two decades. The same has happened because of its intervention in the Syrian Civil War. The toughest contemporary challenge Hezbollah and its *muqawama* project face is the blurring of the boundaries between Lebanese politics and resistance to foreign forces. In turn, the project's success is greatly dependent on the organization's ability to reinstate these boundaries.

The more Hezbollah seeks to expand its hold over the Lebanese arena, the more it needs to downplay its religious profile, provided that this does not completely detach it from the faith-based roots of its power. These roots include the seemingly inexhaustible reserve of active Shi'ite resistance and the organization's intimate relation with its "natural" surroundings, both of which provide a stable basis of support essential to the organization. The Hezbollah counterhegemonic project requires perpetual fine-tuning between openness and expansiveness toward other forces, on the one hand, and the maintenance of its basic identity, on the other. The difficulty of accomplishing both is evident in at least two events over the past decade.

The first occurred when the organization felt obliged to use weapons in internecine strife with al-Mustaqbal and other opponents in May 2008. It was a key symbolic test of Hezbollah's ability to refrain from using overt force to pursue its objectives. The incident revealed the holes in its project. The very use of force, though moderate, demonstrated that the organization had not yet succeeded in permeating all strata of Lebanese society and that the pockets of resistance to its project were not at all small.

The second event is related to the war in neighboring Syria. This civil war reasserted (as the Lebanese Civil War did but even more so) the power of religious-communal tensions in both Syria and Lebanon, a fact always playing against the brand of hegemonic politics that Hezbollah has chosen to follow because the arena is one of "war of all against all" and blitzkrieg, in Gramscian terms. Despite the damage to Hezbollah's image, at least in many Arabs' eyes, sustained by its intervention in Syria, Hezbollah has used the Syrian war to foreground commonalities with potential partners among local and regional minorities. It has likewise used the war to make overtures to secularists, left-wing movements, and nationalist forces in the Arab world that see Islamic State as well Israel and the United States as the embodiment of evil and a threat to religious and ideological pluralism in the Levant. How far Hezbollah has been successful in this attempt remains unclear, given both the threats and the opportunities facing it. Hezbollah's success also depends on its ability to develop an alternative vision of an open and embracing Islamism to counter, not mirror, Islamic State and other jihadist movements.

Notes

Bibliography

Index

Notes

Introduction

1. Shawn T. Flanigan and Mounah Abdel-Samad, "Hezbollah's Social Jihad: Nonprofits as Resistance Organizations," *Middle East Policy* 16, no. 2 (Summer 2009): 122–37.

2. Ranstrup Magnus, *Hizb'Allah in Lebanon: The Politics of Western Hostage Crisis* (Basingstoke, UK: Palgrave Macmillan, 1997).

3. Wadah Shararah, *The State of Hezbollah: Lebanon, an Islamic Society* (in Arabic) (Beirut: Al-Nahar, 1996).

4. Masoud Asad Allahi, *The Islamists in a Multicultural Society* (in Arabic) (Beirut: Al-Arabiya lil-'Oloum, 2004); Eitan Azani, *Hezbollah: The Story of the Party of God, from Revolution to Institutionalization* (New York: Palgrave Macmillan, 2009).

5. Ghassan 'Azi, *Hezbollah: From the Ideological Dream . . . to Political Pragmatism* (in Arabic) (Kuwait City: Qirtas, 1998); Augustus R. Norton, *Hezbollah: A Short History* (Princeton, NJ: Princeton Univ. Press, 2007).

6. Amal Sa'd-Ghrayeb, *Hezbollah: Politics and Religion* (Beirut: Al-Kitab al-'Arabi, 2002).

7. Ahmad Nizar Hamzeh, *In the Path of Hizbullah* (Syracuse, NY: Syracuse Univ. Press, 2004).

8. Eyal Zisser, *Lebanon: Blood in the Cedars* (Tel Aviv: Kav Adom, 2009).

9. Michael Milstein, Muqawama: *The Emergence of the Resistance Challenge and Its Influence on the Perception of Israeli National Security* (in Hebrew) (Tel Aviv: Institute for National Security Studies, 2009).

10. Joseph Alagha, *The Shifts in Hizbullah's Ideology: Religious Ideology, Political Ideology, and Political Program* (Leiden: ISIM and Amsterdam Univ. Press, 2006), and *Hizbullah's Identity Construction* (Amsterdam: Amsterdam Univ. Press, 2011).

11. Samer Abboud and Benjamin J. Muller, *Rethinking Hizballah: Legitimacy, Authority, Violence* (Farnham, UK: Ashgate, 2012).

12. James Worrall, Simon Mabon, and Gurdon Clubb, *Hezbollah: From Islamic Resistance to Government* (Santa Barbara, CA: Praeger, 2016).

13. Rula Jurdi Abisaab and Malek Abisaab, *The Shi'ites of Lebanon: Modernism, Communism, and Hizbullah's Islamists* (Syracuse, NY: Syracuse Univ. Press, 2014).

14. Joseph Daher, *Hezbollah: The Political Economy of Lebanon's Party of God* (London: Pluto Press, 2016), 205.

15. Bashir Saade, *Hizbullah and the Politics of Remembrance: Writing the Lebanese Nation* (Cambridge: Cambridge Univ. Press, 2016), 161, 167.

16. Lina Khatib, Dina Matar, and Atef Alshaer, *The Hizbullah Phenomenon: Politics and Communication* (New York: Oxford Univ. Press, 2014).

17. Zahera Harb, *Channels of Resistance in Lebanon: Liberation Propaganda, Hezbollah, and the Media* (London: I. B Tauris, 2011).

18. Perry Anderson, "The Antinomies of Antonio Gramsci," *New Left Review* 1, no. 100 (Nov.–Dec. 1976): 5–78.

19. Vladimir Lenin, "Two Tactics of Social-Democracy in the Democratic Revolution," in *Lenin: Marx–Engels the Marxism* (in Arabic) (Moscow: Al-Tiba'a wal-Nashr bi-Allughat al-Ajnabiyya, n.d.), 212–27.

20. Lenin, "Two Tactics of Social-Democracy in the Democratic Revolution."

21. Anderson, "The Antinomies of Antonio Gramsci," 20.

22. Antonio Gramsci, *Selections from the Prison Notebooks*, ed. Quintin Hoare and Geoffrey N. Smith (1971; reprint, London: Lawrence and Wishart, 1992), 235.

23. Gwyn A. Williams, "Concept of 'Egemonia' in the Thought of Antonio Gramsci: Some Notes on Interpretation," *Journal of History of Ideas* 21, no. 4 (Oct.–Dec. 1960): 587.

24. Jeremy Lester, *Dialogue of Negation: Debates on Hegemony in Russia and the West* (London: Pluto Press, 2000), 61–63.

25. Robert W. Cox, "Gramsci, Hegemony, and International Relations: An Essay in Method," in *Gramsci, Historical Materialism, and International Relations*, ed. Stephen Gill (Cambridge: Cambridge Univ. Press, 1993), 56.

26. Lester, *Dialogue of Negation*, 61.

27. Gramsci, *Selections*, 5.

28. Dani Filc, *Populism and Hegemony in Israel* (in Hebrew) (Tel Aviv: Resling, 2006), 210.

29. Gramsci, *Selections*, 129.

30. Antonio Gramsci, *Prison Notebooks*, vol. 1, ed. Josef A. Buttigieg, trans. Josef A. Buttigieg and Antonio Callari (New York: Columbia Univ. Press, 1992), 136, 137.

31. Gramsci, *Prison Notebooks*, 1:132–33.

32. Peter D. Thomas, "Hegemony, Passive Revolution, and the Modern Prince," *Thesis Eleven* 117, no. 20 (Aug. 2013): 26.

33. Roger Simon, *Gramsci's Political Thought: An Introduction* (London: Lawrence and Wishart, 1982), 43.

34. Ernesto Laclau and Chantal Mouffe, *Hegemony and Socialist Strategy: Towards a Radical Democratic Politics* (London: Verso, 1985).

35. Laclau and Mouffe, *Hegemony and Socialist Strategy*, 105.

36. Laclau and Mouffe, *Hegemony and Socialist Strategy.*

37. Neelam Srivastava and Baidik Bhattacharya, "Introduction: The Postcolonial Gramsci," in *The Postcolonial Gramsci*, ed. Neelam Srivastava and Baidik Bhattacharya (London: Routledge Taylor & Francis Group, 2013), 7–10.

38. Thomas J. Butko, "Revelation or Revolution: A Gramscian Approach to the Rise of Political Islam," *British Journal of Middle Eastern Studies* 31, no. 1 (May 2004): 41–62.

1. The Essence of *Muqawama*

1. Antonio Gramsci, *On Hegemony: A Selection from the Prison Notebooks* (in Hebrew) (Tel Aviv: Resling, 2004), 158. All translations from Arabic and Hebrew are mine, with assistance from Ruba Simaan, unless otherwise indicated in note citations.

2. Laclau and Mouffe, *Hegemony and Socialist Strategy.*

3. Ibn Manzur, *Dictionary of the Tongue of the Arabs* (in Arabic) (Cairo: Dar al-M'arif, n.d.), s.v. "جهد."

4. This problematic definition of *jihad* is discussed in Roxanne L. Euben, "Killing (for) Politics: Jihad, Martyrdom, and Political Action," *Political Theory* 30, no. 1 (Feb. 2002): 4–35.

5. Rudolph Peters, *Jihad in Classical and Modern Islam: A Reader* (Princeton, NJ: Markus Wiener, 1996), 1.

6. Peters, *Jihad in Classical and Modern Islam*, 6.

7. Euben, "Killing (for) Politics," 14.

8. Ahmad bin 'Abdul Halim ibn Taymiyyah, *Ibn Taymiyyah Studies Compilation* (in Arabic), ed. Muhammad Ezer Shams (Mecca: Alaam al-Fawaid, 2003), 298.

9. Peters, *Jihad in Classical and Modern Islam*, 7.

10. Mehdi Abedi and Gary Legenhausen, introduction to *Jihad and Shahadat: Struggle and Martyrdom in Islam*, ed. Mehdi Abedi and Gary Legenhausen (Houston: Institute for Research and Islamic Studies, 1986), 15.

11. Rola el-Husseini, "Resistance, Jihad, and Martyrdom in Contemporary Lebanese Shi'a Discourse," *Middle East Journal* 62, no. 3 (2008): 401.

12. Quoted in Na'im Qasim, *Hezbollah: Its Approach, Experience, and Future* (in Arabic) (Beirut: Al-Hadi, 2005), 44.

13. Euben, "Killing (for) Politics," 12.

14. *The Intermediate Lexicon* (in Arabic), 4th ed. (Cairo: Majma' al-Logha al-'Arabiyya, 2004), s.v. "شهد."

15. *The Intermediate Lexicon*, s.v. "شهد."

16. Wafa' al-Drisi, *The Martyr through the Interpretation of al-Tabari* (in Arabic) (Beirut: Al-Intishar al-'Arabi, 2008), 32–34.

17. Ibn-Jarir al-Tabari, *Collection of Statements on Interpretation of Verses of the Qur'an* (in Arabic), vol. 5 (Beirut: Al-Fikr, 2001), 203.

18. Al-Drisi, *The Martyr through the Interpretation of al-Tabari*, 27.

19. Najeeb Nur Eddine, *The Ideology of Rejection and Resistance: A Socio-political Research on the Shi'ite Refusal* (in Arabic) (Beirut: Al-Hadi, 2004), 338.

20. Ibn Manzur, *Dictionary of the Tongue of the Arabs*, s.v. "Fada."

21. *The Intermediate Lexicon*, s.v. "Fada."

22. "The Palestinian Anthem," Palestinian News and Info Agency—Wafa, n.d., at http://www.wafainfo.ps/atemplate.aspx?id=2353.

23. Ibn Manzur, *Dictionary of the Tongue of the Arabs*, s.v. "صمد."

24. *The Intermediate Lexicon*, s.v. "صمد."

25. *The Intermediate Lexicon*, s.v. "صمد."

26. Helena Lindholm-Schulz, *The Reconstruction of Palestinian Nationalism: Between Revolution and Statehood* (Manchester, UK: Manchester Univ., 1999), quoted in Laleh Khalili, *Heroes and Martyrs of Palestine: The Politics of National Commemoration* (New York: Cambridge Univ. Press, 2007), 99.

27. Lindholm-Schulz, *The Reconstruction of Palestinian Nationalism*, 54.

28. El-Husseini, "Resistance, Jihad, and Martyrdom," 407.

29. *The Intermediate Lexicon*, s.v. "منع."

30. *The Intermediate Lexicon*, s.v. "منع."

31. *The Intermediate Lexicon*, s.v. "منع."

32. Larbi Sadiqi, "Reshaping the Democratic Resistance: Narratives from Hamas and Hezbollah" (in Arabic), *Al-Mustaqbal al-'Arabi* 377 (July 2010): 71.

33. Eyal Zisser, "Syria in the Face of the Israeli Challenge: Between Passive Resistance (*Munan'a*) and Active Resistance (*Muqawama*)" (in Hebrew), *Strategic Updates* 12 (2009): 68.

34. Zisser, "Syria in the Face of the Israeli Challenge," 73.

35. Na'im Qasim, *The Values of the* Muqawama: *The Choice of Martyrdom and of Life* (in Arabic) (Beirut: Al-Hadi, 2008), 5.

36. Ibn Manzur, *Dictionary of the Tongue of the Arabs*, s.v. "قوم" and "قوم."

37. Jamal al-Din al-Afghani, *The Complete Works* (in Arabic), ed. Muhammad 'Amarah (Cairo: Al-Katib al-'Arabi, n.d.), 447.

38. Al-Afghani, *The Complete Works*, 450–51.

39. Michael Milstein, Muqawama: *The Emergence of the Resistance Challenge and Its Influence on the Perception of Israeli National Security* (in Hebrew) (Tel Aviv: Institute for National Security Studies, 2009), 21.

40. Milstein, *Muqawama*, 22.

41. Mu'een A. Mahmoud, *The Fedae'i Activism* (in Arabic) (Beirut: Al-Maktab al-Tijari, 1969), 24–34.

42. Baruch Kimmerling and Joel S. Migdal, *Palestinians: The Making of a People* (in Hebrew) (Jerusalem: Keter, 1999), 92.

43. Emile Touma, *The Roots of the Palestinian Case*, vol. 4 of *Emile Touma: The Complete Collection* (in Arabic) (Haifa, Israel: Emile Touma Institute for Political and Social Studies, 1995), 115–19.

44. Touma, *The Roots of the Palestinian Case*, 116.

45. Kimmerling and Migdal, *Palestinians*, 103.

46. Kimmerling and Migdal, *Palestinians*, 101.

47. Kimmerling and Migdal, *Palestinians*, 97.

48. Rosemary Sayigh, *The Palestinians: From Peasants to Revolutionaries* (London: Zed Books, 2007), 79.

49. Kimmerling and Migdal, *Palestinians*, 124–25, 132.

50. Kimmerling and Migdal, *Palestinians*, 146.

51. Kimmerling and Migdal, *Palestinians*, 148.

52. Tawfiq Kanaaneh, *Autobiography* (in Arabic) (Acre, Israel: Abu Rahmoun Press, 2009), 50.

53. Kanaaneh, *Autobiography*, 50.

54. Eli Rekhes, *The Arab Minority in Israel: Between Communism and Arab Nationalism* (in Hebrew) (Tel Aviv: Moshe Dayan Center, 1993), 82.

55. Lindholm-Schulz, *The Reconstruction of Palestinian Nationalism*, 54.

56. Yazid Sayigh, *Armed Struggle and the Search for State: The Palestinian National Movement 1948–1993* (in Arabic) (Beirut: Institute for Palestine Studies, 2003), 229.

57. Kimmerling and Migdal, *Palestinians*, 188.

58. Kimmerling and Migdal, *Palestinians*, 192–93.

59. Y. Sayigh, *Armed Struggle*, 132–44.

60. Y. Sayigh, *Armed Struggle*, 144–59; Riyad el-Rayyis and Dunia Nahas, *Guerrillas for Palestine* (London: Portico, 1976), 13–16.

61. Y. Sayigh, *Armed Struggle*, 144–45.

62. Translated and quoted in el-Rayyis and Nahas, *Guerrillas for Palestine*, 27.

63. Cited in Y. Sayigh, *Armed Struggle*, 154.

64. Quoted in Sadiqi, "Reshaping the Democratic Resistance," 68.

65. R. Sayigh, *The Palestinians*, 150–51.

2. The Shattered Hegemony and the Beginning of Hezbollah

1. William Harris, *The New Face of Lebanon: History's Revenge* (Princeton, NJ: Marcus Wiener, 2006), 68.

2. Kamal Salibi, *The Modern History of Lebanon* (in Arabic) (Beirut: Al-Nahar, 1967), 201–5.

3. Carolyn Gates, *The Merchant Republic of Lebanon: Rise of an Open Economy* (London: Center for Lebanese Studies, 1998), 17.

4. Meir Zmir, *The Establishment of Modern Lebanon* (in Hebrew) (Tel Aviv: Ma'arachot and Israeli Ministry of Defense, 1993), 49–104.

5. Zisser, *Lebanon: Blood in the Cedars*, 34.

6. Theodor Hanf, *Lebanon: Coexistence in Times of War—from the Collapse of a State to the Emergence of a Nation* (in Arabic) (Paris: Euro-Arab Center for Studies, 1993), 92.

7. Fawwaz Trabulsi, *The Modern History of Lebanon: From the Emirate to the Ta'if Agreement* (in Arabic) (Beirut: Riyyad al-Rayess, 2008), 137.

8. Quoted in Hanf, *Lebanon*, 103.

9. Gates, *The Merchant Republic of Lebanon*, 80–90; Roger Owen, "The Economic History of Lebanon, 1943–1974: Its Salient Features," in *Toward a Viable Lebanon*, ed. Halim Barakat (Washington, DC: Center for Contemporary Arab Studies, 1988), 27–41.

10. Gates, *The Merchant Republic of Lebanon*, 2.

11. Trabulsi, *The Modern History of Lebanon*, 154–56.

12. Asher Kaufman, *Reviving Phoenicia: The Search for Identity in Lebanon* (London: I. B. Tauris, 2004), 87.

13. Trabulsi, *The Modern History of Lebanon*, 155–56.

14. Kaufman, *Reviving Phoenicia*, 153.

15. Kaufman, *Reviving Phoenicia*, 145.

16. Trabulsi, *The Modern History of Lebanon*, 155–56.

17. Kamal Salibi, *A House of Many Mansions: The History of Lebanon Reconsidered* (London: I. B. Tauris, 1988), 178.

18. Kaufman, *Reviving Phoenicia*, 162.

19. Kaufman, *Reviving Phoenicia*, 159–69.

20. Quoted in Hanf, *Lebanon*, 99.

21. Kamal Dib, *Warlords and Merchants: The Lebanese Business and Political Establishment* (Reading, UK: Ithaca Press, 2004), 77.

22. Salibi, *The Modern History of Lebanon*, 217.

23. Trabulsi, *The Modern History of Lebanon*, 158.

24. Philip Hitti, *Lebanon in History: From the Earliest Times to the Present* (in Arabic) (Beirut: Franklin Institution for Publications, 1959), 610.

25. Gates, *The Merchant Republic of Lebanon*, 89.

26. Such as Kamal Hamdan, Fawwaz Trabulsi, Theodor Hanf, David Gordon, Roger Owen, and Kamal Dib.

27. Hanf, *Lebanon*, 102–3; Owen, "The Economic History of Lebanon," 28.

28. Kamal Hamdan, *The Lebanese Crisis: Religious Groups, Social Classes, and the National Identity* (in Arabic) (Beirut: Al-Farabi, 1998); Trabulsi, *The Modern History of Lebanon*, 192.

29. Trabulsi, *The Modern History of Lebanon*, 193.

30. Gates, *The Merchant Republic of Lebanon*, 95.

31. Hamdan, *The Lebanese Crisis*, 88.

32. Gates, *The Merchant Republic of Lebanon*, 33.

33. Hamdan, *The Lebanese Crisis*, 89.

34. Hamdan, *The Lebanese Crisis*, 94.

35. Gates, *The Merchant Republic of Lebanon*, 59.

36. Trabulsi, *The Modern History of Lebanon*, 196.

37. Trabulsi, *The Modern History of Lebanon*, 196.

38. Trabulsi, *The Modern History of Lebanon*, 198.

39. Gates, *The Merchant Republic of Lebanon*, 88.

40. Hamdan, *The Lebanese Crisis*, 95.

41. Trabulsi, *The Modern History of Lebanon*, 288.

42. This change is further elaborated later in this chapter. See also Fuad Ajami, *The Vanished Imam: Musa al-Sadr and the Shi'a in Lebanon* (Tel Aviv: Aam Oved, 1986); Hamdan, *The Lebanese Crisis*; and Trabulsi, *The Modern History of Lebanon*.

43. Trabulsi, *The Modern History of Lebanon*, 196.

44. Hamdan, *The Lebanese Crisis*, 115.

45. Hanf, *Lebanon*, 139.

46. Quoted in Hanf, *Lebanon*, 140.

47. Hanf, *Lebanon*, 139.

48. Hanf, *Lebanon*, 133.

49. A famous statement made by Pierre Gemayel, founder of the Phalanges Party and one of the Lebanese right-wing leaders.

50. Ussama Makdisi, *The Culture of Sectarianism: Community, History, and Violence in Nineteenth-Century Lebanon* (Berkeley: Univ. of California Press, 2000), 3.

51. Trabulsi, *The Modern History of Lebanon*, 414–15.

52. Hamdan, *The Lebanese Strike*, 163.

53. Data from the Central Bureau of Statistics in Lebanon, cited in Hamdan, *The Lebanese Strike*, 162.

54. Mahdi 'Amel, *In the Sectarian State* (in Arabic) (Beirut: Al-Farabi, 1986), 212.

55. Muhammad Ali Khalidi, *The Palestinian Refugees in Lebanon* (Beirut: Institute for Palestine Studies, 2001), 1.

56. Rami Siklawi, "The Dynamics of Palestinian Political Endurance in Lebanon," *Middle East Journal* 64, no. 4 (2010): 598.

57. Ahmad Beydoun, "The South Lebanon Border Zone: A Local Perspective," *Journal of Palestinian Studies* 21, no. 3 (Spring 1992): 35–36.

58. Trabulsi, *The Modern History of Lebanon*, 192.

59. Trabulsi, *The Modern History of Lebanon*, 193; Hamdan, *The Lebanese Crisis*, 87.

60. Rosemary Sayigh, cited in Siklawi, "The Dynamics of Palestinian Political Endurance," 599.

61. Sandra Mackey, *Lebanon: Death of a Nation* (New York: Congdon & Weed, 1989), 132.

62. Trabulsi, *The Modern History of Lebanon*, 220–36.

63. Abisaab and Abisaab, *The Shi'ites of Lebanon*, 23.

64. Norton, *Hezbollah*, 12–14.

65. Mackey, *Lebanon*, 131.

66. Mackey, *Lebanon*, 131.

67. Yuval Arnon-Ohana and Arieh Yudfat, *PLO: A Portrait of an Organization* (in Hebrew) (Tel Aviv: Ma'arev Library, 1985), 138; Trabulsi, *The Modern History of Lebanon*, 262.

68. John K. Cooley, "The Palestinians," in *Lebanon in Crisis: Participants and Issues*, ed. Edward Haley and Lewis W. Snider (Syracuse, NY: Syracuse Univ. Press, 1979), 29–31.

69. Siklawi, "The Dynamics of Palestinian Political Endurance," 604–5.

70. Hamdan, *The Lebanese Crisis*, 206–7.

71. Trabulsi, *The Modern History of Lebanon*, 288–89; Mackey, *Death of a Nation*, 138.

72. Cooley, "The Palestinians," 53.

73. This movement was not initially Shi'ite; it became so later.

74. Shimon Shapira, *Hezbollah: Between Iran and Lebanon* (in Hebrew) (Tel Aviv: Hakibbutz Hameuchad, 2000), 45–46; Trabulsi, *The Modern History of Lebanon*, 316.

75. Trabulsi, *The Modern History of Lebanon*, 352.

76. Y. Sayegh, *Armed Struggle*, 518–27; Khalili, *Heroes and Martyrs of Palestine*, 47.

77. Hamdan, *The Lebanese Crisis*, 207.

78. Kamal Salibi, "Tribal Origins of the Religious Sects in the Arab East," in *Toward a Viable Lebanon*, ed. Hale Barakat (Washington, DC: Center for Contemporary Arab Studies, 1988), 24–25.

79. Albert Hourani, "From Jabal 'Āmil to Persia," *Bulletin of the School of Oriental and African Studies, University of London* 49, no. 1 (1986): 133; Majed Halawi, *A Lebanon Defied: Musa al-Sadr and the Shi'a Community* (Boulder, CO: Westview Press, 1992), 29.

80. Rodger Shanahan, *The Shi'a of Lebanon: Clans, Parties, and Clerics* (London: Tauris Academic Studies, 2005), 13.

81. Rula Jurdi Abisaab, "Shi'ite Beginnings and Scholastic Tradition on Jabal 'Amil in Lebanon," *Muslim World* 89, no. 1 (Jan. 1999): 4.

82. Josef al-Agha, *Hezbollah: The Political and Ideological History* (in Arabic) (Baghdad: Dirasat 'Iraqiyya, 2008), 24.

83. Al-Agha, *Hezbollah*, 24.

84. Muhammad Jaber al-Safa, *The History of Jabal 'Amel* (in Arabic) (Beirut: Ma'ajam Matn al-Lugha, n.d.), 135–40.

85. Al-Safa, *The History of Jabal 'Amel*, 146

86. Abisaab and Abisaab, *The Shi'ites of Lebanon*, 19.

87. Muhammad Murad, "The Development of Political Options among the Shi'ites since the Emergence of the Modern Lebanese State to Date" (in Arabic), *Shuaoun al-awsat* 132 (Apr. 2009): 157.

88. Halawi, *A Lebanon Defied*, 52.

89. Halawi, *A Lebanon Defied*, 42.

90. Sa'doun Hamada, *The Shi'ite History in Lebanon* (in Arabic), vol. 1 (Beirut: Al-Khal, 2008), 8–9.

91. Halawi, *A Lebanon Defied*, 52.

92. Trabulsi, *The Modern History of Lebanon*, 283.

93. Trabulsi, *The Modern History of Lebanon*, 285.

94. Hamdan, *The Lebanese Crisis*, 101.

95. Waddah Shararah, *The State of Hezbollah: Lebanon, an Islamic Society* (in Arabic) (Beirut: Al-Nahar, 1996), 5.

96. Abisaab and Abisaab, *The Shi'ites of Lebanon*, 5.

97. Ajami, *The Vanished Imam*, 146–50.

98. Hanf, *Lebanon*, 141.

99. Zisser, *Lebanon: Blood in the Cedars*, 59.

100. Augustus R. Norton, *Amal and the Shi'a: Struggle for the Soul of Lebanon* (Austin: Univ. of Texas Press, 1987), 28.

101. Shanahan, *The Shi'a of Lebanon*, 71–77.

102. Ajami, *The Vanished Imam*.

103. Shapira, *Hezbollah*, 28–29.

104. Roschanack Shaery-Eisenlohr, *Shi'ite Lebanon: Transnational Religion and the Making of National Identity* (New York: Columbia Univ. Press, 2008), 25.

105. As summarized by Hussein al-Husseini, cited in Ajami, *The Vanished Imam*, 81.

106. Norton, *Amal and the Shi'a*, 60.

107. Norton, *Amal and the Shi'a*, 61.

108. Norton, *Amal and the Shi'a*, 67.

109. Zisser, *Lebanon: Blood in the Cedars*, 59.

110. Abisaab and Abisaab, *The Shi'ites of Lebanon*, 108; Sa'ad-Ghrayeb, *Hezbollah*, 17.

111. Hamzeh, *In the Path of Hizbullah*, 15–19.

112. Shanahan, *The Shi'a of Lebanon*, 129.

113. Shanahan, *The Shi'a of Lebanon*, 117.

114. Quoted in Ajami, *The Vanished Imam*, 82–83.

115. Shararah, *The State of Hezbollah*, 67–69.

116. Hamzeh, *In the Path of Hizbullah*, 15–17.

117. Al-Agha, *Hezbollah*, 56; also see Shapira, *Hezbollah*.

118. Muhammad Fneish (one of Hezbollah's leaders), interview, cited in Sa'ad-Ghrayeb, *Hezbollah*, 25.

119. Shanahan, *The Shi'a of Lebanon*, 113.

120. Shanahan, *The Shi'a of Lebanon*, 113.

121. Shapira, *Hezbollah*, 101–2.

122. Hamzeh, *In the Path of Hizbullah*, 24.

123. Elie Kadourie, *Nationalism* (London: Anchor Press, 1966), 9; see also Erika Harrus, *Nationalism: Theories and Cases* (Edinburgh: Edinburgh Univ. Press, 2009), 62.

124. Zisser, *Lebanon: Blood in the Cedars*, 199.

125. Rula Jurdi Abisaab, "The Cleric as Organic Intellectual: Revolutionary Shi'ism in the Lebanese *Hawzas*," in *Distant Relations: Iran and Lebanon in the Last 500 Years*, ed. H. E. Chehabi (London: Centre for Lebanese Studies and I. B. Tauris, 2006), 233.

126. Shapira, *Hezbollah*, 110–11.

127. Shapira, *Hezbollah*, 112.

128. Shapira, *Hezbollah*, 113.

129. Shapira, *Hezbollah*, 120.

130. Shapira, *Hezbollah*, 117–19.

131. Shapira, *Hezbollah*, 113.

132. Shararah, *The State of Hezbollah*, 160.

3. The *Muqawama* Thought

1. Bernard Lewis, "The Shi'a in Islamic History," in *Shi'ism, Resistance, and Revolution*, ed. Martin Kramer (Boulder, CO: Westview Press, 1987), 21.

2. Husayn Murawwa, *Materialist Trends in the Islamic Arab Philosophy* (in Arabic) (Beirut: Al-Farabi, 1988), 493–94.

3. Touma, *The Roots of the Palestinian Case*, 167–79.

4. Ahmad al-Kateb, *Development of the Shi'ite Political Thought: From 'Ashura' to the Guardianship of the Islamic Jurist* (in Arabic) (Beirut: Al-Jadeed, 1998), 271.

5. Al-Kateb, *Development of the Shi'ite Political Thought*, 325.

6. Al-Kateb, *Development of the Shi'ite Political Thought*, 399.

7. Nikki R. Keddie, *Iran: Religion, Politics, and Society* (London: Frank Cass, 1980), 94–98.

8. Fu'ad Ibrahim, *The Faqih and the State: The Shi'ite Political Thought* (in Arabic) (Beirut: Al-Kunouz al-Adabiyya, 1998), 209.

9. Nikki R. Keddie, *Roots of Revolution: An Interpretive History of Modern Iran* (New Haven, CT: Yale Univ. Press, 1981), 65–67.

10. Ervand Abrahamian, *Iran between Two Revolutions* (Princeton, NJ: Princeton Univ. Press, 1982), 80.

11. Said A. Arjomand, *The Turban for the Crown: The Islamic Revolution in Iran* (Oxford: Oxford Univ. Press, 1988), 35.

12. Nikki R. Keddie, *Modern Iran: Roots and Results of Revolution* (New Haven, CT: Yale Univ. Press, 2003), 66–67.

13. Keddie, *Roots of Revolution*, 87.

14. Keddie, *Roots of Revolution*, 111.

15. Keddie, *Roots of Revolution*, 132–42.

16. Keddie, *Roots of Revolution*, 132–42; Ibrahim, *The Faqih and the State*, 271.

17. Abrahamian, *Iran between Two Revolutions*, 423–24.

18. Keddie, *Roots of Revolution*, 157–58.

19. Abrahamian, *Iran between Two Revolutions*, 426–27.

20. Abrahamian, *Iran between Two Revolutions*, 496–573.

21. Keddie, *Modern Iran*, 215–16.

22. Keddie, *Modern Iran*, 238.

23. Khalil Ali Haidar, *The Turban and the Scepter: The Shi'ite Referential Authority in Iraq and Iran* (in Arabic) (Kuwait City: Qirtas, 1997), 204.

24. T. M. Aziz, "The Rule of Muhammad Baqir al-Sadr in Shii Political Activism in Iraq from 1958 to 1980," *International Journal in Middle East Studies* 25, no. 2 (May 1993): 208.

25. Hanna Batatu, *Iraq: The Social Classes and the Revolutionary Movements from the Ottoman Empire to the Establishment of the Republic* (in Arabic) (Beirut: Moasasat al-Abhath al-Arabiya, 1995).

26. Abdulaziz A. Sachedina, "Activist Shi'ism in Iran, Iraq, and Lebanon," in *Encyclopedia of Jihad*, ed. Raj Pruthi (New Delhi: Anmol, 2002), 987.

27. Hanna Batatu, "Shi'i Organizations in Iraq: Al-Da'wah al-Islamiyah and al-Mujahidin," in *Shi'ism and Social Protest*, ed. Juan Cole and Nikki R. Keddie (New Haven, CT: Yale Univ. Press, 1986), 182.

28. Batatu, "Shi'i Organizations in Iraq," 182.

29. Quoted in Batatu, "Shi'i Organizations in Iraq," 199.

30. Batatu, "Shi'i Organizations in Iraq," 192.

31. Muhammad Baqir al-Sadr, *Fadak in History* (in Arabic) (1955; reprint, n.p.: Ghadir Center for Islamic Studies, 1994), 17–32.

32. Rachel Kanz-Feder, "Fatima's Revolutionary Image in *Fadak fi al-Tarikh* (1955): The Inception of Muhammad Baqir al-Sadr's Activism," *British Journal of Middle Eastern Studies* 41, no. 1 (2014): 79–96.

33. Baqir al-Sadr, *Fadak in History*, 32.

34. Baqir al-Sadr, *Fadak in History*, 48.

35. Aziz, "The Rule of Muhammad Baqir al-Sadr," 207.

36. Batatu, "Shi'i Organizations in Iraq," 192.

37. Heinz Halm, *Shi'ism* (in Arabic), trans. Muhammad Kbebo (1988; reprint, Baghdad: Al-Warraq, 2011), 144.

38. Ruhollah Khomeini, *Islam and Revolution: Writings and Declarations of Imam Khomeini (1941–1980)*, ed. and trans. Hamid Algar (Berkeley, CA: Mizan Press, 1989), 170.

39. Halm, *Shi'ism*, 144.

40. Dustin Byrd, *Ayatollah Khomeini and the Anatomy of the Islamic Revolution in Iran: Toward a Theory of Prophetic Charisma* (Lanham, MD: Univ. Press of America, 2011), 6.

41. Baqer Moin, *Khomeini: Life of the Ayatollah* (New York: Thomas Dunne Books, 1999), 101–6.

42. Ervand Abrahamian, *Khomeinism: Essays on the Islamic Republic* (Berkeley: Univ. of California Press, 1993), 11.

43. Ruhollah Khomeini, *The Islamic Government* (in Arabic) (Beirut: Al-Tali'a, 1979).

44. Al-Kateb, *Development of the Shi'ite Political Thought*, 414.

45. Khomeini, *The Islamic Government*, 25–27.

46. Khomeini, *The Islamic Government*, 25–27.

47. Al-Kateb, *Development of the Shi'ite Political Thought*, 418–20.

48. Khomeini, *The Islamic Government*, 49.

49. Ibrahim, *The Faqih and the State*, 287–88; Ahmad al-Kateb, *Political Shi'ism and "Religious Shi'ism"* (in Arabic) (Beirut: Al-Intishal al 'Arabi, 2009), 381.

50. Al-Kateb, *Development of the Shi'ite Political Thought*, 424–47.

51. Abrahamian, *Khomeinism*, 17.

52. Mansoor Moaddel, *Class, Politics, and Ideology in the Iranian Revolution* (New York: Columbia Univ. Press, 1992), 257–62.

53. Zeev Sternhell, Mario Schneider, and Maya Ashri, *The Foundations of Fascism: A Cultural Dimension to the Political Revolution* (in Hebrew) (Tel Aviv: Am Oved, 1992), 93, 94.

54. Adel Ra'ouf, *Imam Khomeini: The Discourse, the State, and the Consciousness* (in Arabic) (Damascus: Iraqi Media and Studies Center, 2001).

55. Khomeini, *The Islamic Government*, 21–22.

56. Hamid Algar, introduction to Ali Shari'ati, *On the Sociology of Islam: Lectures by Ali Shari'ati*, trans. and ed. Hamid Algar (Berkeley, CA: Mizan Press, 1979), 16.

57. Abedi and Legenhausen, introduction to *Jihad and Shahadat*, ed. Abedi and Legenhausen, 35.

58. Abedi and Legenhausen, introduction to *Jihad and Shahadat*, 31.

59. Ali Rahnema, "Ali Shari'ati: Teacher, Preacher, Rebel," in *Pioneers of Islamic Revival*, ed. Ali Rahnema (New York: Zed Books, 2005), 209.

60. Hamid Dabashi, *Shi'ism: A Religion of Protest* (Cambridge, MA: Belknap Press of Harvard Univ. Press, 2011), 53–54.

61. Abdulaziz Sachedina, "Ali Shariati: Ideologue of the Iranian Revolution," in *Voices of Resurgent Islam*, ed. John L. Esposito (Oxford: Oxford Univ. Press, 1983), 205–11.

62. 'Ali Shari'ati, "Red Shi'ism versus Black Shi'ism," in *That Is How 'Ali Shari'ati Spoke: An Idea and a Revolution in the Advancement of the Islamic Movement and a Collection of His Writings* (in Arabic), ed. Fadel Rasoul (Beirut: Al-Kalima, 1982), 185–86.

63. Shari'ati, "Red Shi'ism versus Black Shi'ism," 185–86.

64. Halm, *Shi'ism*, 140.

65. Ervand Abrahamian, *Radical Islam: The Iranian Mojahedin* (London: I. B. Tauris, 1989), 107.

66. Byrd, *Ayatollah Khomeini and the Anatomy of the Islamic Revolution*, 97.

67. ʻAli Shariʻati, "Where Shall We Begin?," lecture, Iran Chamber Society, no date given, Iran Chamber Society website, at http://iranchamber.com/personalities/ashariati/works/where_shall_we_begin.php.

68. ʻAli Shariʻati, "Revolutionary Asceticism or Sufism in the Sense of Isolation?," in *That Is How ʻAli Shariʻati Spoke*, 205–6.

69. Elisheva Machlis, "ʻAli Shariʻati and the Notion of Tawhid: Re-exploring the Question of God's Unity," *Die Welt des Islams* 54, no. 2 (2014): 183–211.

70. Machlis, "ʻAli Shariʻati and the Notion of Tawhid," 192.

71. Ali Shariʻati, "The World-View of Tawhid," in *On the Sociology of Islam*, 82.

72. Machlis, "ʻAli Shariʻati and the Notion of Tawhid," 202–4.

73. Shariʻati, "Revolutionary Asceticism or Sufism in the Sense of Isolation?," 207.

74. Ali Shariʻati, "The Dialectic of Sociology," in *On the Sociology of Islam*, 116–17.

75. Shariʻati, "The Dialectic of Sociology," 111–12.

76. Shariʻati, "The Dialectic of Sociology," 116.

77. Norton, *Amal and the Shiʻa*, 39.

78. Ajami, *The Vanished Imam*, 33.

79. Norton, *Amal and the Shiʻa*, 39.

80. Ajami, *The Vanished Imam*, 98–100.

81. Shanahan, *The Shiʻa of Lebanon*, 147.

82. Shanahan, *The Shiʻa of Lebanon*, 41.

83. Quoted in Ajami, *The Vanished Imam*, 144.

84. Nur Eddine, *The Ideology of Rejection and Resistance*, 268.

85. Nur Eddine, *The Ideology of Rejection and Resistance*, 268.

86. Ajami, *The Vanished Imam*, 142–43.

87. Musa al-Sadr, speech, *al-Nahar*, Feb. 18, 1974.

88. Ajami, *The Vanished Imam*, 156.

89. Nur Eddine, *The Ideology of Rejection and Resistance*, 273.

90. Norton, *Amal and the Shiʻa*, 42.

91. Shapira, *Hezbollah*, 102–3.

92. Shapira, *Hezbollah*, 110–12, 117–20.

93. Nur Eddine, *The Ideology of Rejection and Resistance*, 345.

94. Nur Eddine, *The Ideology of Rejection and Resistance*, 345.

95. Shapira, *Hezbollah*, 151.

96. Nur Eddine, *The Ideology of Rejection and Resistance*, 348.

97. Mohammad Husayn Fadlallah, *The Power of Will* (in Arabic), ed. Naguib Nour al-Din (Beirut: Al-Malek, 2000), 42–43.

98. Fadlallah, *The Power of Will*, 18.

99. Quoted in Jamal Sankari, *A Journey of a Shiʻite Leader: Al-Sayyed Mohammad Husayn Fadlallah* (in Arabic) (Beirut: Al-Saki, 2008), 317.

100. Sankari, *A Journey of a Shi'ite Leader*, 353–57.

101. Sankari, *A Journey of a Shi'ite Leader*, 329.

4. The *Muqawama* of Hezbollah

1. Ibrahim al-Haydari, *The Tragedy of Karbala': The Sociology of the Shi'ite Discourse* (in Arabic) (Beirut: Al-Saqi, 1999), 91.

2. Moojan Momen, *An Introduction to Shi'i Islam: The History and Doctrines of Twelver Shi'ism* (New Haven, CT: Yale Univ. Press, 1985), 28.

3. Al-Haydari, *The Tragedy of Karbala'*, 91.

4. Momen, *An Introduction*, 30–31.

5. Mohsen al-Amin, quoted in Nur Eddine, *The Ideology of Rejection and Resistance*, 251.

6. Nur Eddine, *The Ideology of Rejection and Resistance*, 253.

7. Ralph Rizqallah, *The Blood Day: 'Ashura' Scene in Jabal 'Amel. A Psychological and Social Approach to the Killing of Imam Husayn* (in Arabic) (1977; reprint, Beirut: Dar al-Tali'a, 1997).

8. Rizqallah, *The Blood Day.*

9. Rizqallah, *The Blood Day*, 137.

10. *Al-'Ahd*, "Muslims Guardian about 'Ashura' Ceremonies and the Virtues of Commemoration" (in Arabic), June 17, 1994.

11. Shaery-Eisenlohr, *Shi'ite Lebanon*, 135.

12. Dabashi, *Shi'ism*, 80.

13. Guy Rocher, quoted in Rizqallah, *The Blood Day*, 118–19, my translation.

14. As explained in Sternhell, Schneider, and Ashri, *The Foundations of Fascism*, 93.

15. Ruhollah Khomeini, *The Renaissance of 'Ashura'* (in Arabic), n.d, http://www.imam-khomeini.com/web1/arabic/showitem.aspx?cid=2189&h=19&f=20&pid=2525.

16. Khomeini, *The Renaissance of 'Ashura'*.

17. Hamid Dabashi, *Theology of Discontent: The Ideological Foundation of the Islamic Revolution in Iran* (New Brunswick, NJ: Transaction, 2006).

18. El-Hussein, "Resistance, Jihad, and Martyrdom."

19. Hamid Dabashi, *Islamic Liberation Theology: Resisting the Empire* (London: Routledge, 2008), 96, 68.

20. Dabashi, *Islamic Liberation Theology*, 71.

21. Dabashi, *Islamic Liberation Theology*, 154.

22. Dabashi, *Islamic Liberation Theology*, 202.

23. Hamzeh, *In the Path of Hezbollah*, 31.

24. Jason Wimberly, "Wilayat al-Faqih in Hizballah's Web of Concepts: A Perspective on Ideology," *Middle Eastern Studies* 51, no. 5 (2015): 687–710.

25. Wimberly, "Wilayat al-Faqih in Hizballah's Web of Concepts," 695.

26. Hassan Nasrallah, quoted in Hamzeh, *In the Path of Hezbollah*, 36.

27. Qasim, *Hezbollah*, 69, 70.

28. Qasim, *Hezbollah*, 75–76.

29. Qasim, *Hezbollah*, 77.

30. Abed Kanaaneh, "From Jihad to Muqawamah: The Case of Hezbollah in Lebanon," *Journal of the Irish Society for the Academic Studies of Religion* 6 (2018): 38–59.

31. Hassan Nasrallah, press conference, Nov. 30, 2009, in *Hizbullah's Documents: From the 1985 Open Letter to the 2009 Manifesto*, [ed. and trans.] Joseph Alagha (Amsterdam: Pallas and Amsterdam Univ. Press, 2011), 138.

32. For "Al-Risala al-maftuha" (The open letter), Feb. 16, 1985, I used the version given in al-Agha, *Hezbollah*, 434–52.

33. For "Al-Wathiqa al-siyassiya" (The political document), Nov. 30, 2009, I used the copy given at the Hezbollah website at http://www.moqawama.org/essaydetailsf.php?eid=16245&fid=47.

34. Na'im Qasim, foreword to *The Values of the* Muqawama: *The Choices of Martyrdom and Life* (in Arabic) (Beirut: Dar al-Hadi, 2008), 6.

35. Qasim, foreword to *The Values of the* Muqawama, 6.

36. On this point, see Saade, *Hizbullah and the Politics of Remembrance*.

37. Alagha, *Hizbullah's Identity Construction*, 43–44.

38. Hamzeh, *In the Path of Hezbollah*, 113.

39. Alagha, *Hizbullah's Identity Construction*, 43–44.

40. Ayatollah Mohammad Husayn Fadlallah, comprehensive interview, *al-'Ahd*, Mar. 10, 1989.

41. Fadlallah, comprehensive interview, *al-'Ahd*, Mar. 10, 1989.

42. Na'im Qasim, comprehensive interview, al-Mayadeen television network, Feb. 2, 2016.

43. Hassan Nassrallah, "The Terrorist Expiatory Project Threatens the Region and the World" (in Arabic), *al-'Alam*, Oct. 15, 2015. http://www.alalam.ir/news/1750378.

44. Ernesto Laclau, *Politics and Ideology in Marxist Theory: Capitalism, Fascism, Populism* (London: Verso, 1979).

45. Rudiger Dornbuch and Sebastian Edwards, "The Macroeconomics of Populism," in *The Macroeconomics of Populism in Latin America*, ed. Rudiger Dornbuch and Sebastian Edwards (Chicago: Univ. of Chicago Press, 1991), 9–10.

46. Quoted in al-Agha, *Hezbollah*, 207.

47. *Al-'Ahd*, "Hizballah's Electoral Platform for the Parliamentary Elections of 1992" (in Arabic), July 7, 1992.

48. Hezbollah platform, 1996, Hezbollah website, at https://www.moqawama.org/essaydetails.php?eid=11253&cid=109.

49. Hezbollah platform, June 4, 2009, Hezbollah website, at http://www.moqawama.org/essaydetailsf.php?eid=14229&fid=45.

50. Hezbollah platform, 1996; Hezbollah platform, 2009.

51. *Al-'Ahd*, "The Proletariat, the Fuel of War, and the Victim of the 'Ta'if Agreement'" (in Arabic), May 1, 1992; *al-'Ahd*, "What Does Rafiq Hariri Want from Lebanon" (in Arabic), Mar. 26, 1993; *al-'Ahd*, "That Is How Hariri Buys Lebanon . . . and for Whom Does He Buy It?" (in Arabic), Apr. 9, 1993.

52. Elizabeth Nugent, "Hezbollah in Lebanese Domestic Politics: Islamism, Nationalism, and Parliamentary Opposition," MA thesis, Georgetown Univ., 2010, 52–53.

53. Nugent, "Hezbollah in Lebanese Domestic Politics," 63.

54. Nugent, "Hezbollah in Lebanese Domestic Politics," 52.

55. *Al-'Ahd*, "Nasrallah: If We Asked to Choose between the *Muqawama* and the Parliamentary Representation, We Will Definitely Renounce the Latter" (in Arabic), Sept. 25, 1992.

56. Ajami, *The Vanished Imam*.

57. Shaery-Eisenlohr, *Shi'ite Lebanon*, 32.

58. Norton, *Amal and the Shi'a*, 61.

59. Norton, *Amal and the Shi'a*, 67.

60. Muhammad Ra'd, quoted in Sa'ad-Ghrayeb, *Hezbollah*, 99.

61. *Al-'Ahd*, "The Communist Party Wants to Be an Instrument of Sedition against Muslims and Its Elements Assassinate the Mujahid 'Ali Shehadeh in an Armed Ambush" (in Arabic), Feb. 28, 1986.

62. *Al-'Ahd*, "Martyrdom of the Islamic Resistance Operations Officer: Suspicious Attacks against Hezbollah in the Western Biqa'" (in Arabic), June 13, 1986.

63. Abisaab and Abisaab, *The Shi'ites of Lebanon*, 133.

64. Abisaab and Abisaab, *The Shi'ites of Lebanon*, 133–34; Norton, *Hezbollah*, 105–6.

65. Zisser, *Lebanon: Blood in the Cedars*, 222–23.

66. The survey is cited in Imad Salamey and Frederic Pearson, "Hezbollah: A Proletarian Party with an Islamic Manifesto—a Sociopolitical Analysis of Islamist Populism in Lebanon and the Middle East," *Small Wars & Insurgencies* 18, no. 3 (Sept. 2007): 421–22.

67. Hamzeh, *In the Path of Hezbollah*, 43.

68. Shararah, *The State of Hezbollah*.

69. Na'im Qasim, *The* Muqawama *Society: The Martyrdom Will and the Production of Victory* (in Arabic) (Beirut: Ma'had al-Ma'arif al-Hikmiyya lil-Dirasat al-Dinniyya wal-Falsafiyya, 2008).

70. Al-Agha, *Hezbollah*, 293–94.

71. Flanigan and Abdel-Samad, "Hezbollah's Social Jihad," 128.

72. Flanigan and Abdel-Samad, "Hezbollah's Social Jihad," 128.

73. Flanigan and Abdel-Samad, "Hezbollah's Social Jihad," 128.

74. Qasim, *The* Muqawama *Society*, 27.

75. Flanigan and Abdel-Samad, "Hezbollah's Social Jihad," 127.

76. Qasim, *The* Muqawama *Society*, 28.

77. Al Mayadeen TV, "A Comprehensive Interview with Hizballah's Secretary-General, Na'im Qasim," part 4 (in Arabic), Jan. 19, 2016.

78. Islamic Charitable Emdad Committee, "About Us," website, http://www.alemdad.net/article.php?id=144&cid=517#.VqdxJ_l97IU.

79. Shapira, *Hezbollah*, 146.

80. Shaery-Eisenlohr, *Shi'ite Lebanon*, 164.

81. Lara Deeb, *An Enchanted Modern: Gender and Public Piety in Shi'i Lebanon* (Princeton, NJ: Princeton Univ. Press, 2006), 90.

82. Flanigan and Abdel-Samad, "Hezbollah's Social Jihad," 126.

83. Hamzeh, *In the Path of Hezbollah*, 55–58.

84. Hamzeh, *In the Path of Hezbollah*, 57.

5. The *Muqawama* as a Counterhegemonic Project

1. Norberto Bobbio, "Gramsci and the Conception of Civil Society," in *Gramsci and Marxist Theory*, ed. Chantal Mouffe (London: Routledge and Kegan Paul, 1979), 39.

2. Anne Showstack Sassoon, *Gramsci and Contemporary Politics: Beyond Pessimism of the Intellect* (London: Routledge, 2000), 45. See also Anderson, "The Antinomies of Antonio Gramsci," and Christine Buci-Glucksmann, *Gramsci and the State* (London: Lawrence and Wishart, 1980), 7–8.

3. Thomas, "Hegemony, Passive Revolution, and the Modern Prince," 27.

4. Thomas, "Hegemony, Passive Revolution, and the Modern Prince," 28.

5. Gramsci, *Selections*, 181–82.

6. Shafiq Jaradi, the organizers' foreword to *The Values of the* Muqawama (in Arabic), ed. Qasim, 2.

7. Na'im Qasim, foreword to *The Values of the* Muqawama, ed. Qasim, 5.

8. Hassan Jonny, "The Legitimacy of the *Muqawama* in Light of the Law," in *The Values of the* Muqawama, ed. Qasim, 51.

9. Munir Shafiq, "The *Muqawama* Following the End of the Cold War," in *The Values of the* Muqawama, ed. Qasim, 255.

10. 'Adnan al-Sayyed Husayn, "The Source of Authority of the *Muqawama* Culture in a Pluralistic Society," in *The Values of the* Muqawama, ed. Qasim, 69, 72.

11. Georges Massouh, "The Meaning of Life in the Christian Perception," in *The Values of the* Muqawama, ed. Qasim, 187, 191–92.

12. Shafiq Jaradi, ed., *The Resistance Triumph: The Essence of Victory and Its Political Implications* (in Arabic) (Beirut: al-Markiz al-Islami lil-Dirasat al-Fikriyya, 2007).

13. Salim Elias, *The Encyclopedia of the Lebanese Resistance: Hezbollah under the Leadership of Sayyed Hassan Nasrallah* (in Arabic), 12 vols. (Beirut: Al-Markaz al-Thaqafi al-Lubnani, 2006), 2:77–99.

14. *Encyclopedia of Nasrallah: The Man Who Embodies a Nation* (in Arabic) (Beirut: Manshurat al-Fajir, 2006).

15. Hassan Fadlallah, *A War of Wills: The Battle between the* Muqawama *and the Israeli Occupier in Lebanon* (in Arabic) (Beirut: Al-Hadi, 1998).

16. Hassan Fadlallah, *The Fall of Illusion: The Defeat of the Occupation and the Victory of the* Muqawama (in Arabic) (Beirut: Al-Hadi, 2001), 219–23.

17. Abir Hamdar, "'We Are All Hizbullah Now': Narrating the Party of God," *Journal for Cultural Research* 18, no. 2 (2014): 158–70.

18. De Gaulle Abu Tas, *Without Handcuffs*, quoted and translated in Hamdar, "'We Are All Hizbullah Now,'" 167, brackets around ellipses included in Hamdar's translation, indicating his insertion of ellipses.

19. Abu Tas, *Without Handcuffs*, quoted and translated in Hamdar, "'We Are All Hizbullah Now,'" 166, 167, all ellipses in original novel.

20. 'Abd-el-Ilah Belkziz, *The State of Siege*, quoted and translated in Hamdar, "'We Are All Hizbullah Now,'" 167–68, ellipses in original.

21. The United Nations report is cited in Thanassis Cambanis, "Hizbollah Mahdi Schools Mix Maths with Doctrine," *Financial Times*, Oct. 20, 2013.

22. *Al-'Ahd*, "In Light of Official Neglect and the Government's Policy of Ignorance: Opening the Mahdi Schools" (in Arabic), Oct. 15, 1993.

23. *Al-'Ahd*, "In Light of Official Neglect."

24. Flanigan and Abdel-Samad, "Hezbollah's Social Jihad."

25. Shaery-Eisenlohr, *Shi'ite Lebanon*, 63, 65.

26. *Al-'Ahd*, "In Light of Official Neglect."

27. *Al-'Ahd*, "Nasrallah: Our Struggle with the Enemy Is Not Based Just on the Rifle, but on Science and Knowledge" (in Arabic), Dec. 26, 1997.

28. Shaery-Eisenlohr, *Shi'ite Lebanon*, 63.

29. Shaery-Eisenlohr, *Shi'ite Lebanon*, 70.

30. Ibrahim al-Amin, speech, in *Al-'Ahd*, Feb. 12, 1988.

31. *Al-'Ahd*, "Competition Results: Feather for Resistance" (in Arabic), Mar. 5, 1999.

32. "My Beirut" (in English), *Ajyal al-Mustafa* 2 (1996): 31, provided in Shaery-Eisenlohr, *Shi'ite Lebanon*, 67.

33. Tal Pavel, "Hezbollah's Image and Plain Activism on the Internet, as Reflected in Its Different Electronic Websites" (in Hebrew), MA thesis, Hebrew Univ. of Jerusalem, 2003.

34. Hezbollah, "Resistance and Occupation" (in Arabic), Hezbollah website, at http://www.moqawama.org/fileessays.php?fid=27.

35. Hezbollah, "A Tourist Landmark on the *Muqawama*" (in Arabic), Hezbollah website, at http://www.moqawama.org/essaydetailsf.php?eid=16910&fid=46 .

36. Hezbollah, "*Muqawama* Games" (in Arabic), Hezbollah website, at http://www.moqawama.org/pagedetails.php?pid=4.

37. Hezbollah, "Play and Resist!" (in Arabic), portal, Hezbollah website, at http://games.moqawama.org/.

38. Al-Manar TV, "About" (in Arabic), al-Manar website, at http://www.almanar.com.lb/about.

39. Al-Manar TV, "About."

40. Anne Marie Baylouny, "Not Your Father's Islamist TV: Changing Programming on Hizbullah's al-Manar," *Arab Media & Society* 9 (Fall 2009), at http://faculty.nps.edu/ambaylou/baylouny%20manar%20AMS%20fall%2009%20copy.pdf.

41. Baylouny, "Not Your Father's Islamist TV."

42. Baylouny, "Not Your Father's Islamist TV."

43. Al-Manar TV, *The Victors*, series in Arabic, http://www.almanar.com.lb/adetails.php?eid=189659&st=%C7%E1%DB%C7%E1%C8%E6%E4&cid=24&fromval=3&frid=41&seccatid=101.

44. *The Greatest Victory Documented*, music video in Arabic, n.d., YouTube, at https://www.youtube.com/watch?v=EE_5nRwV3E8.

45. *Your Victory Shook the World*, music video in Arabic, n.d., YouTube, at https://www.youtube.com/watch?v=IneNiXHcMnM.

46. *We All Are the Resistance, We All Are for the Homeland*, music video in Arabic, n.d., YouTube, at https://www.youtube.com/watch?v=0xpI_nT28zM.

47. *My Homeland! The Land of Light!*, music video in Arabic, May 25, 2015, YouTube, at https://www.youtube.com/watch?v=PXATop1ypdc.

48. *Al-'Ahd*, Hezbollah posters, Nov. 4, 1997.

49. *We Will Not Be Subjugated by the Occupier*, music video in Arabic, n.d., YouTube, at https://www.youtube.com/watch?v=LOw-KCLRNJ0.

50. Abboud and Muller, *Rethinking Hizballah*, 54–55.

51. Abdel Halim Hafiz, "Keep the Weapons Ready" (in Arabic), song used in Hezbollah video, n.d., YouTube, at https://www.youtube.com/watch?v=PwArGXf97wE.

52. "The Victory of the Arabs" (in Arabic), song used in Hezbollah videos, n.d., YouTube, at https://www.youtube.com/watch?v=ycu1_ooHvnE.

53. Hezbollah video featuring Julia Boutros's song "My Loved Ones" (in Arabic), n.d., YouTube, https://www.youtube.com/watch?v=TkTqtStlBx0.

54. Quoted in *al-Akhbar*, "Ziad: Those Who Attack 'al-Sayyid' and 'al-Sayyida,' Defend Israel" (in Arabic), Dec. 20, 2013.

55. Quoted and translated in Mona Harb and Lara Deeb, "Culture as History and Landscape: Hizballah's Efforts to Shape an Islamic Milieu in Lebanon," *Arab Studies Journal* 19, no. 1 (Spring 2011): 29.

56. Harb and Deeb, "Culture as History and Landscape," 16, 17, 20.

57. Harb and Deeb, "Culture as History and Landscape," 18.

58. Harb and Deeb, "Culture as History and Landscape," 19–20.

59. Harb and Deeb, "Culture as History and Landscape," 21.

60. Mleeta website, n.d., http://www.mleeta.com/mleeta/definition0.html.

61. Harb and Deeb, "Culture as History and Landscape," 24.

62. Mleeta website, n.d., http://www.mleeta.com/mleeta/definition2.html.

63. Harb and Deeb, "Culture as History and Landscape," 24.

64. Quoted and translated in Harb and Deeb, "Culture as History and Landscape," 27.

65. Elias, *Encyclopaedia of the Lebanese Resistance*, 12:66–67.

66. Noah Feldman, "Beirut Is the New Beirut," *Wall Street Journal*, Dec. 2, 2010.

67. *Al-Akhbar*, "'Al-Akhbar' between Project and Implementation" (in Arabic), Mar. 27, 2012.

68. "About *al-Akhbar*," *al-Akhbar* website, n.d., https://www.al-akhbar.com/about.

69. The period preceding the Lebanon War in July 2006.

70. Joseph Samaha, "The Right Time" (in Arabic), *al-Akhbar*, Aug. 14, 2006.

71. Ziad Rahbani, statement (in Arabic), *al-Akhbar*, Apr. 5, 2007.

72. *Al-Akhbar*, "'Ali Saleh: The Terminator of the Merkava Myth" (in Arabic), July 12, 2012.

73. *Al-Akhbar*, "July 2006–2011: Here Is Maroun al-Ras" (in Arabic), special edition on the anniversary of the end of the Lebanon War of 2006, July 12, 2011.

74. The use of Jabal 'Amel instead of southern Lebanon is very important, for Jabal 'Amel has religious connotations associated with Shi'a Islam, whereas the name "southern Lebanon" includes the name "Lebanon," whose existence is not considered legitimate.

75. Hassan Nasrallah, speech, *al-'Ahd*, May 24, 1985.

76. Hassan Nasrallah, speech, *al-'Ahd*, Dec. 10, 1991.

77. Hassan Nasrallah, speech at a conference in September 1986 commemorating the disappearance of Imam Musa al-Sadr, *al-'Ahd*, Sept. 5, 1986.

78. Nasrallah, speech, *al-'Ahd*, Sept. 1986.

79. Hassan Nasrallah, interview, *al-'Ahd*, Feb. 28, 1992; this interview was originally conducted by *al-Safir* newspaper.

80. Hassan Nasrallah, interview, *al-Diyar*, June 21, 1992.

81. Hassan Nasrallah, speech at the Second National Islamic Conference, Beirut, *al-'Ahd*, Oct. 31, 1997.

82. *Al-'Ahd*, "An Inclusive National Cadre toward a Confrontation with the Enemy" (in Arabic), Nov. 7, 1997.

83. "Nasrallah's Speech, May 26, 2000," Hezbollah website, at http://www.moqawama.org/essaydetails.php?eid=16927&cid=141.

84. *Nasrallah's Speech ("The Divine Victory"), September 22, 2006* (in Arabic), video, at https://www.youtube.com/watch?v=KurXHcmjsOc.

85. *Nasrallah's Speech ("The Divine Victory"), September 22, 2006.*

86. Chronology of events (1975–2010), in *Hizbullah's Documents*, [ed. and trans.] Alagha, 175.

87. Hassan Nasrallah, press conference, May 8, 2008, Lebanese-Canadian Coordinating Council website, http://www.10452lccc.com/hezbollah07/nasrallah8.5.08.speech.htm.

88. Hassan Nasrallah, press conference following the publication of "The Political Document," Nov. 30, 2009, in *Hizbullah's Documents*, [ed. and trans.] al-Alagha, 141.

89. Nasrallah, press conference following the publication of "The Public Document," Nov. 30, 2009, 141.

90. Nahid Hittir, *Husayn Nasrallah and the National Liberation Issues* (in Arabic) (Beirut: Maislaoun lil-Dirasat wal-I'lam, 2016), 105, 106. Hittir was assassinated by an Islamist activist in Jordan after publishing a caricature of ISIS on September 25, 2016.

91. *Nasrallah's 'Ashura' Speech on October 23, 2015*, video, YouTube, at https://www.youtube.com/watch?v=uZ1jrRKXB0Q.

92. *Nasrallah's 'Ashura' Speech on October 23, 2015.*

93. *Nasrallah's 'Ashura' Speech on October 23, 2015.*

94. *Nasrallah's Interview with RT*, Apr. 17, 2012, video, YouTube, at https://www.youtube.com/watch?v=46eKtrVU7nY.

Conclusion

1. Hassan Nasrallah, speech, Feb. 16, 2007, Hezbollah media-relations website, at https://mediarelations-lb.org/post.php?id=3944.

Bibliography

Sources in English

Abboud, Samer, and Benjamin J. Muller. *Rethinking Hizballah: Legitimacy, Authority, Violence*. Farnham, UK: Ashgate, 2012.

Abedi, Mehdi, and Gary Legenhausen. Introduction to *Jihad and Shahadat: Struggle and Martyrdom in Islam*, edited by Mehdi Abedi and Gary Legenhausen, 1–46. Houston: Institute for Research and Islamic Studies, 1986.

———, eds. *Jihad and Shahadat: Struggle and Martyrdom in Islam*. Houston: Institute for Research and Islamic Studies, 1986.

Abisaab, Rula Jurdi. "The Cleric as Organic Intellectual: Revolutionary Shiʿism in the Lebanese *Hawzas*." In *Distant Relations: Iran and Lebanon in the Last 500 Years*, edited by H. E. Chehabi, 231–58. London: Centre for Lebanese Studies and I. B. Tauris, 2006.

———. "Shiʿite Beginnings and Scholastic Tradition on Jabal ʿAmil in Lebanon." *Muslim World* 89, no. 1 (Jan. 1999): 1–21.

Abisaab, Rula Jurdi, and Malek Abisaab. *The Shiʿites of Lebanon: Modernism, Communism, and Hizbullah's Islamists*. Syracuse, NY: Syracuse Univ. Press, 2014.

Abrahamian, Ervand. *Iran between Two Revolutions*. Princeton, NJ: Princeton Univ. Press, 1982.

———. *Khomeinism: Essays on the Islamic Republic*. Berkeley: Univ. of California Press, 1993.

———. *Radical Islam: The Iranian Mojahedin*. London: I. B. Tauris, 1989.

Abu Khalil, Asaʿd. "Ideology and Practice of Hizballah in Lebanon: Islamization of Leninist Organizational Principles." *Middle Eastern Studies* 27, no. 3 (1991): 390–403.

Adamson, Walter L. *Hegemony and Revolution: A Study of Antonio Gramsci's Political and Cultural Theory*. Berkeley: Univ. of California Press, 1980.

Alagha, Joseph, [ed. and trans.]. *Hizbullah's Documents: From the 1985 Open Letter to the 2009 Manifesto*. Amsterdam: Pallas and Amsterdam Univ. Press, 2011.

———. *Hizbullah's Identity Construction*. Amsterdam: Amsterdam Univ. Press, 2011.

———. *The Shifts in Hizbullah's Ideology: Religious Ideology, Political Ideology, and Political Program*. Leiden: ISIM and Amsterdam Univ. Press, 2006.

Algar, Hamid. Introduction to Ali Shari'ati, *On the Sociology of Islam: Lectures by Ali Shari'ati*, translated and edited by Hamid Algar, 11–38. Berkeley, CA: Mizan Press, 1979.

Ajemian, Pete. "Resistance beyond Time and Space: Hezbollah's Media Campaigns." *Arab Media and Society* 5 (Spring 2008): 1–17.

Anderson, Perry. "The Antinomies of Antonio Gramsci." *New Left Review* 1, no. 100 (Nov.–Dec. 1976): 5–78.

Arjomand, Said A. *The Turban for the Crown: The Islamic Revolution in Iran*. Oxford: Oxford Univ. Press, 1988.

Azani, Eitan. *Hezbollah: The Story of the Party of God, from Revolution to Institutionalization*. New York: Palgrave Macmillan, 2009.

Aziz, T. M. "The Rule of Muhammad Baqir al-Sadr in Shi'i Political Activism in Iraq from 1958 to 1980." *International Journal in Middle East Studies* 25, no. 2 (May 1993): 207–22.

Batatu, Hanna. "Shi'i Organizations in Iraq: Al-Da'wah al-Islamiyah and al-Mujahidin." In *Shi'ism and Social Protest*, edited by Juan Cole and Nikki R. Keddie, 179–200. New Haven, CT: Yale Univ. Press, 1986.

Baylouny, Anne Marie. "Not Your Father's Islamist TV: Changing Programming on Hizbullah's al-Manar." *Arab Media and Society* 9 (Fall 2009). At http://faculty.nps.edu/ambaylou/baylouny%20manar%20AMS%20fall%2009%20copy.pdf.

Beydoun, Ahmad. "The South Lebanon Border Zone: A Local Perspective." *Journal of Palestinian Studies* 21, no. 3 (Spring 1992): 35–53.

Bobbio, Norberto. "Gramsci and the Conception of Civil Society." In *Gramsci and Marxist Theory*, edited by Chantal Mouffe, 21–47. London: Routledge & Kegan Paul, 1979.

Buchta, Wilfried. *Who Rules Iran? The Structure of Power in the Islamic Republic*. Washington, DC: Washington Institute for Near East Policy; Sankt Augustin, Germany: Konrad Adenauer Stiftung, 2000.

Buci-Glucksmann, Christine. *Gramsci and the State*. London: Lawrence and Wishart, 1980.

Butko, Thomas J. "Revelation or Revolution: A Gramscian Approach to the Rise of Political Islam." *British Journal of Middle Eastern Studies* 31, no. 1 (May 2004): 41–62.

Buttigieg, Joseph A. "Subaltern Social Groups in Antonio Gramsci's *Prison Notebooks*." In *The Political Philosophies of Antonio Gramsci and B. R. Ambedkar: Itineraries of Dalits and Subalterns*, edited by Cazimo Zene, 35–42. London: Routledge Taylor & Francis Group, 2013.

Byrd, Dustin. *Ayatollah Khomeini and the Anatomy of the Islamic Revolution in Iran: Toward a Theory of Prophetic Charisma*. Lanham, MD: Univ. Press of America, 2011.

Cambanis, Thanassis. "Hizbollah Mahdi Schools Mix Maths with Doctrine." *Financial Times*, Oct. 20, 2013.

Cooley, John K. "The Palestinians." In *Lebanon in Crisis: Participants and Issues*, edited by Edward Haley and Lewis W. Snider, 31–54. Syracuse, NY: Syracuse Univ. Press, 1979.

Coutinho, Carlos Nelson. *Gramsci's Political Thought*. Leiden: Brill, 2012.

Cox, Robert W. "Gramsci, Hegemony, and International Relations: An Essay in Method." In *Gramsci, Historical Materialism, and International Relations*, edited by Stephen Gill, 49–66. Cambridge: Cambridge Univ. Press, 1993.

Crehan, Kate. "Living Subalternity: Antonio Gramsci's Concept of Common Sense." In *The Political Philosophies of Antonio Gramsci and B. R. Ambedkar: Itineraries of Dalits and Subalterns*, edited by Cazimo Zene, 103–15. London: Routledge Taylor & Francis Group, 2013.

Dabashi, Hamid. *Islamic Liberation Theology: Resisting the Empire*. London: Routledge, 2008.

———. *Shi'ism: A Religion of Protest*. Cambridge, MA: Belknap Press of Harvard Univ. Press, 2011.

———. *Theology of Discontent: The Ideological Foundation of the Islamic Revolution in Iran*. New Brunswick, NJ: Transaction, 2006.

Daher, Joseph. *Hezbollah: The Political Economy of Lebanon's Party of God*. London: Pluto Press, 2016.

Deeb, Lara. *An Enchanted Modern: Gender and Public Piety in Shi'i Lebanon*. Princeton, NJ: Princeton Univ. Press, 2006.

Dib, Kamal. *Warlords and Merchants: The Lebanese Business and Political Establishment*. Reading, UK: Ithaca Press, 2004.

Dornbuch, Rudiger, and Sebastian Edwards. "The Macroeconomics of Populism." In *The Macroeconomics of Populism in Latin America*, edited by

Rudiger Dornbuch and Sebastian Edwards, 7–13. Chicago: Univ. of Chicago Press, 1991.

Euben, Roxanne L. "Killing (for) Politics: Jihad, Martyrdom, and Political Action." *Political Theory* 30, no. 1 (Feb. 2002): 4–35.

Feldman, Noah. "Beirut Is the New Beirut." *Wall Street Journal*, Dec. 2, 2010.

Firro, Kais. *Inventing Lebanon: Nationalism and the State under the Mandate.* London: I. B. Tauris, 2003.

Flanigan, Shawn T., and Mounah Abdel-Samad. "Hezbollah's Social Jihad: Nonprofits as Resistance Organizations." *Middle East Policy* 16, no. 2 (Summer 2009): 122–37.

Gates, Carolyn. *The Merchant Republic of Lebanon: Rise of an Open Economy.* London: Center for Lebanese Studies, 1998.

Geis, Michael. *The Language of Politics.* New York: Springer, 1987.

Gillespie, Joan. *Algeria: Rebellion and Revolution.* London: Ernest Benn, 1960.

Gramsci, Antonio. *Prison Notebooks.* Vol. 1. Edited by Josef A. Buttigieg. Translated by Josef A. Buttigieg and Antonio Callari. New York: Columbia Univ. Press, 1992.

———. *Selections from the Prison Notebooks.* Edited by Quintin Hoare and Geoffrey N. Smith. 1971. Reprint. New York: International, 1992.

Green, Marcus E. "On the Postcolonial Image of Gramsci." *Postcolonial Studies* 16, no. 1 (2013): 90–101.

———. "Race, Class, and Religion: Gramsci's Conception of Subalternity." In *The Political Philosophies of Antonio Gramsci and B. R. Ambedkar: Itineraries of Dalits and Subalterns*, edited by Cazimo Zene, 116–29. London: Routledge Taylor & Francis Group, 2013.

———. "Rethinking the Subaltern and the Question of Censorship in Gramsci's *Prison Notebooks*." *Postcolonial Studies* 14, no. 4 (2011): 387–404.

Hage Ali, Mohanad. *Nationalism, Transnationalism, and Political Islam: Hizbullah's Institutional Identity.* London: Palgrave Macmillan, 2017.

Halawi, Majed. *A Lebanon Defied: Musa al-Sadr and the Shi'a Community.* Boulder, CO: Westview Press, 1992.

Hamdar, Abir. "'We Are All Hizbullah Now': Narrating the Party of God." *Journal for Cultural Research* 18, no. 2 (2014): 158–70.

Hamzeh, Ahmad Nizar. *In the Path of Hizbullah.* Syracuse, NY: Syracuse Univ. Press, 2004.

———. "Lebanon's Hizballah: From Islamic Revolution to Parliamentary Accommodation." *Third World Quarterly* 14, no. 2 (1993): 321–37.

Harb, Mona, and Lara Deeb. "Culture as History and Landscape: Hizballah's Efforts to Shape an Islamic Milieu in Lebanon." *Arab Studies Journal* 19, no. 1 (Spring 2011): 10–41.

Harb, Zahera. *Channels of Resistance in Lebanon: Liberation Propaganda, Hezbollah, and the Media*. London: I. B. Tauris, 2011.

Harris, William. *The New Face of Lebanon: History's Revenge*. Princeton, NJ: Marcus Wiener, 2006.

Harrus, Erika. *Nationalism: Theories and Cases*. Edinburgh: Edinburgh Univ. Press, 2009.

Hourani, Albert. "From Jabal 'Āmil to Persia." *Bulletin of the School of Oriental and African Studies, University of London* 49, no. 1 (1986): 133–40.

Hoveyda, Fereydoun. *The Shah and the Ayatollah: Iranian Mythology and Islamic Revolution*. London: Praeger, 2003.

El-Husseini, Rola. "Resistance, Jihad, and Martyrdom in Contemporary Lebanese Shi'a Discourse." *Middle East Journal* 62, no. 3 (2008): 399–414.

Kadourie, Elie. *Nationalism*. London: Anchor Press, 1966.

Kanaaneh, Abed. "From Jihad to Muqawamah: The Case of Hezbollah in Lebanon." *Journal of the Irish Society for the Academic Studies of Religion* 6 (2018): 38–59.

Kanz-Feder, Rachel. "Fatima's Revolutionary Image in *Fadak fi al-Tarikh* (1955): The Inception of Muhammad Baqir al-Sadr's Activism." *British Journal of Middle Eastern Studies* 41, no. 1 (2014): 79–96.

Kaufman, Asher. *Reviving Phoenicia: The Search for Identity in Lebanon*. London: I. B. Tauris, 2004.

Keddie, Nikki R. *Iran: Religion, Politics, and Society*. London: Frank Cass, 1980.

———. *Modern Iran: Roots and Results of Revolution*. New Haven, CT: Yale Univ. Press, 2003.

———. *Roots of Revolution: An Interpretive History of Modern Iran*. New Haven, CT: Yale Univ. Press, 1981.

Khalidi, Muhammad Ali. *The Palestinian Refugees in Lebanon*. Beirut: Institute for Palestine Studies, 2001.

Khalidi, Walid. *Conflict and Violence in Lebanon: Confrontation in the Middle East*. Cambridge, MA: Harvard Univ. Press, 1979.

Khalili, Laleh. *Heroes and Martyrs of Palestine: The Politics of National Commemoration*. New York: Cambridge Univ. Press, 2007.

Khatib, Lina, Dina Matar, and Atef Alshaer. *The Hizbullah Phenomenon: Politics and Communication*. New York: Oxford Univ. Press, 2014.

Khomeini, Ruhollah. *Islam and Revolution: Writings and Declarations of Imam Khomeini (1941–1980)*. Edited and translated by Hamid Algar. Berkeley, CA: Mizan Press, 1989.

Kimmerling, Baruch, and Joel S. Migdal. *Palestinians: The Making of a People*. Cambridge, MA: Harvard Univ. Press, 1994.

Laclau, Ernesto. *Politics and Ideology in Marxist Theory: Capitalism, Fascism, Populism*. London: Verso, 1979.

Laclau, Ernesto, and Chantal Mouffe. *Hegemony and Socialist Strategy: Towards a Radical Democratic Politics*. London: Verso, 1985.

Lester, Jeremy. *Dialogue of Negation: Debates on Hegemony in Russia and the West*. London: Pluto Press, 2000.

Lewis, Bernard. *The Political Language of Islam*. Chicago: Univ. of Chicago Press, 1988.

———. "The Shi'a in Islamic History." In *Shi'ism, Resistance, and Revolution*, edited by Martin Kramer, 21–30. Boulder, CO: Westview Press, 1987.

Lindholm-Schulz, Helena. *The Reconstruction of Palestinian Nationalism: Between Revolution and Statehood*. Manchester, UK: Manchester Univ. Press, 1999.

Machlis, Elisheva. "'Ali Shari'ati and the Notion of Tawhid: Re-exploring the Question of God's Unity." *Die Welt des Islams* 54, no. 2 (2014): 183–211.

Mackey, Sandra. *Lebanon: Death of a Nation*. New York: Congdon & Weed, 1989.

Magnus, Ranstrup. *Hizb'Allah in Lebanon: The Politics of Western Hostage Crisis*. Basingstoke, UK: Palgrave Macmillan, 1997.

Makdisi, Ussama. *The Culture of Sectarianism: Community, History, and Violence in Nineteenth-Century Lebanon*. Berkeley: Univ. of California Press, 2000.

Moaddel, Mansoor. *Class, Politics, and Ideology in the Iranian Revolution*. New York: Columbia Univ. Press, 1992.

Moin, Baqer. *Khomeini: Life of the Ayatollah*. New York: Thomas Dunne Books, 1999.

Momen, Moojan. *An Introduction to Shi'i Islam: The History and Doctrines of Twelver Shi'ism*. New Haven, CT: Yale Univ. Press, 1985.

Norton, Augustus R. *Amal and the Shi'a: Struggle for the Soul of Lebanon*. Austin: Univ. of Texas Press, 1987.

———. *Hezbollah: A Short History*. Princeton, NJ: Princeton Univ. Press, 2007.

Nugent, Elizabeth. "Hizbullah in Lebanese Domestic Politics: Islamism, Nationalism, and Parliamentary Opposition." MA thesis, Georgetown Univ., 2010.

Olmert, Joseph. “The Shiʿis and the Lebanese State.” In *Shiʿism, Resistance, and Revolution*, edited by Martin Kramer, 189–202. Boulder, CO: Westview Press, 1987.

Owen, Roger. “The Economic History of Lebanon, 1943–1974: Its Salient Features.” In *Toward a Viable Lebanon*, edited by Halim Barakat, 27–41. Washington, DC: Center for Contemporary Arab Studies, 1988.

Pasha, Mustapha Kamal. “Islam, ‘Soft’ Orientalism, and Hegemony: A Gramscian Rereading.” *Critical Review of International Social and Political Philosophy* 8, no. 4 (2005): 543–58.

Peters, Rudolph. *Jihad in Classical and Modern Islam: A Reader.* Princeton, NJ: Markus Wiener, 1996.

Phares, Walid. *Lebanese Christian Nationalism: The Rise and Fall of an Ethnic Resistance.* Boulder, CO: Lynne Rienner, 1995.

Rahnema, Ali. “Ali Shariʿati: Teacher, Preacher, Rebel.” In *Pioneers of Islamic Revival*, edited by Ali Rahnema, 208–50. New York: Zed Books, 2005.

Ram, Haggay. *Myth and Mobilization in Revolutionary Iran: The Use of the Friday Congregational Sermon.* Washington, DC: American Univ. Press, 1994.

El-Rayyis, Riyad, and Dunia Nahas. *Guerrillas for Palestine.* London: Portico, 1976.

Saade, Bashir. *Hizbullah and the Politics of Remembrance: Writing the Lebanese Nation.* Cambridge: Cambridge Univ. Press, 2016.

Sachedina, Abdulaziz A. “Activist Shiʿism in Iran, Iraq, and Lebanon.” In *Encyclopaedia of Jihad*, edited by Raj Pruthi, 958–1054. New Delhi: Anmol, 2002.

———. “Ali Shariati: Ideologue of the Iranian Revolution.” In *Voices of Resurgent Islam*, edited by John L. Esposito, 205–11. Oxford: Oxford Univ. Press, 1983.

Salamey, Imad, and Frederic Pearson. “Hezbollah: A Proletarian Party with an Islamic Manifesto—a Sociopolitical Analysis of Islamist Populism in Lebanon and the Middle East.” *Small Wars and Insurgencies* 18, no. 3 (Sept. 2007): 416–38.

Salibi, Kamal. *A House of Many Mansions: The History of Lebanon Reconsidered.* London: I. B. Tauris, 1988.

———. “Tribal Origins of the Religious Sects in the Arab East.” In *Toward a Viable Lebanon*, edited by Barakat Hale, 15–26. Washington, DC: Center for Contemporary Arab Studies, 1988.

Sayigh, Rosemary. *The Palestinians: From Peasants to Revolutionaries.* London: Zed Books, 2007.

Shaery-Eisenlohr, Roschanack. *Shi'ite Lebanon: Transnational Religion and the Making of National Identity.* New York: Columbia Univ. Press, 2008.

Shanahan, Rodger. *The Shi'a of Lebanon: Clans, Parties, and Clerics.* London: Tauris Academic Studies, 2005.

Shari'ati, Ali. "The Dialectic of Sociology." In *On the Sociology of Islam: Lectures by Ali Shari'ati*, translated and edited by Hamid Algar, 111–18. Berkeley, CA: Mizan Press, 1979.

———. "Shahadat." In *Jihad and Shahadat: Struggle and Martyrdom in Islam*, edited by Mehdi Abedi and Gary Legenhausen, 153–229. Houston: Institute for Research and Islamic Studies, 1986.

———. "Where Shall We Begin?" Lecture, Iran Chamber Society, no date given. Iran Chamber Society website, at http://iranchamber.com/personalities/ashariati/works/where_shall_we_begin.php.

———. "The World-View of Tawhid." In *On the Sociology of Islam: Lectures by Ali Shari'ati*, translated and edited by Hamid Algar, 82–87. Berkeley, CA: Mizan Press, 1979.

Showstack-Sassoon, Anne. *Gramsci and Contemporary Politics: Beyond Pessimism of the Intellect.* London: Routledge, 2000.

Siklawi, Rami. "The Dynamics of Palestinian Political Endurance in Lebanon." *Middle East Journal* 64, no. 4 (2010): 597–611.

Simon, Roger. *Gramsci's Political Thought: An Introduction.* London: Lawrence and Wishart, 1982.

Srivastava, Neelam, and Baidik Bhattacharya. "Introduction: The Postcolonial Gramsci." In *The Postcolonial Gramsci*, edited by Neelam Srivastava and Baidik Bhattacharya, 1–14. London: Routledge Taylor & Francis Group, 2013.

———, eds. *The Postcolonial Gramsci.* London: Routledge Taylor & Francis Group, 2013.

Texier, Jacques. "Gramsci, Theoretician of the Superstructures." In *Gramsci and Marxist Theory*, edited by Chantal Mouffe, 48–79. London: Routledge & Kegan Paul, 1979.

Thomas, Peter D. "Hegemony, Passive Revolution, and the Modern Prince." *Thesis Eleven* 117, no. 1 (Aug. 2013): 20–39.

Williams, Gwyn A. "Concept of 'Egemonia' in the Thought of Antonio Gramsci: Some Notes on Interpretation." *Journal of the History of Ideas* 21, no. 4 (Oct.–Dec. 1960): 586–99.

Wimberly, Jason. "Wilayat al-Faqih in Hizballah's Web of Concepts: A Perspective on Ideology." *Middle Eastern Studies* 51, no. 5 (2015): 687–710.

Worrall, James, Simon Mabon, and Gurdon Clubb. *Hezbollah: From Islamic Resistance to Government*. Santa Barbara, CA: Praeger, 2016.

Zisser, Eyal. *Lebanon—the Challenge of Independence*. London: I. B. Tauris, 2000.

Sources in Arabic

Note: I have translated into English the titles of all of the Arabic-language works in this section.

Al-Afghani, Jamal al-Din. *The Complete Works*. Edited by Muhammad ʻAmarah. Cairo: Al-Katib al-ʻArabi, n.d.

Al-Agha, Josef. *Hezbollah: The Political and Ideological History 1978–2008*. Baghdad: Dirasat ʻIraqiyya, 2008.

ʻAmel, Mahdi. *In the Sectarian State*. Beirut: Al-Farabi, 1986.

Asad Allahi, Masoud. *The Islamists in a Multicultural Society*. Beirut: Al-Arabiya lil-ʻOloum, 2004.

ʻAzi, Ghassan, *Hezbollah: From the Ideological Dream . . . to Political Pragmatism*. Kuwait City: Qirtas, 1998.

Baqir al-Sadr, Muhammad. *Fadak in History*. 1955. Reprint. N.p.: Ghadir Center for Islamic Studies, 1994.

Batatu, Hanna. *Iraq: The Social Classes and the Revolutionary Movements from the Ottoman Empire to the Establishment of the Republic*. Beirut: Moasasat al-Abhath al-Arabiya, 1995.

Al-Drisi, Wafaʼ. *The Martyr through the Interpretation of al-Tabari*. Beirut: Al-Intishar al-ʻArabi, 2008.

Elias, Salim. *The Encyclopedia of the Lebanese Resistance: Hezbollah under the Leadership of Sayyed Hassan Nasrallah*. 12 vols. Beirut: Al-Markez al-Thaqafi al-Lubnani, 2006.

Encyclopedia of Nasrallah: The Man Who Embodies a Nation. Beirut: Manshurat al-Fajir, 2006.

Fadlallah, Hassan. *The Fall of Illusion: The Defeat of the Occupation and the Victory of the* Muqawama. Beirut: Al-Hadi, 2001.

———. *A War of Wills: The Battle between the* Muqawama *and the Israeli Occupier in Lebanon*. Beirut: Al-Hadi, 1998.

Fadlallah, Muhammad Husayn. *The Power of Will*. Edited by Naguib Nour al-Din. Beirut: Al-Malek, 2000.

Haidar, Khalil Ali. *The Turban and the Scepter: The Shiʻite Referential Authority in Iraq and Iran*. Kuwait City: Qirtas, 1997.

Halm, Heinz. *Shi'ism*. Translated by Muhammad Kbebo. 1988. Reprint. Baghdad: Al-Warraq, 2011.

Hamada, Sa'doun. *The Shi'ite History in Lebanon*. Vol. 1. Beirut: Al-Khal, 2008.

Hamdan, Kamal. *The Lebanese Crisis: Religious Groups, Social Classes, and the National Identity*. Beirut: Al-Farabi, 1998.

Hanf, Theodor. *Lebanon: Coexistence in Times of War—from the Collapse of a State to the Emergence of a Nation*. Paris: Euro-Arab Center for Studies, 1993.

Al-Haydari, Ibrahim. *The Tragedy of Karbala': The Sociology of the Shi'ite Discourse*. Beirut: Al-Saqi, 1999.

Hitti, Philip. *Lebanon in History: From the Earliest Times to the Present*. Beirut: Franklin Institution for Publications, 1959.

Hittir, Nahid. *Hassan Nasrallah and the National Liberation Issues*. Beirut: Maislaoun lil-Dirasat wal-I'lam, 2016.

Al-Husseini, Mazen. *Reading in Gramsci's Thought: Revolution, Power, and the Coalitions*. Jerusalem: Dar al-Tanweer lel-Nashr wal-Markez al-Falasteeni li-Qadayya as-Salam wal-Democratiyya, 2001.

Ibn Taymiyyah, Ahmad bin 'Abdul Halim. *Ibn Taymiyyah Studies Compilation*. Edited by Muhammad Ezer Shams. Mecca: Alaam al-Fawaid, 2003.

Ibrahim, Fu'ad. *The Faqih and the State: The Shi'ite Political Thought*. Beirut: Al-Kunouz al-Adabiyya, 1998.

Jaradi, Shafiq, ed. *The Resistance Triumph: The Essence of Victory and Its Political Implications*. Beirut: Al-Markiz al-Islami lil-Dirasat al-Fikriyya, 2007.

Kanaaneh, Tawfiq. *Autobiography*. Acre, Israel: Abu Rahmoun Press, 2009.

Al-Kateb, Ahmad. *Development of the Shi'ite Political Thought: From 'Ashura' to the Guardianship of the Islamic Jurist*. Beirut: Al-Jadeed, 1998.

———. *Political Shi'ism and "Religious Shi'ism."* Beirut: Al-Intishal al 'Arabi, 2009.

Khomeini, Ruhollah. *The Islamic Government*. Beirut: Al-Tali'a, 1979.

Lenin, Vladimir. "Two Tactics of Social-Democracy in the Democratic Revolution." In *Lenin: Marx–Engels the Marxism*, 212–27. Moscow: Al-Tiba'a wal-Nashr bi-Allughat al-Ajnabiyya, n.d.

Mahmoud, Mu'een A. *The Fedae'i Activism*. Beirut: Al-Maktab al-Tijari, 1969.

Murad, Muhammad "The Development of Political Options among the Shi'ites since the Emergence of the Modern Lebanese State to Date." *Shuaoun al-awsat* 132 (Apr. 2009): 155–71.

Murawwa, Husayn. *Materialist Trends in the Islamic Arab Philosophy*. Beirut: Al-Farabi, 1988.

Nur Eddine, Najeeb. *The Ideology of Rejection and Resistance: A Socio-political Research on the Shi'ite Refusal.* Beirut: Al-Hadi, 2004.

'Otoum, Muhammad. *The Contemporary Political Theory of the Twelver Shi'a.* Amman, Jordan: Al-Bashir, 1988.

Qasim, Na'im. *Hezbollah: Its Approach, Experience, and Future.* Beirut: Al-Hadi, 2006.

———. *The* Muqawama *Society: The Martyrdom Will and the Production of Victory.* Beirut: Ma'had al-Ma'arif al-Hikmiyya lil-Dirasat al-Dinniyya wal-Falsafiyya, 2008.

———, ed. *The Values of the* Muqawama: *The Choice of Martyrdom and of Life.* Beirut: Al-Hadi, 2008.

Ra'ouf, 'Adel. *Imam Khomeini: The Discourse, the State, and the Consciousness.* Damascus: Iraqi Media and Studies Center, 2001.

Rif'at, Sayyed Ahmad. *Islamist Movements in Egypt and Iran.* Cairo: Sina, 1989.

Rizqallah, Ralph. *The Blood Day: 'Ashura' Scene in Jabal 'Amel. A Psychological and Social Approach to the Killing of Imam Husayn.* 1977. Reprint. Beirut: Dar al-Tali'a, 1997.

Sa'd-Ghrayeb, Amal. *Hezbollah: Politics and Religion.* Beirut: Al-Kitab al-'Arabi, 2002.

Sadiqi, Alarbi. "Reshaping the Democratic Resistance: Narratives from Hamas and Hezbollah." *Al-Mustaqbal al-'Arabi* 377 (July 2010): 55–82.

Al-Safa, Muhammad Jaber. *The History of Jabal 'Amel.* Beirut: Ma'ajam Matn al-Lugha, n.d.

Salibi, Kamal. *The Modern History of Lebanon.* Beirut: Al-Nahar, 1967.

Sankari, Jamal. *A Journey of a Shi'ite Leader: Al-Sayyed Muhammad Husayn Fadlallah.* Beirut: Al-Saki, 2008.

Sayigh, Yazid. *Armed Struggle and the Search for State: The Palestinian National Movement 1948–1993.* Beirut: Institute for Palestine Studies, 2003.

Shararah, Wadah. *The State of Hezbollah: Lebanon, an Islamic Society.* Beirut: Al-Nahar, 1996.

Shari'ati, 'Ali. "Red Shiism versus Black Shiism." In *That Is How 'Ali Shari'ati Spoke: An Idea and a Revolution in the Advancement of the Islamic Movement and a Collection of His Writings,* edited by Fadel Rasoul, 183–90. Beirut: Al-Kalima, 1982.

———. "Revolutionary Asceticism or Sufism in the Sense of Isolation?" In *That Is How 'Ali Shari'ati Spoke: An Idea and a Revolution in the Advancement of the Islamic Movement and a Collection of His Writings*, edited by Fadel Rasoul, 204–8. Beirut: Al-Kalima, 1982.

Al-Tabari, Ibn-Jarir. *Collection of Statements on Interpretation of Verses of the Qur'an*. Vol. 5. Beirut: Al-Fikr, 2001.

Touma, Emile. *The Roots of the Palestinian Case*. Vol. 4 of *Emile Touma: The Complete Collection*. Haifa, Israel: Emile Touma Institute for Political and Social Studies, 1995.

Trabulsi, Fawwaz. *The Modern History of Lebanon: From the Emirate to the Ta'if Agreement*. Beirut: Riyyad al-Rayess, 2008.

Sources in Hebrew

Note: I have translated into English the titles of all of the Hebrew-language works in this section.

Ajami, Fuad. *The Vanished Imam: Musa al-Sadr and the Shi'a in Lebanon*. Tel Aviv: Aam Oved, 1986.

Arnon-Ohana, Yuval, and Arieh Yudfat. *PLO: A Portrait of an Organization*. Tel Aviv: Ma'arev Library, 1985.

Filc, Dani. *Populism and Hegemony in Israel*. Tel Aviv: Resling, 2006.

Gramsci, Antonio. *On Hegemony: A Selection from the Prison Notebooks*. Translated into Hebrew by Alon Altras. Tel Aviv: Resling, 2004.

Kimmerling, Baruch, and Joel S. Migdal. *Palestinians: The Making of a People*. Jerusalem: Keter, 1999.

Milstein, Michael. Muqawama: *The Emergence of the Resistance Challenge and Its Influence on the Perception of Israeli National Security*. Tel Aviv: Institute for National Security Studies, 2009.

Pavel, Tal. "Hezbollah's Image and Plain Activism on the Internet, as Reflected in Its Different Electronic Websites." MA thesis, Hebrew Univ. of Jerusalem, 2003.

Rekhes, Eli. *The Arab Minority in Israel: Between Communism and Arab Nationalism*. Tel Aviv: Moshe Dayan Center, 1993.

Shapira, Shimon. *Hezbollah: Between Iran and Lebanon*. Tel Aviv: Hakibbutz Hameuchad, 2000.

Sternhell, Zeev, Mario Schneider, and Maya Ashri. *The Foundations of Fascism: A Cultural Dimension to the Political Revolution*. Tel Aviv: Am Oved, 1992.

Zisser, Eyal. *Lebanon: Blood in the Cedars*. Tel Aviv: Kav Adom, 2009.

———. "Syria in the Face of the Israeli Challenge: Between Passive Resistance (*Mumana'a*) and Active Resistance (*Muqawama*)." *Strategic Updates* 12 (2009): 67–79.

Zmir, Meir. *The Establishment of Modern Lebanon*. Tel Aviv: Ma'arachot and Israeli Ministry of Defense, 1993.

Newspapers and Magazines

Al-'Ahd
Ajyal al-Mustafa
Al-Akhbar
Al-Diyar
Al-Safir
Al-Shira'

Websites

Al-'Ahd. www.alahednews.com.lb.
Al-Akhbar. www.al-akhbar.com.
Al-'Alam Channel. www.alalam.ir.
Al-Emdad organization. www.alemdad.net.
Al-Hay'a al-Sihiyya al-Islamiyya. www.hayaa.org.
Hezbollah. www.moqawama.org.
Imam Khomeini. www.imam-khomeini.com/web1/arabic/default.aspx.
Jihad al-bina' development association. www.jihadbinaa.org.lb.
Islamic Charitable Emdad Committee. www.alemdad.net.
Al-Manar TV. www.almanar.com.lb.
Al-Mayadeen TV. www.almayadeen.net.
Mleeta. mleeta.com/mleeta.
Palestinian News and Info Agency—Wafa. www.wafainfo.ps.
Al-Qard al-Hasan. www.qardhasan.org.
Al-Safir. www.assafir.com.
Al-Shahid association. www.shaheed.com.lb.

Arabic Dictionaries

Note: I have translated into English the titles of the Arabic-language dictionaries in this section.

Ibn Manzur. *Dictionary of the Tongue of the Arabs*. Cairo: Dar al-M'arif, n.d.
The Intermediate Lexicon. 4th ed. Cairo: Majma' al-Logha al-'Arabiyya, 2004.

Index

Abed T. Kanaaneh is a senior lecturer in the Department of Middle Eastern and African History at Tel Aviv University. He was previously a postdoctoral fellow of the Minerva Stiftung in the Department of Middle Eastern and Islamic Studies at Ruhr-University Bochum. He was also a visiting scholar in Middle Eastern, South Asian, and African studies at Columbia University. He holds a BA in political science and communication, an MA in political science from the Hebrew University of Jerusalem, and a PhD in Middle Eastern studies from Tel Aviv University. His research interests include Shi'ite political thought, radical Islamic movements, revolutionary thought in the Middle East, the Arab–Israeli conflict, and Marxism and neo-Marxism in the Middle East.